CHARMING
Bouquets

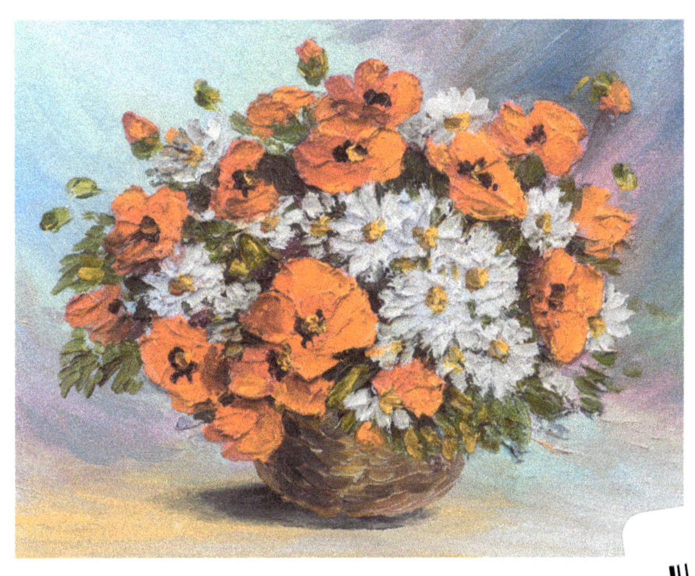

Make-a-Masterpiece
Adult Grayscale Coloring Book
with Color Guides

Linda Wright

About the Author

LINDA WRIGHT discovered the magic of coloring over grayscale years ago when she hand-colored her first black and white photograph. It was astonishingly easy, yet just as astonishingly beautiful. Now, in the midst of a long career in the photo industry, she is happy to bring her experience with imagery to further fruition with her collection of Make-a-Masterpiece Adult Grayscale Coloring Books.

Thank you so much for buying *Charming Bouquets*. May you find hours of fun and relaxation with its pages. If you enjoy this book, please consider leaving a review at your online place of purchase.

Other Adult Grayscale Coloring Books by Linda Wright:

CHARMING
Houses and Gardens

CHARMING
Villas by the Sea

CHARMING
Landscapes

CHARMING
Country Scenes

CHARMING
Blossoms

CHARMING
Flowers

Lindaloo Enterprises
P.O. Box 90135
Santa Barbara, California 93190
sales@lindaloo.com

Version 1.1
ISBN: 978-1-937564-79-7

Welcome!

In this unique coloring book, a Color Guide is printed across from each grayscale image.

Imitate the Color Guide for the ultimate in relaxing coloring! Or...use it for inspiration...and innovate to develop a new color palette.

Ready to Make-a-Masterpiece?

Get started!

Tips & Techniques

The magic of grayscale coloring happens when a transparent medium such as markers or colored pencils is applied to a grayscale image and the shades of gray show through. Even with no shading experience, you will look like a pro!

This Make-a-Masterpiece Adult Grayscale Coloring Book has been created from carefully curated paintings that have been converted into coloring pages. The gray tones for each image have been optimized for beautiful depth and a pleasing pop when colored.

Color Guides are included to enhance your experience and provide for a relaxing coloring process. Across from each grayscale coloring page is a full-size image showing the colors of the original painting. You can match the guides color-for-color or use them as a springboard for innovation. Test Images are also provided so that you can try out your colors on a small version of the artwork before using them on your full-size piece.

There are many ways to approach grayscale coloring. Perhaps you are an experienced colorist with preferred techniques. In that case, dive in! If you are less experienced, read on for some suggestions to make your masterpieces look their best.

Color can be applied in back and forth strokes, continuous circles, lots of tiny dots, hatching, or cross-hatching. Hatching involves drawing a series of parallel lines close together. To cross-hatch, another set of hatch marks is drawn on top, usually in a perpendicular or near-perpendicular direction to the first set. All of these techniques can be used in various combinations to create interesting effects.

Make-a-Masterpiece

This is my favorite method for coloring a stunning masterpiece.

1. Color the subject matter with light or medium-value **markers** following the Color Guide. Dark markers are not good as they will cover up the grayscale shading.

2. Color accents on top with lighter and darker **colored pencils**. The effect is beautiful!

3. Color the background using a palette of colored **chalks** or **eye shadows**. Apply them with makeup sponges or cotton swabs. Pointed "precision tip" cotton swabs are ideal for tight spots.

Voila!

To remove a page for coloring, use a utility knife. Otherwise, place a protective layer of paper or cardstock behind your work to catch any color that bleeds through. To keep your borders free of overspill, low-tack artist tape can be used to mask off the edges.

You may think that some areas of a coloring page look too dark to color—but grab your marker or pencil and go for it! It's surprising how an area that looks dark will accept color and come to life. In my testing, it was only at the grayscale levels used in this book that I was able to consistently get beautiful, rich results that I would be proud to hang on my wall.

Always test your colors and media before applying them to your artwork. The Test Images that I've provided are extremely helpful, so please use them to avoid spoiling a coloring page. Keep a piece of white scrap paper handy, too, and test there first.

The supplies that you use will definitely make a difference. There are many from which to choose and I've not tried them all, but I do have current favorites that work well. For markers, I primarily use Spectrum Noir (pastels, lights and brights) and my big set of Crayola Super Tips. I have also filled in my collection with assorted Copic Markers and Blick Studio Brush Markers that can be purchased individually at dickblick.com. For colored pencils, I use Prismacolor Premier. For backgrounds, I use a palette of Pebbles Chalks. My favorite is the Pearlescent set. The shimmer is slight and I've been able to get the most vivid colors from these. My second choice is the Basic Brights. Pebbles Chalks are economical, convenient and they truly revolutionized my background results. They can even be used to color an entire grayscale image. If you have trouble getting sufficient color from your chalks, roughing up the surface can help. Scratch the surface lightly with a straight pin—just enough to release the amount of chalk you'll use at the time. Practice with chalks on scrap paper to get the feel for them. Press lightly with your applicator for pale tints and more firmly for deeper tones. Apply multiple layers if needed. Another benefit of chalks is that they are erasable! If you don't like the look, use a good, clean eraser.

Keep experimenting with supplies because you just may discover something new that you love. If you have a local art supply store, it's fun to browse and see what's available. One of my secret weapons is a white blender marker from Winsor & Newton which I found that way. Numerous times it has saved areas where I applied a marker that later looked too dark. It also makes nice accents on any color. A white colored pencil can be used in a similar manner. Other unexpected treasures are my fluorescent markers. Initially I disregarded the fluorescents that came in my sets, but when I tested the yellow-green on an image that needed vibrant foliage, it was perfect! The grayscale will tone down your colors, so if you want luminosity, it helps to go extra bright. Opaque gel pens can be used on top of markers for little accents and details.

YouTube.com offers many excellent coloring tutorials. I highly recommend taking a look. There are so many fun techniques and products to try! I collect my favorite coloring products and my favorite YouTube video tutorials on a Pinterest board. Go to Lindaloo Enterprises on Pinterest at www.Pinterest.com/LindalooEnt and find the board named Make-a-Masterpiece. You can also find Make-a-Masterpiece on Facebook. Please visit for inspiration at www.facebook.com/make.a.masterpiece.coloring.books.

Finally, be sure to share your masterpieces with others!

∞ This book is printed on acid-free paper.

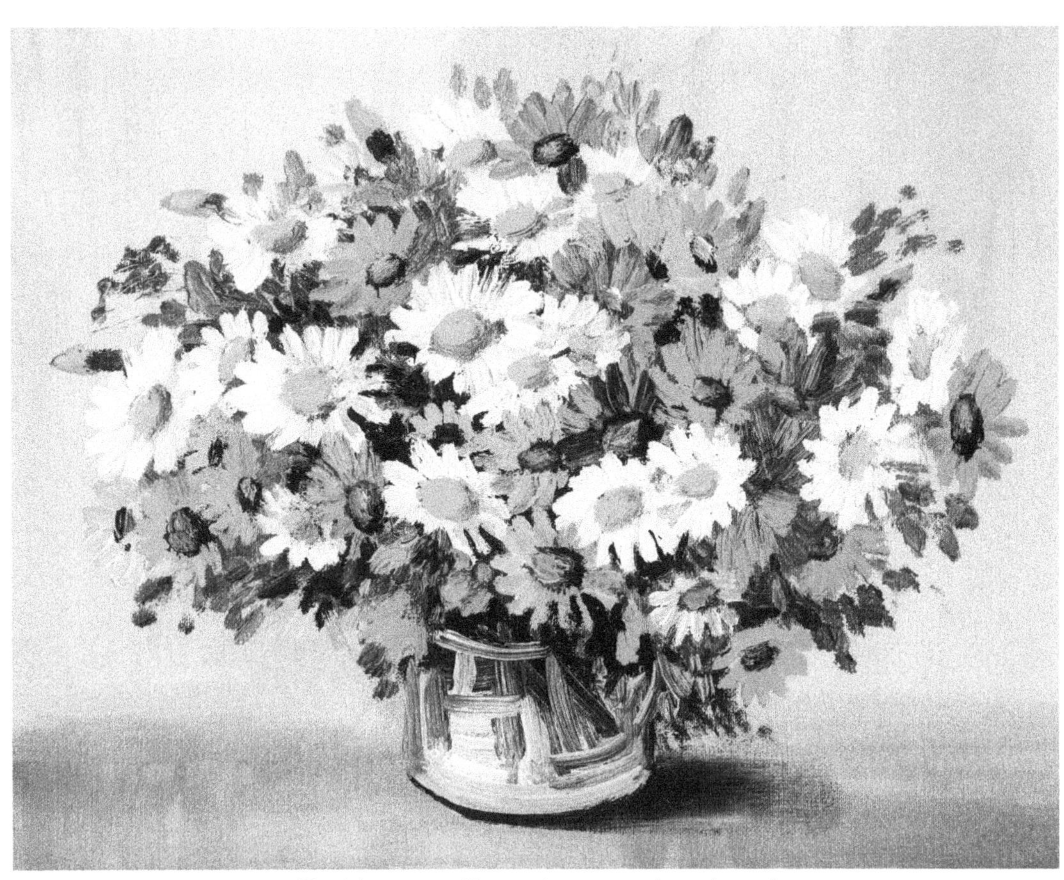

Test Images: Try out your colors here!

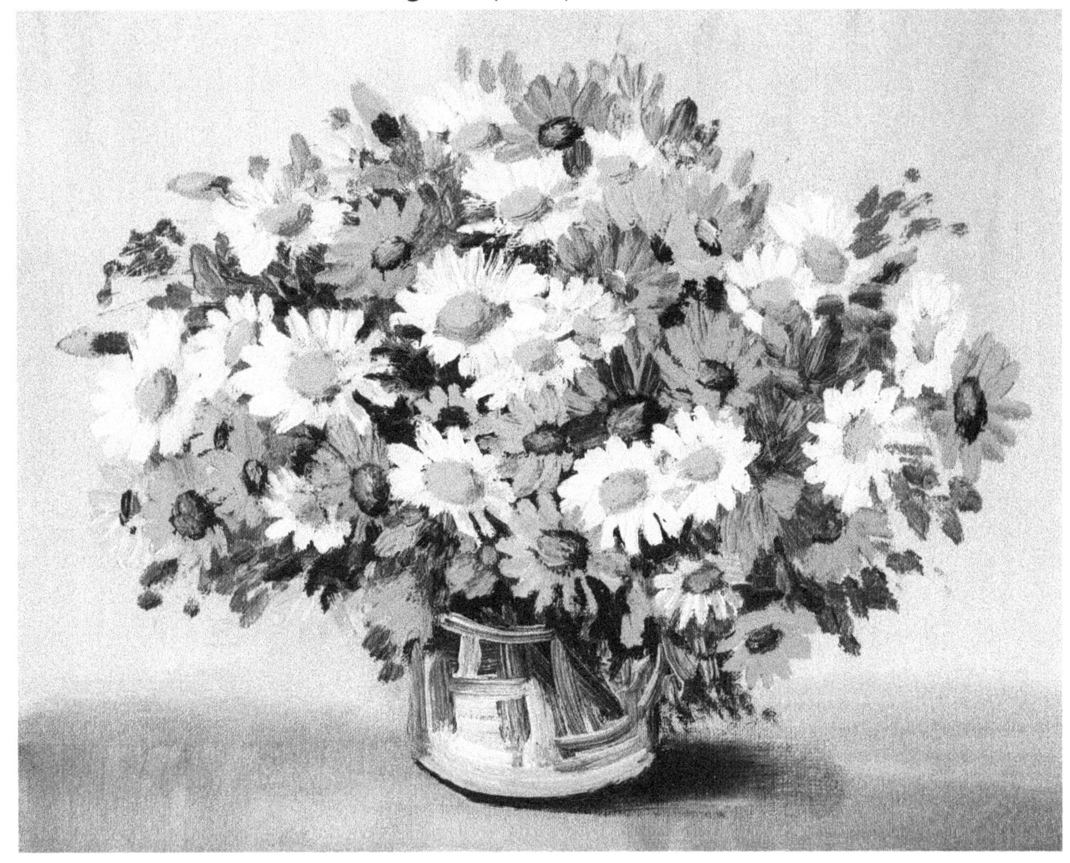

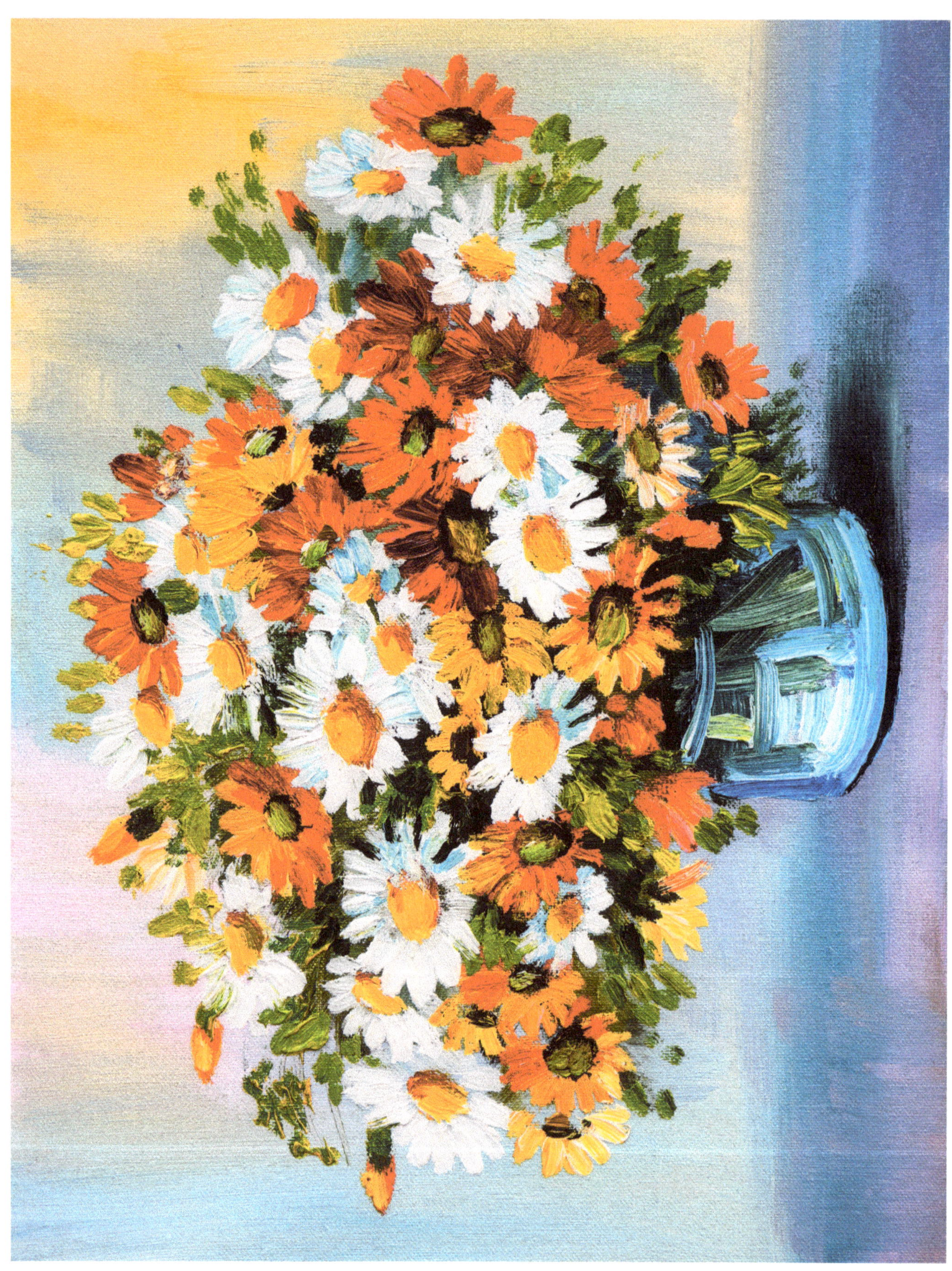

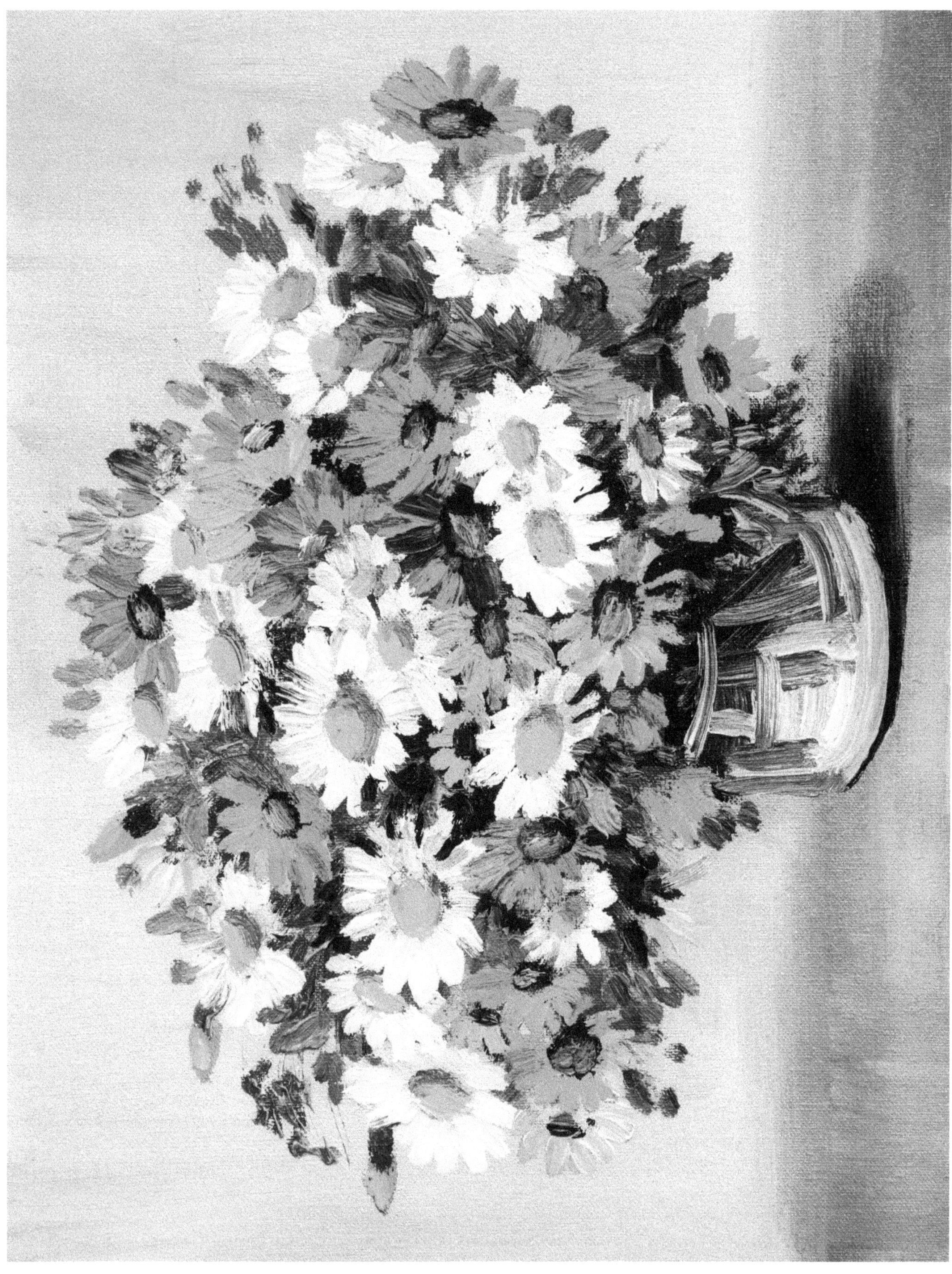

Colored By ______________________________ Date ______________________

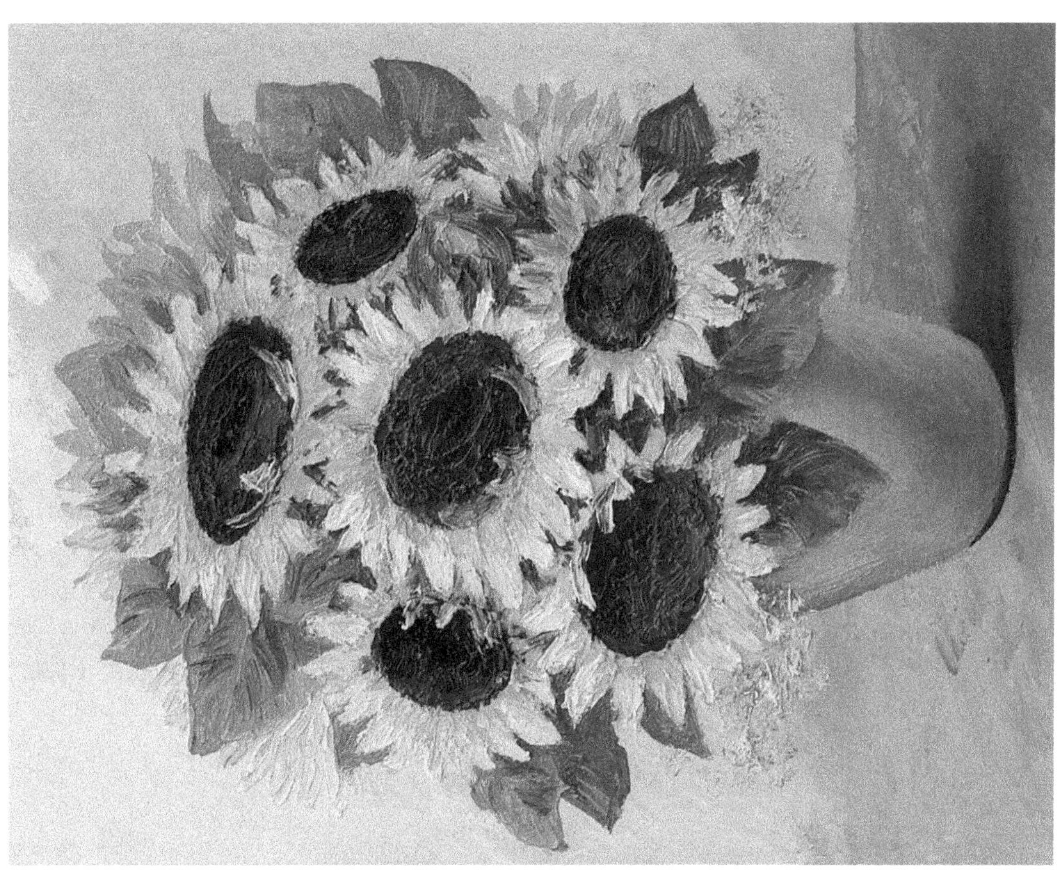

Test Images: Try out your colors here!

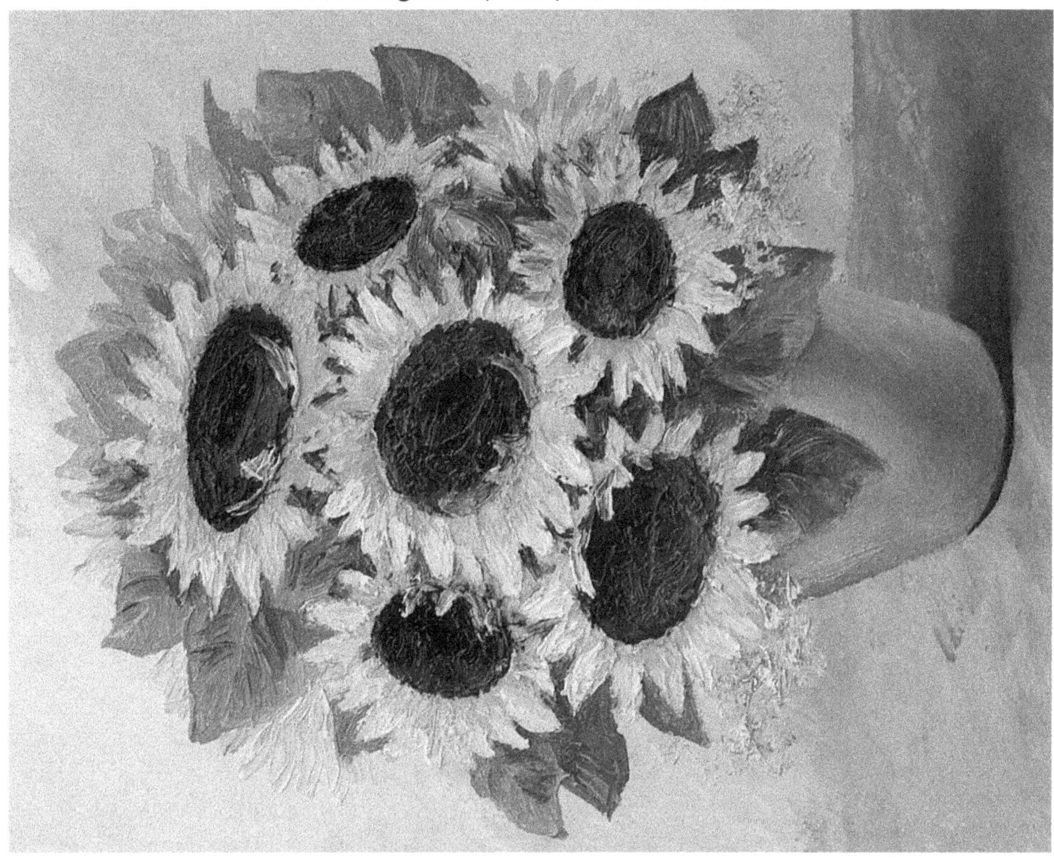

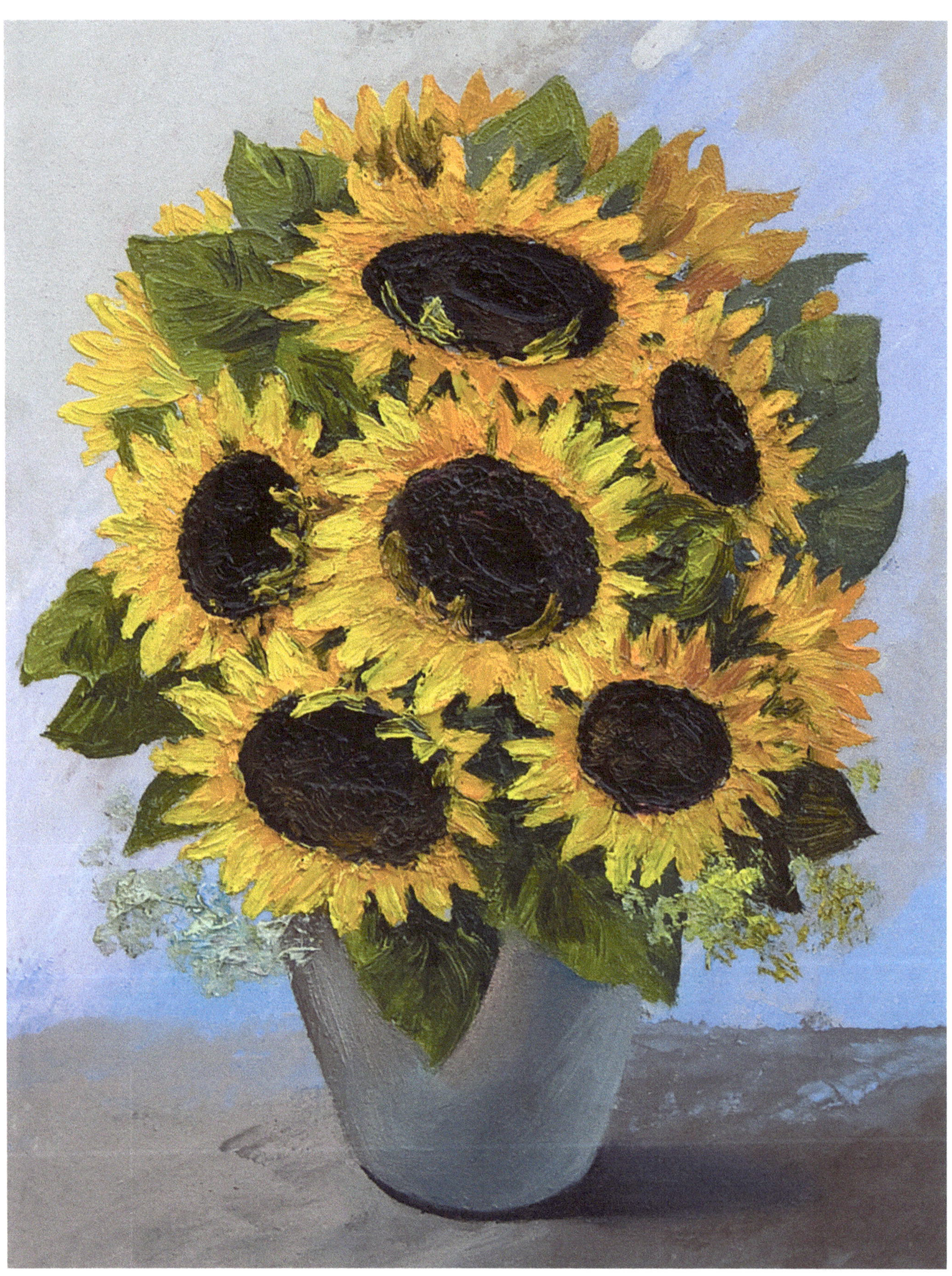

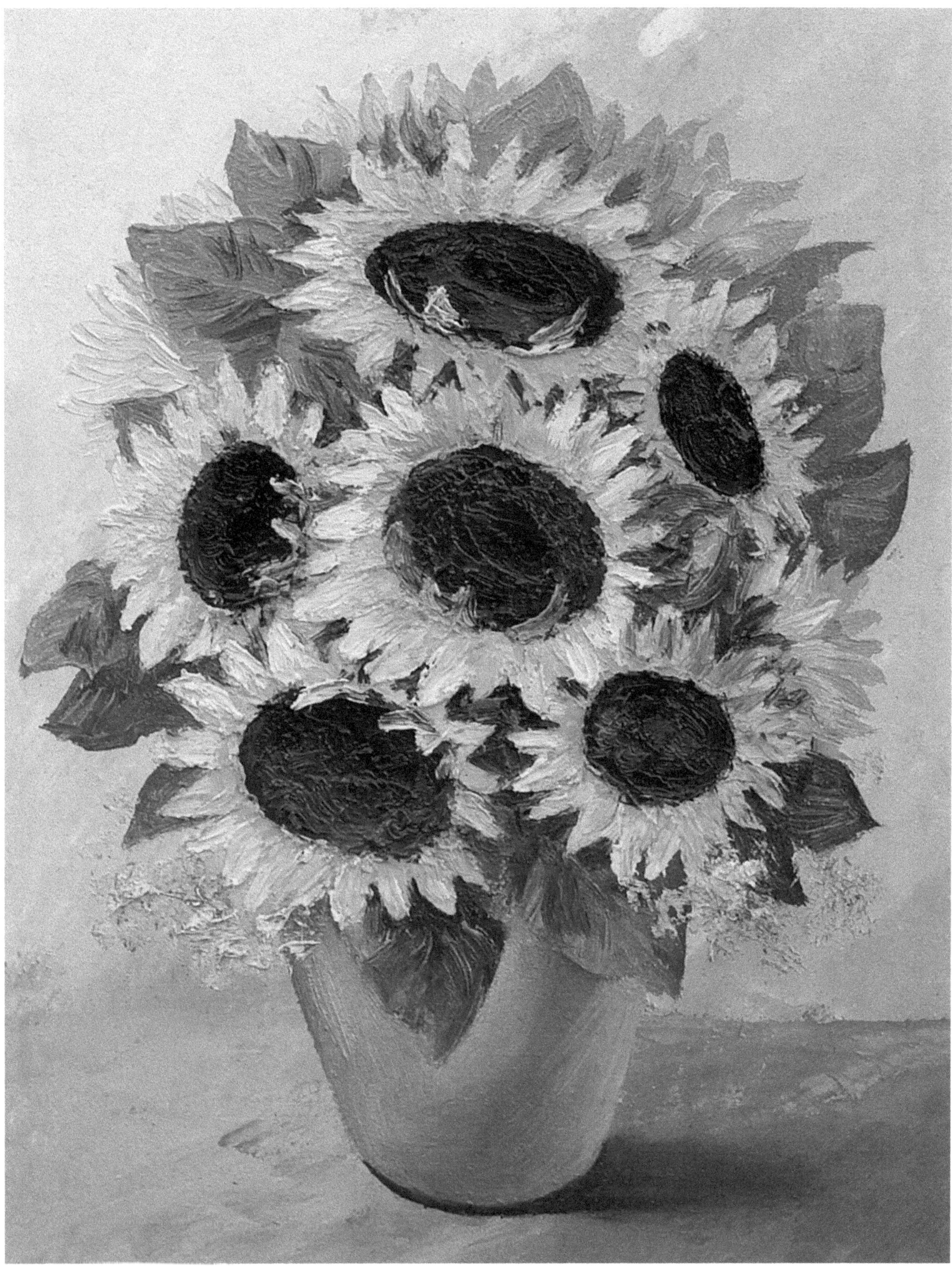

Colored By ____

Date ____

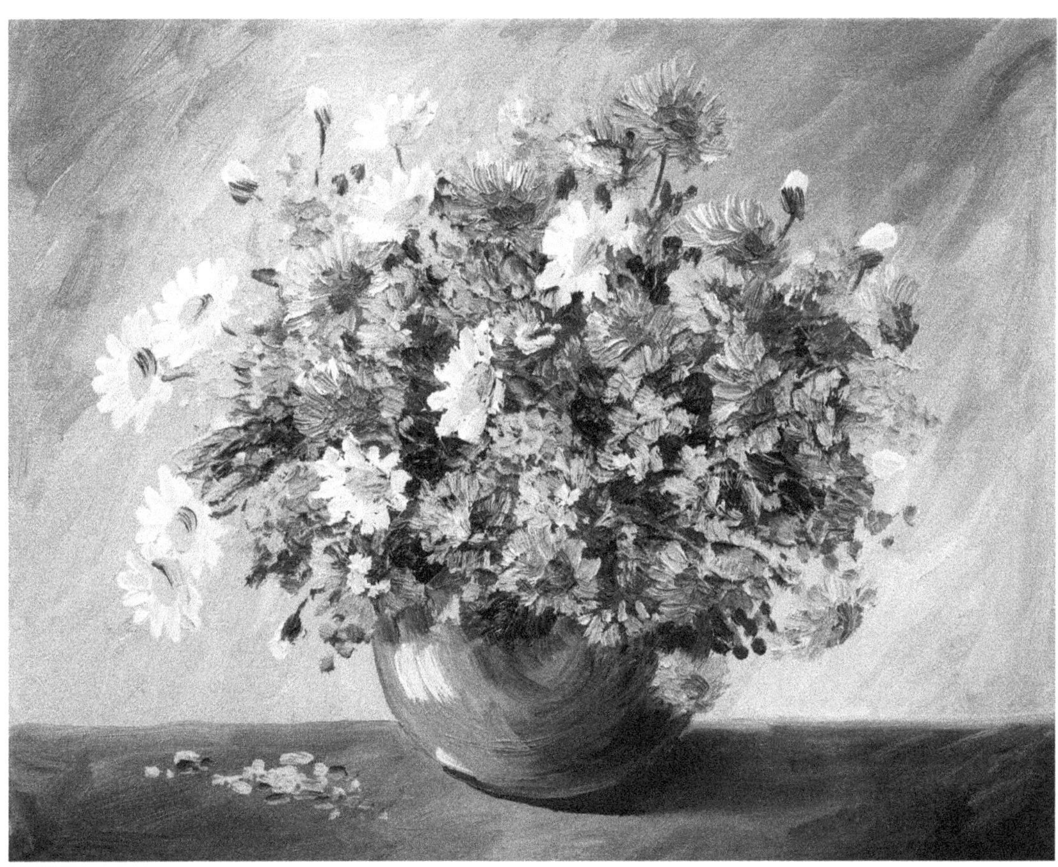

Test Images: Try out your colors here!

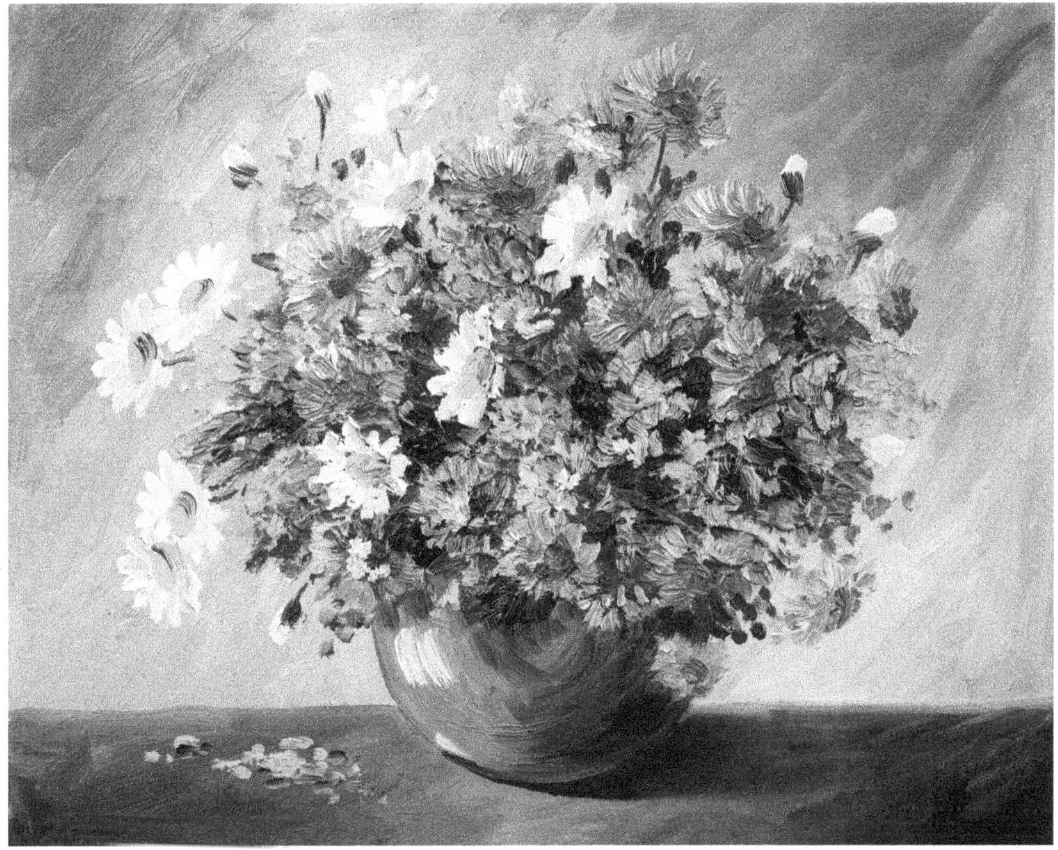

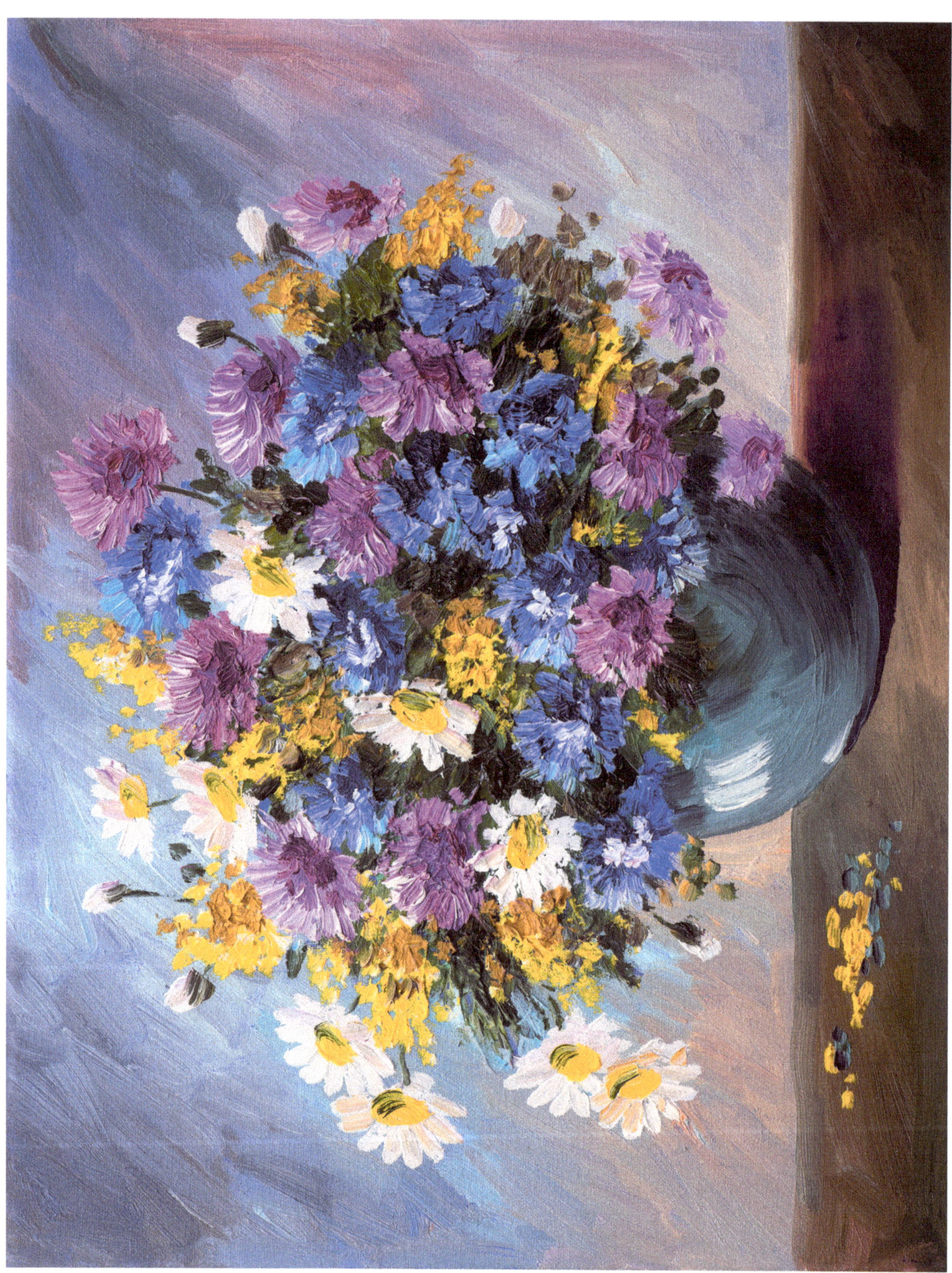

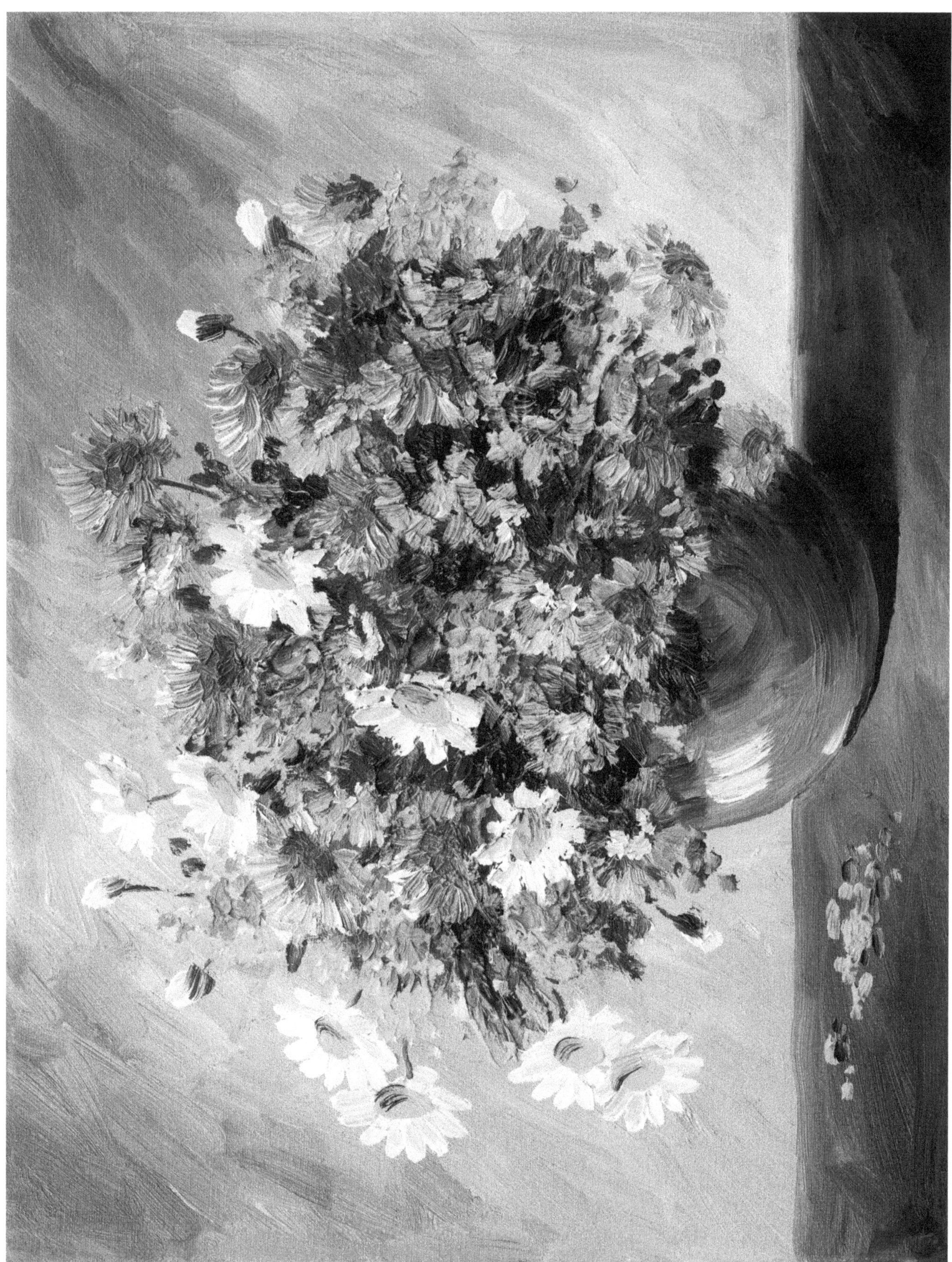

Colored By ______________________________ Date ______________________

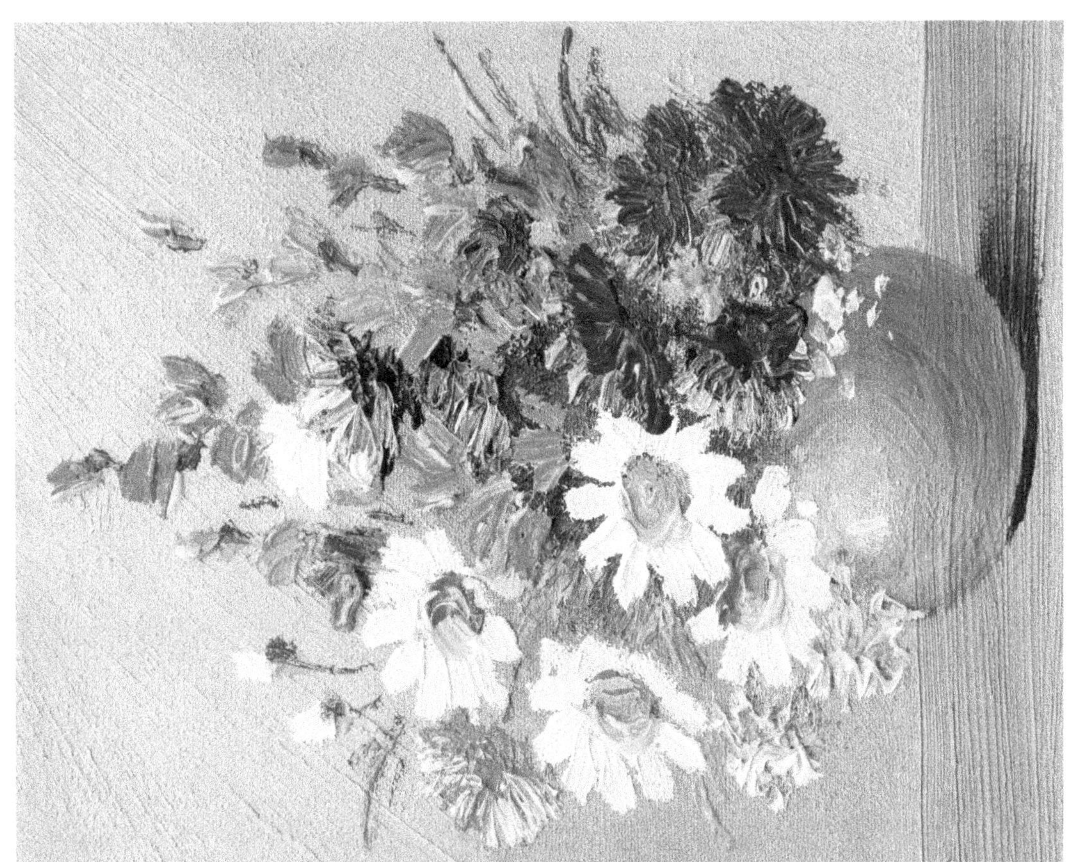

Test Images: Try out your colors here!

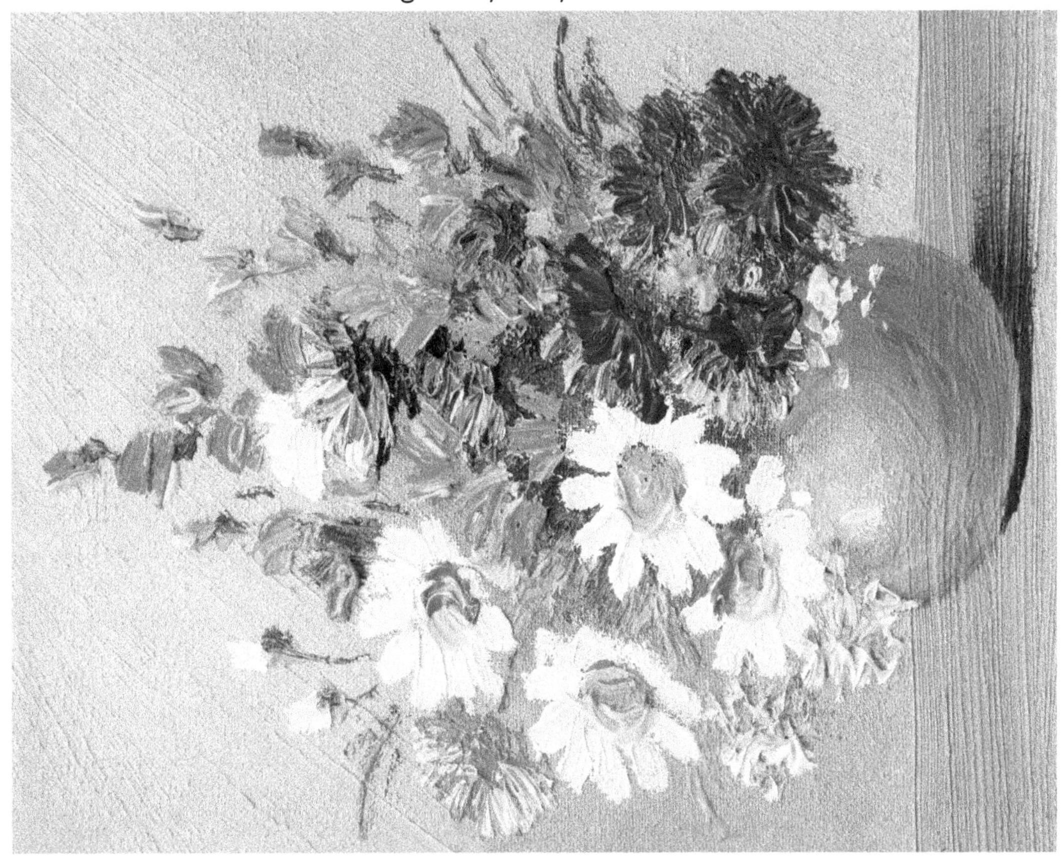

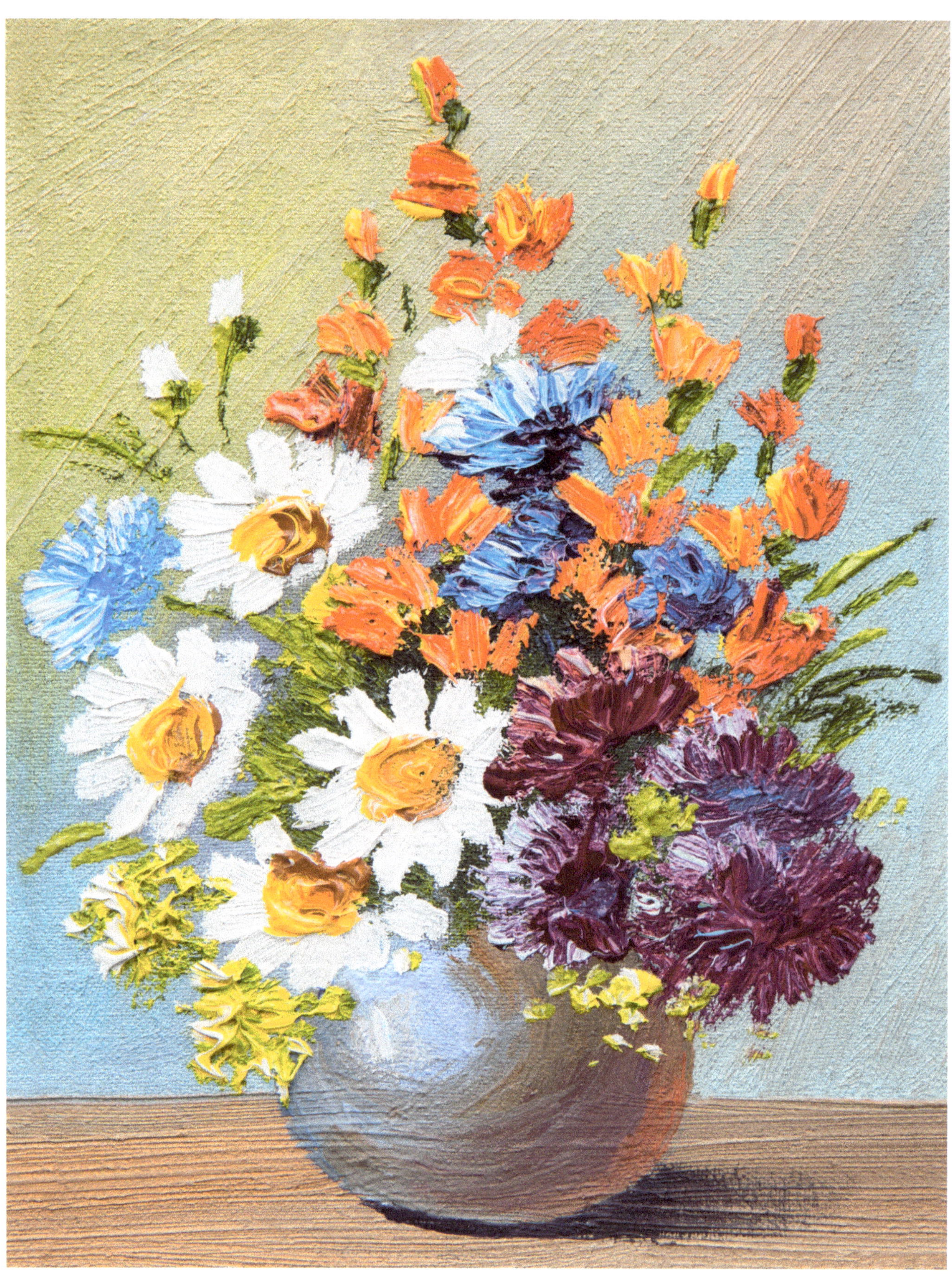

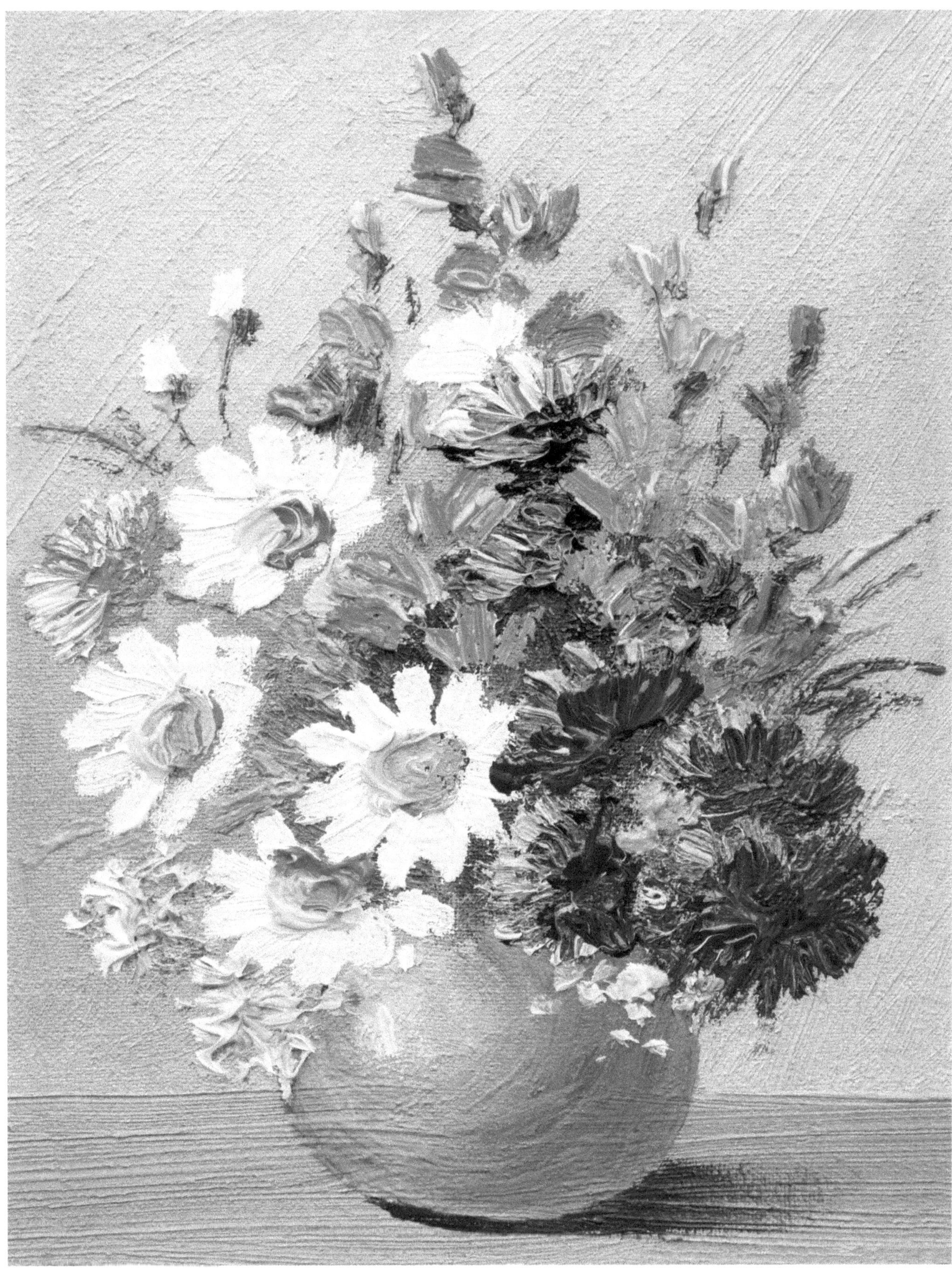

Colored By ______________________________

Date ______________________________

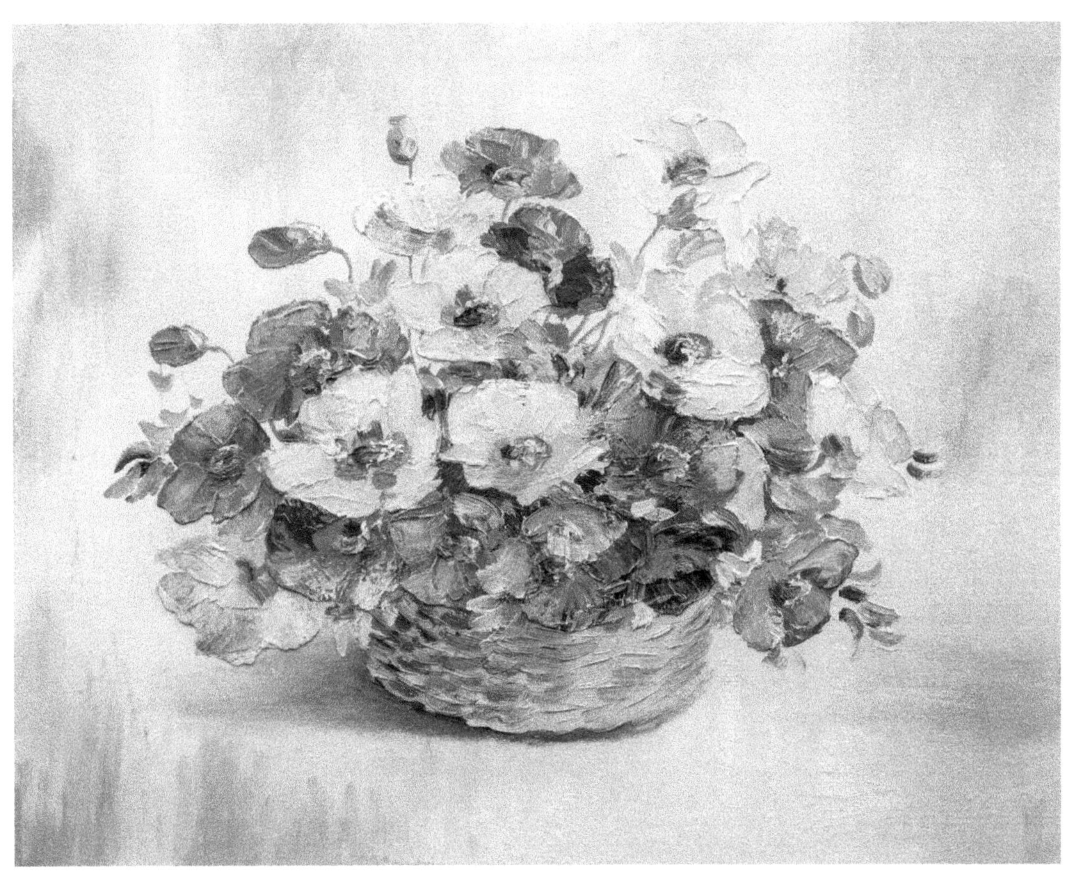

Test Images: Try out your colors here!

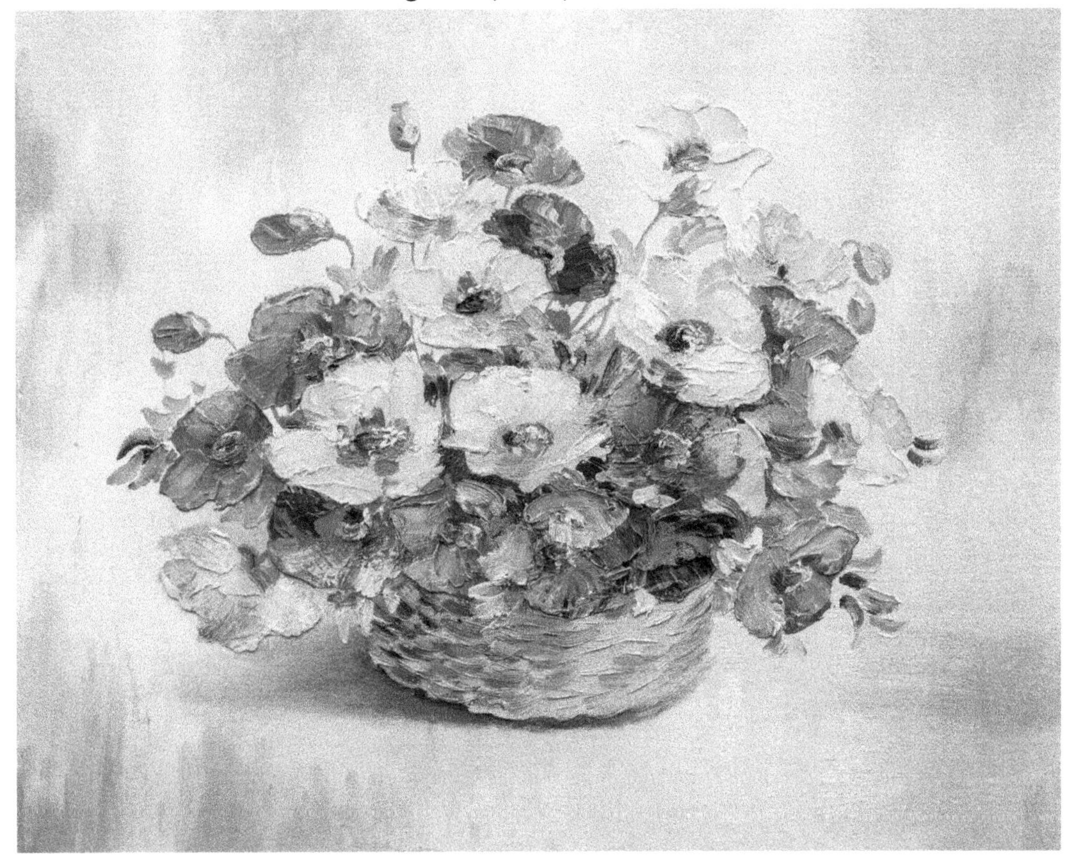

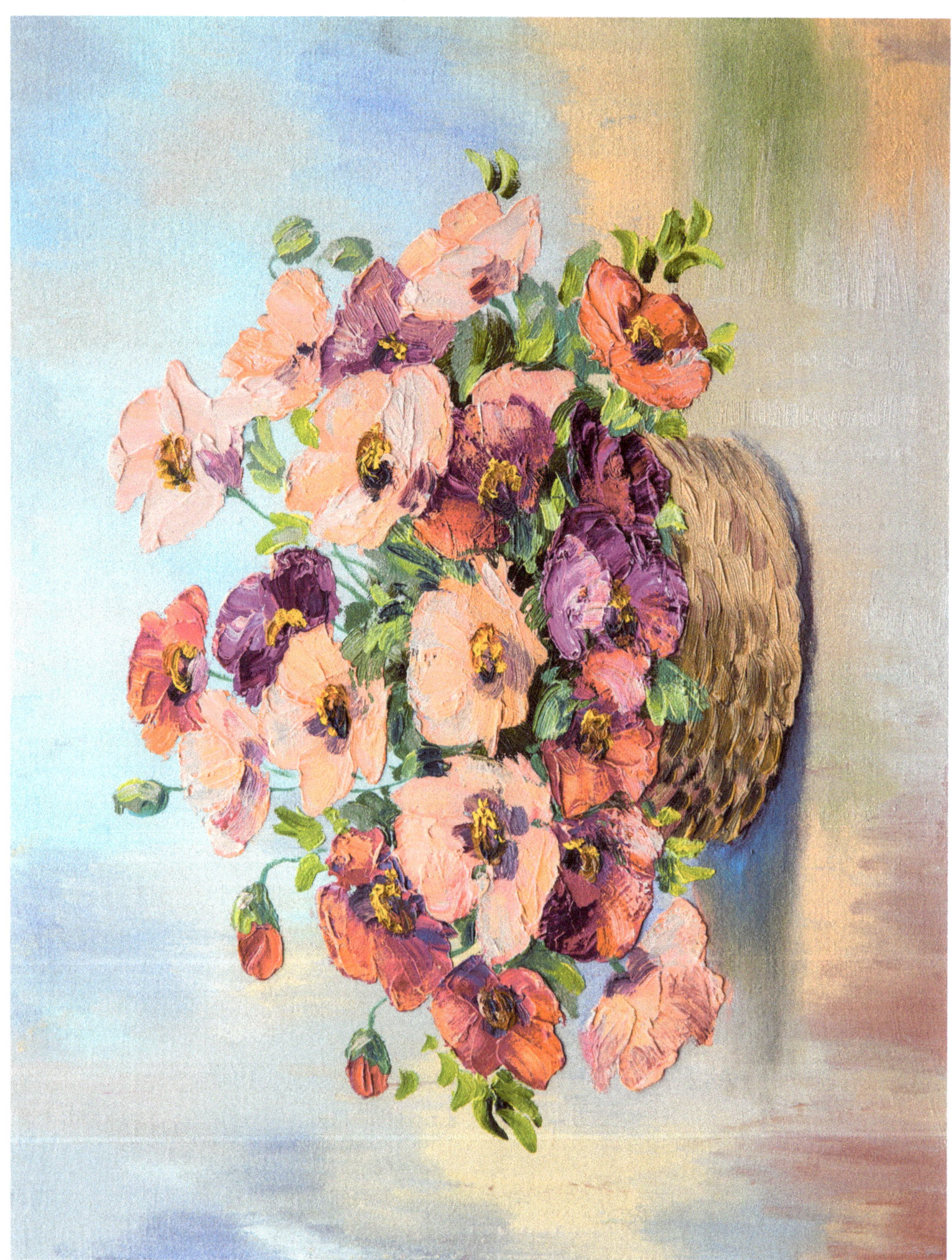

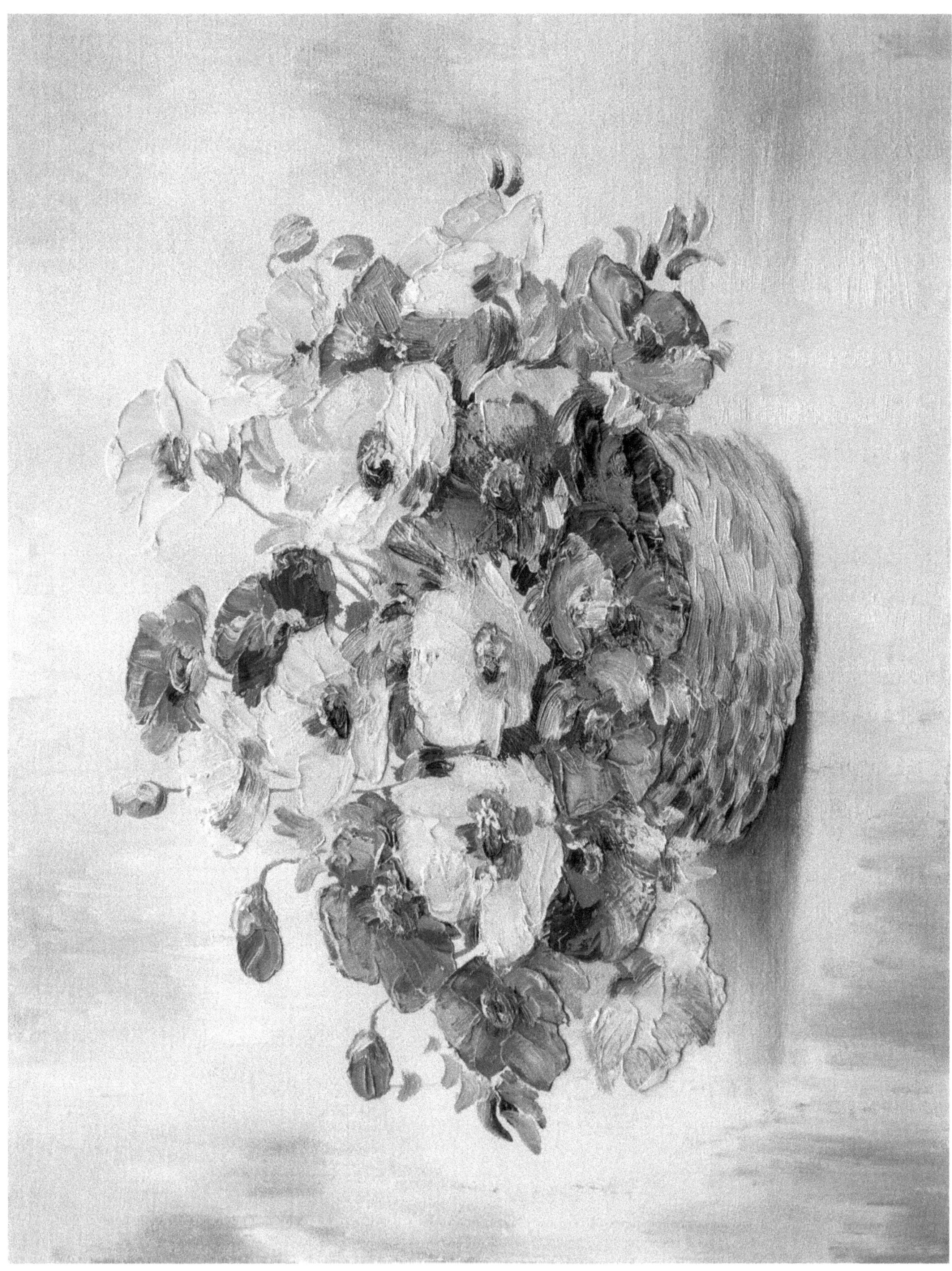

Colored By ______________________________ Date ______________________

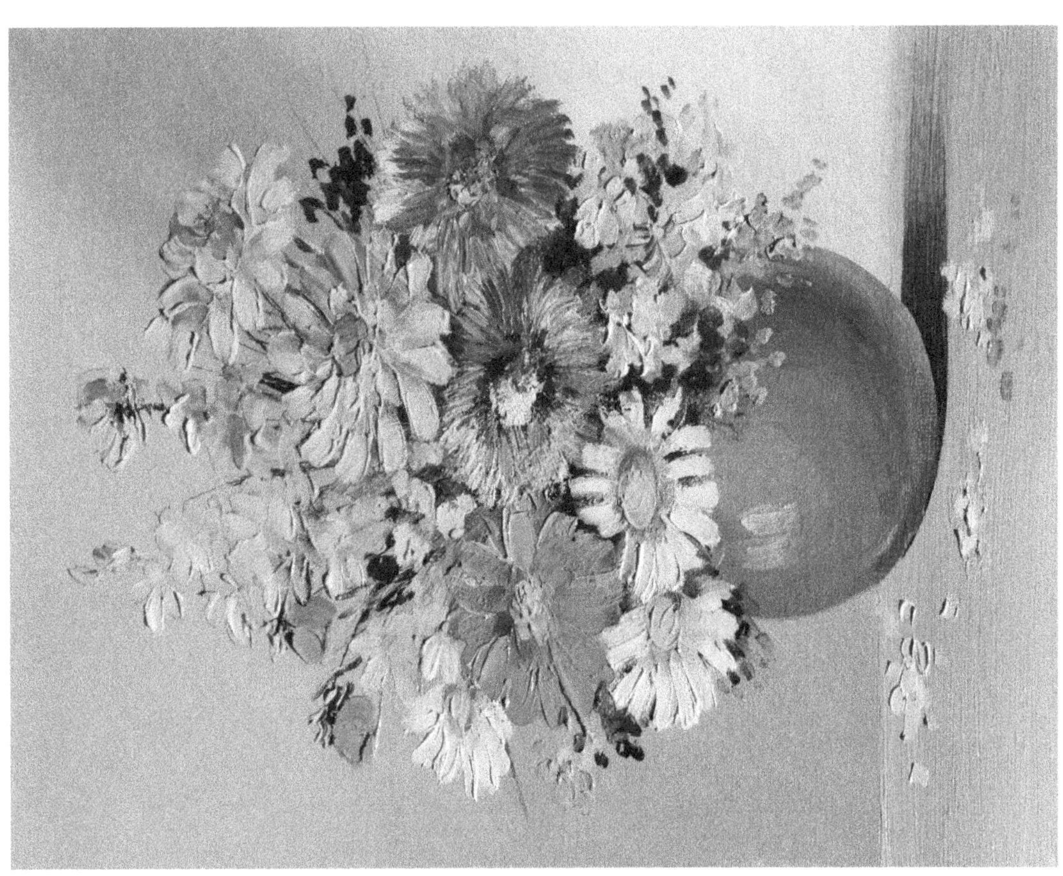

Test Images: Try out your colors here!

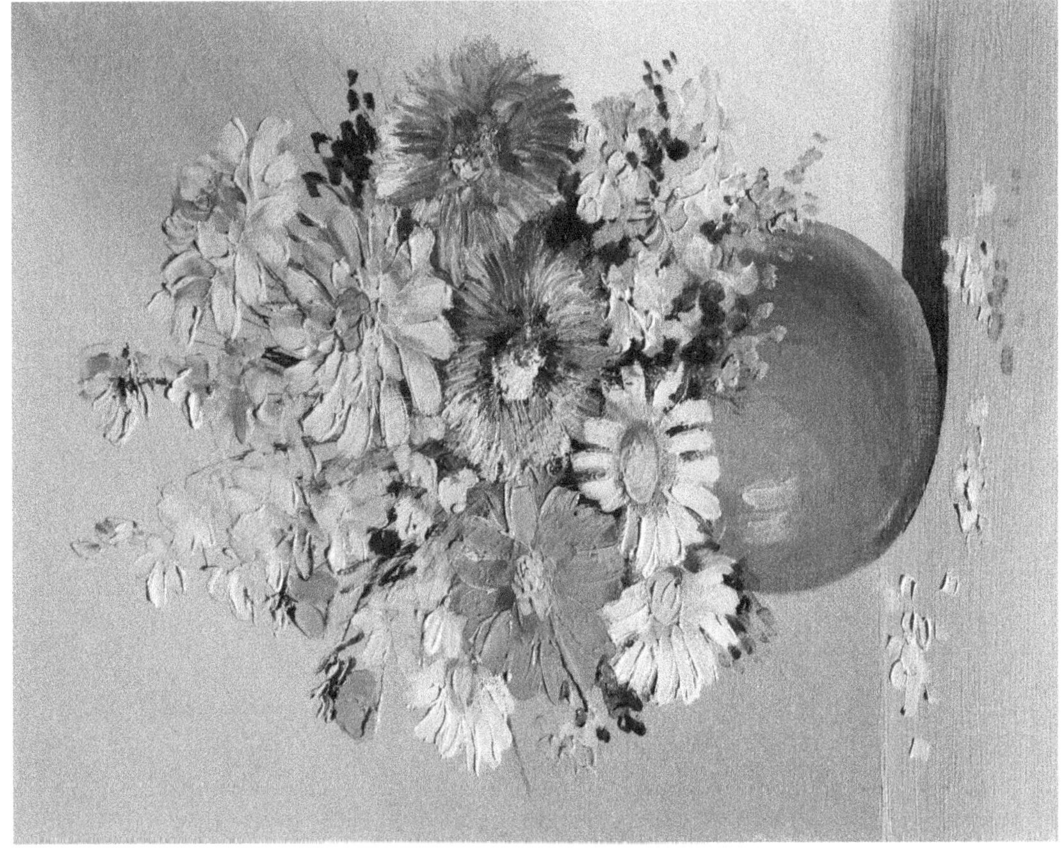

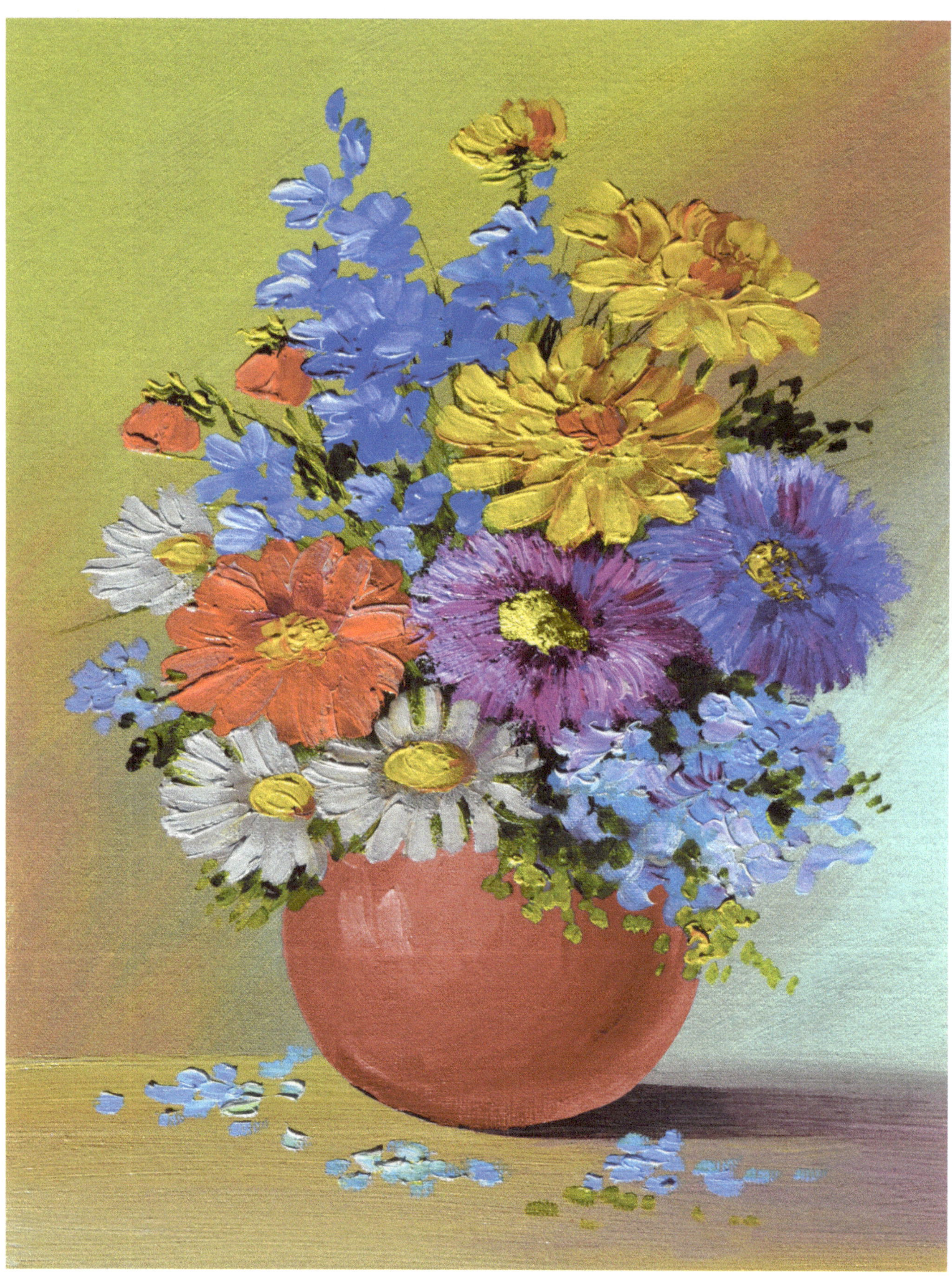

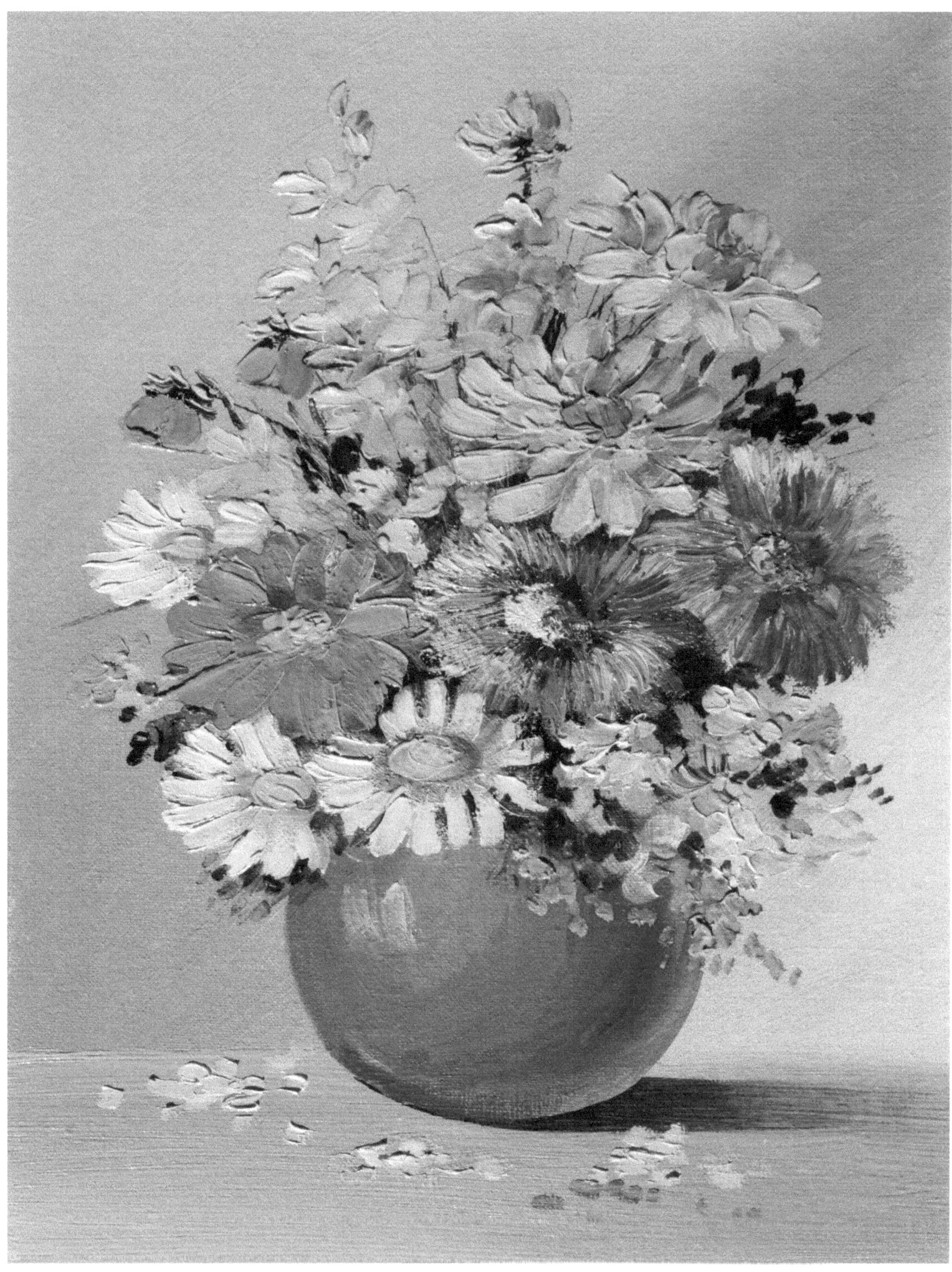

Colored By ____

Date ____

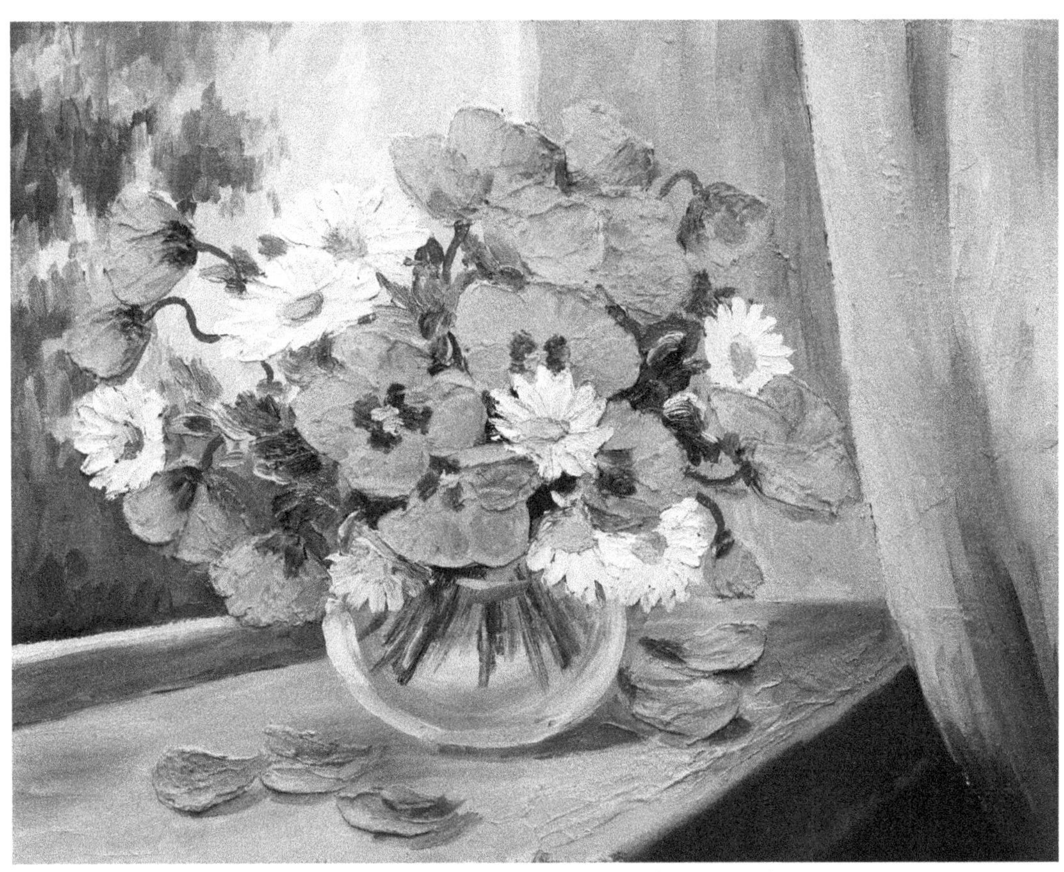

Test Images: Try out your colors here!

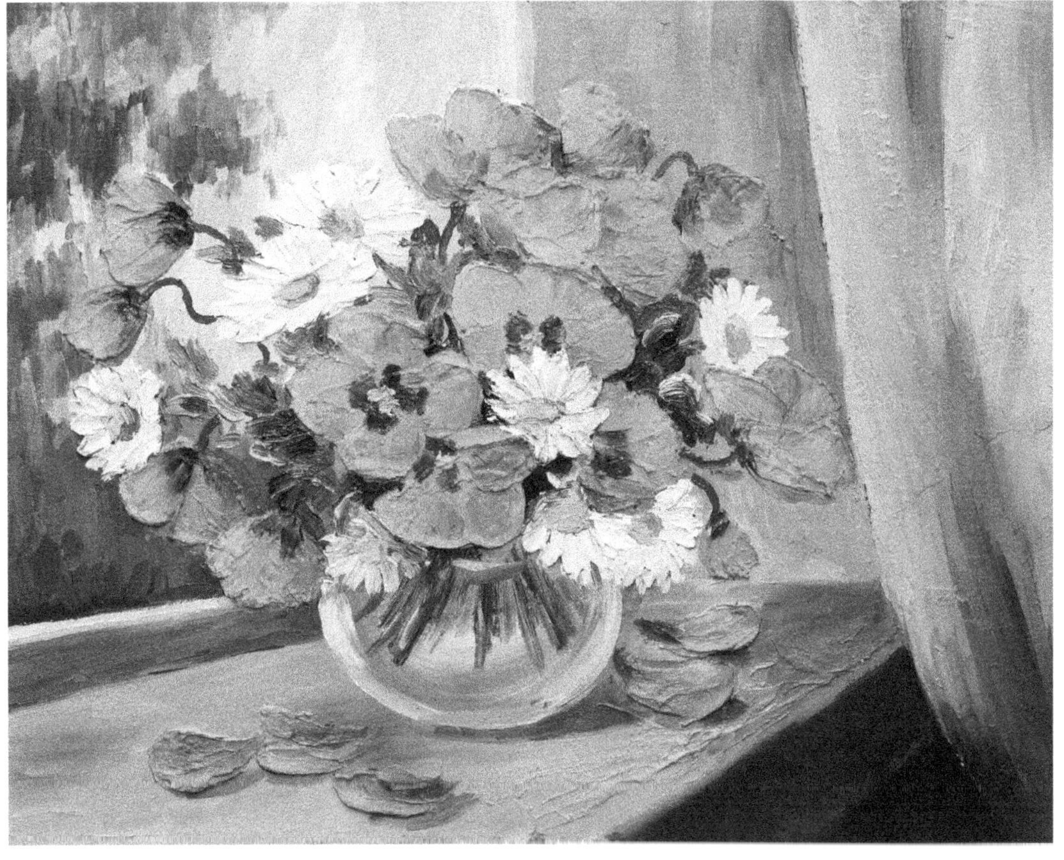

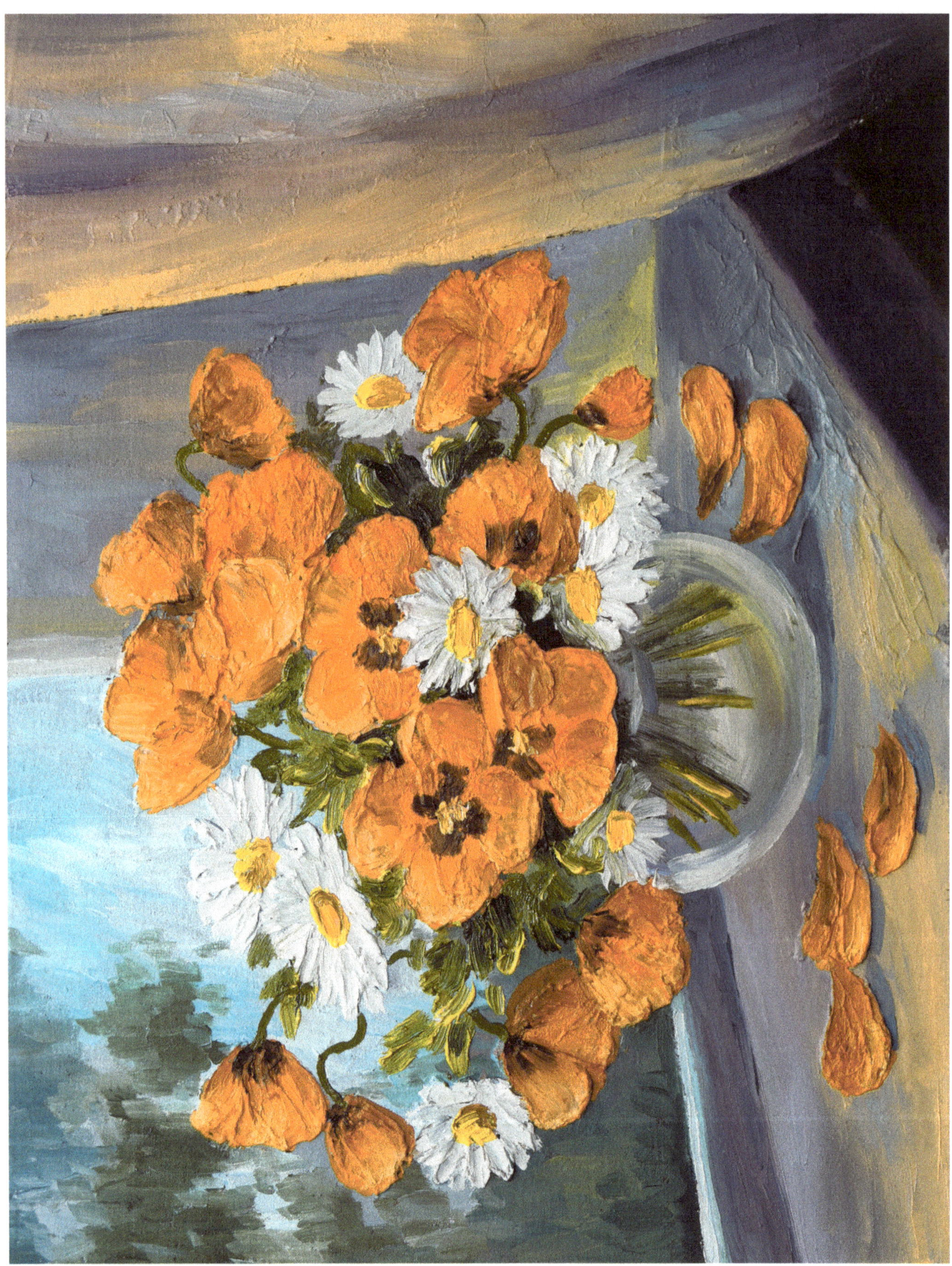

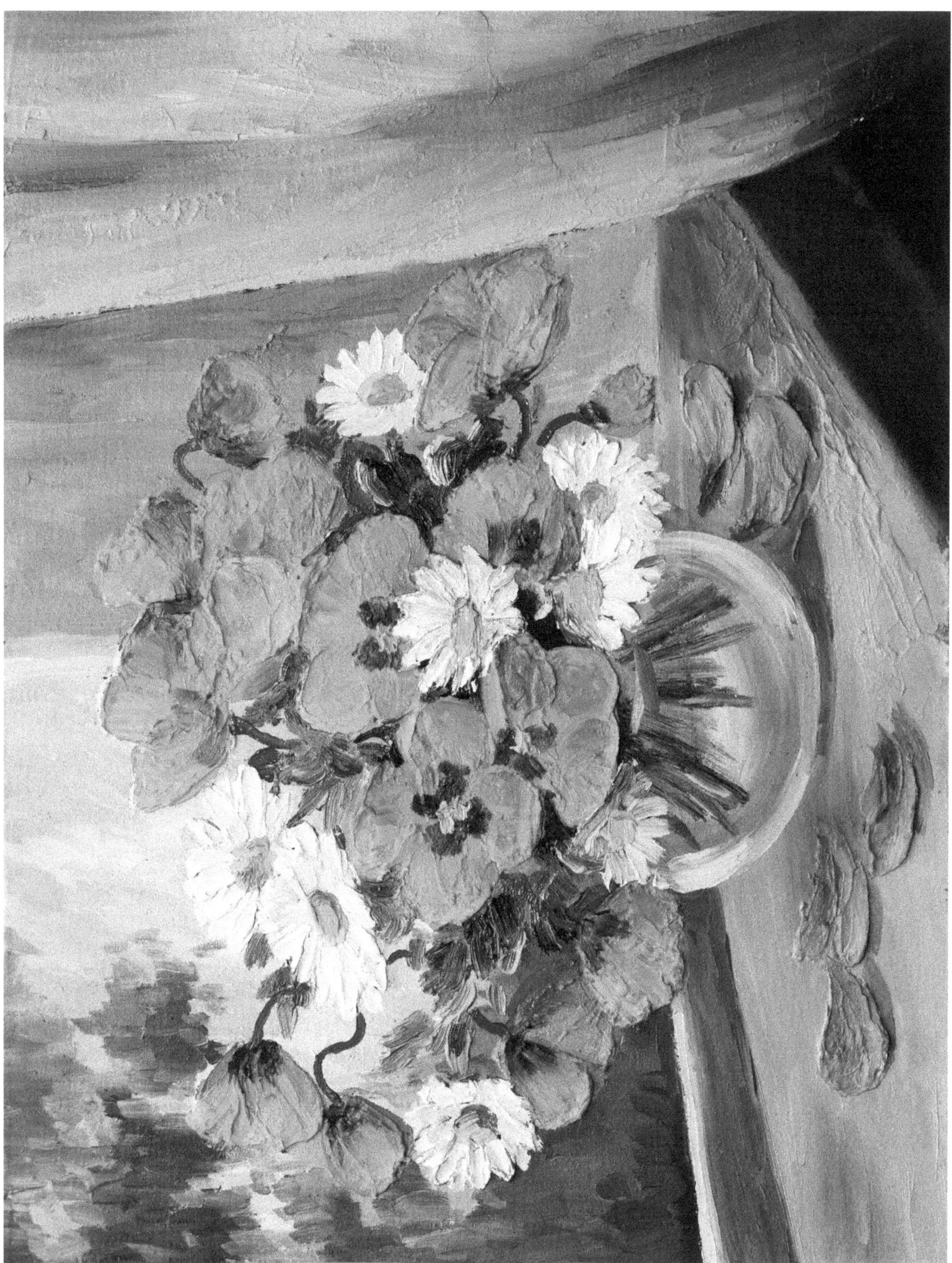

Colored By ______________________________ Date ______________________

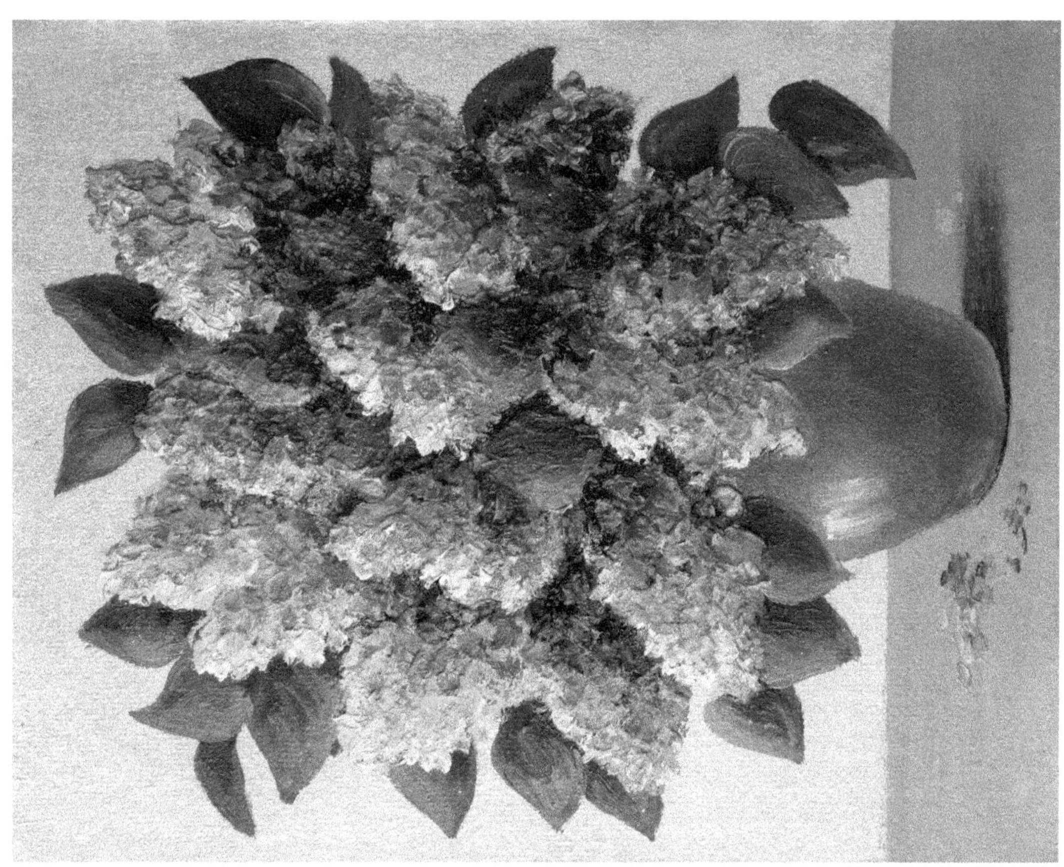

Test Images: Try out your colors here!

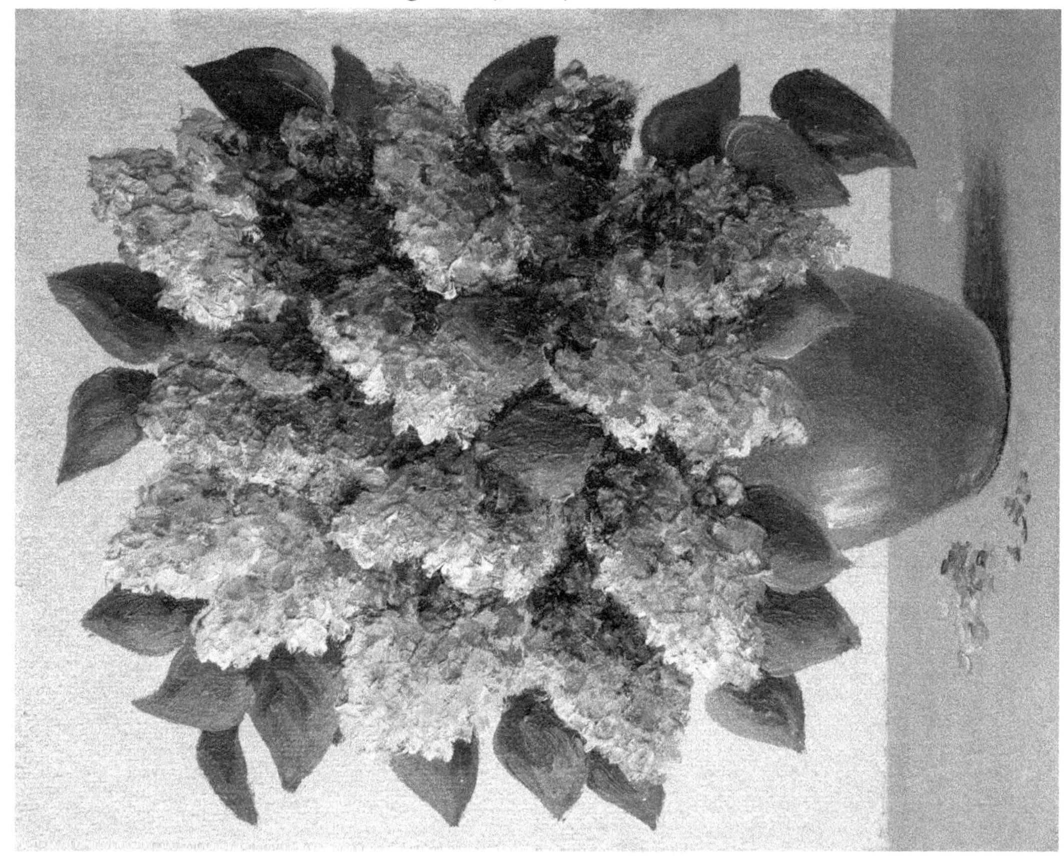

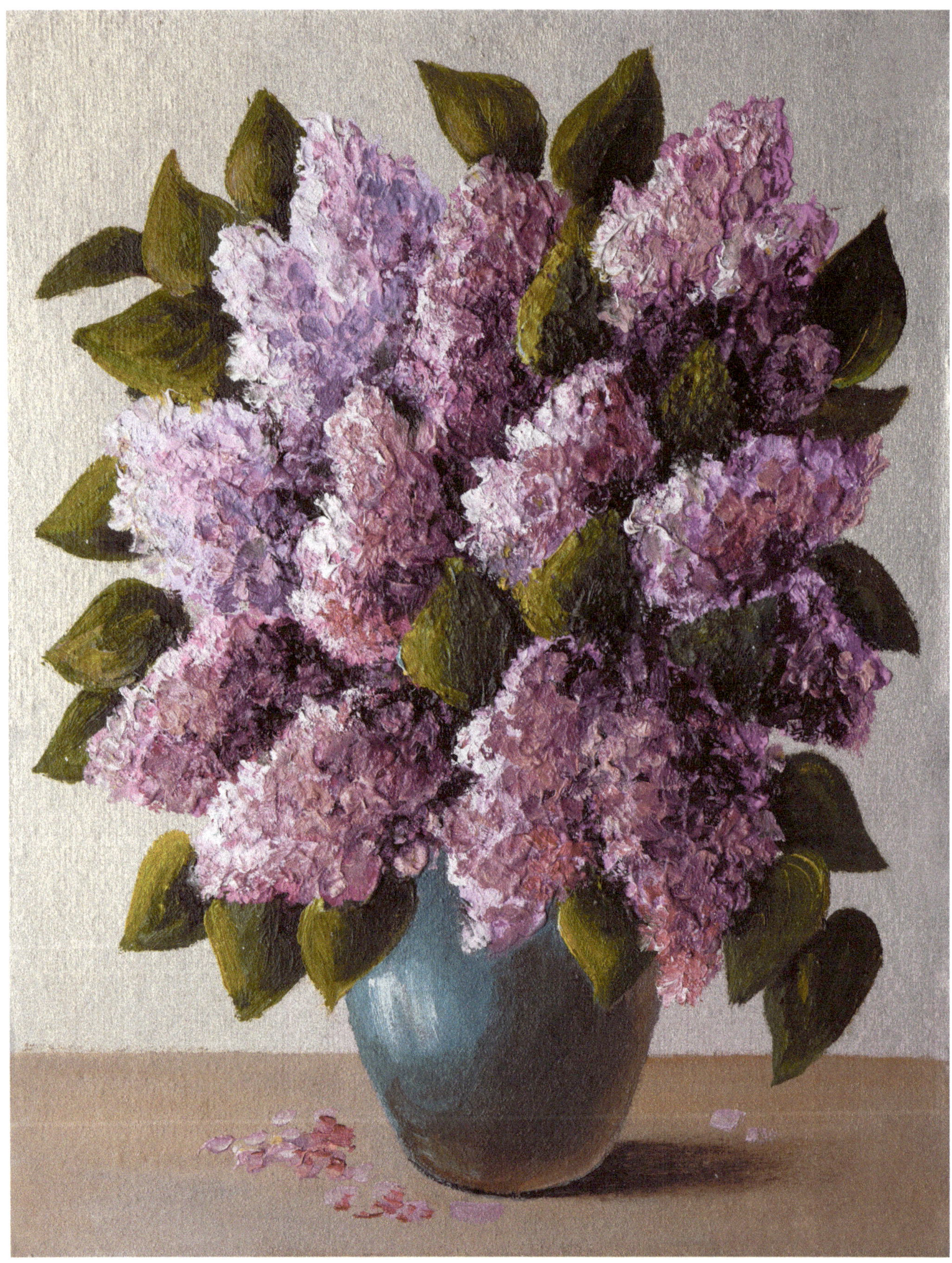

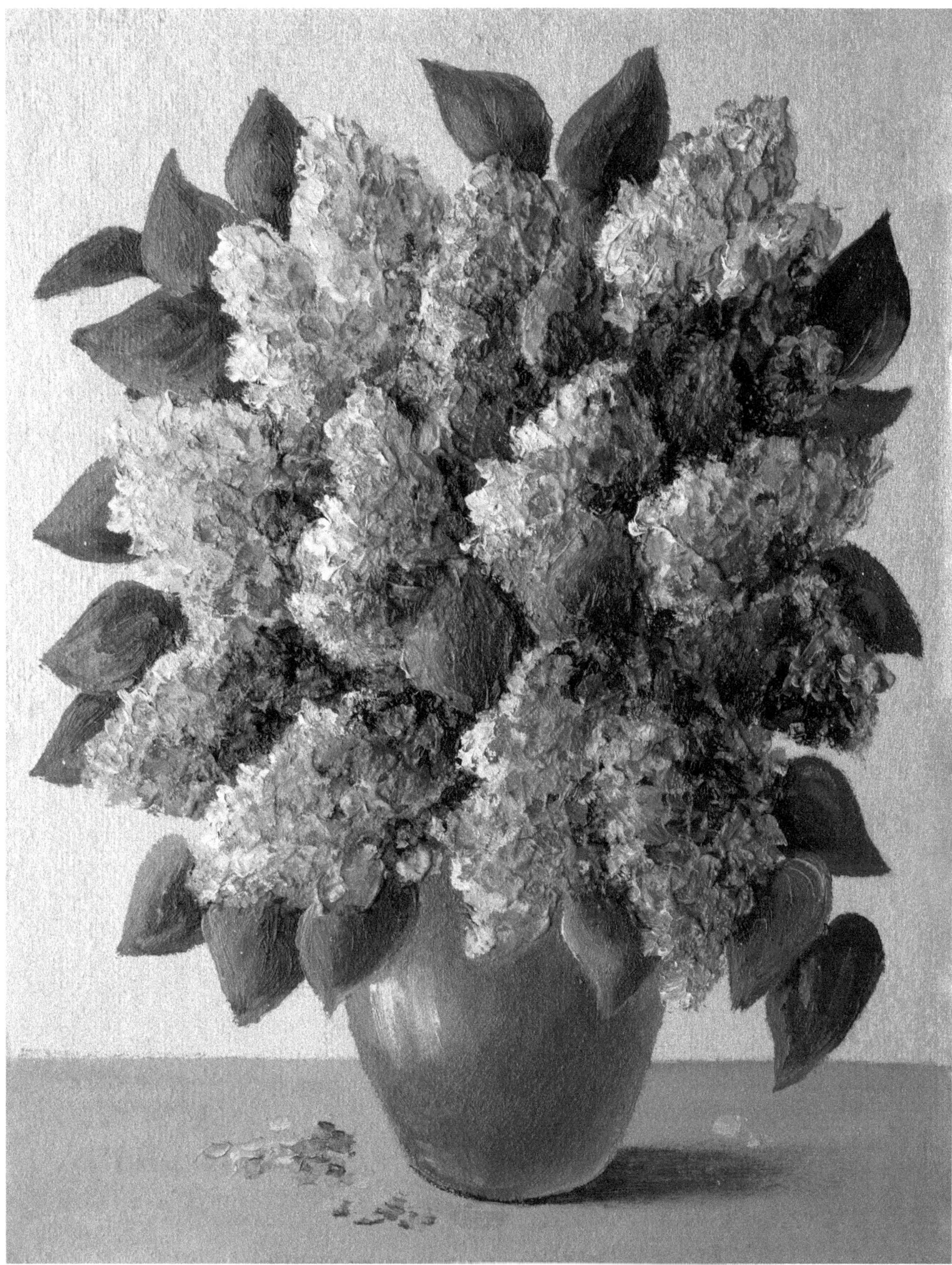

COLORED BY ____

DATE ____

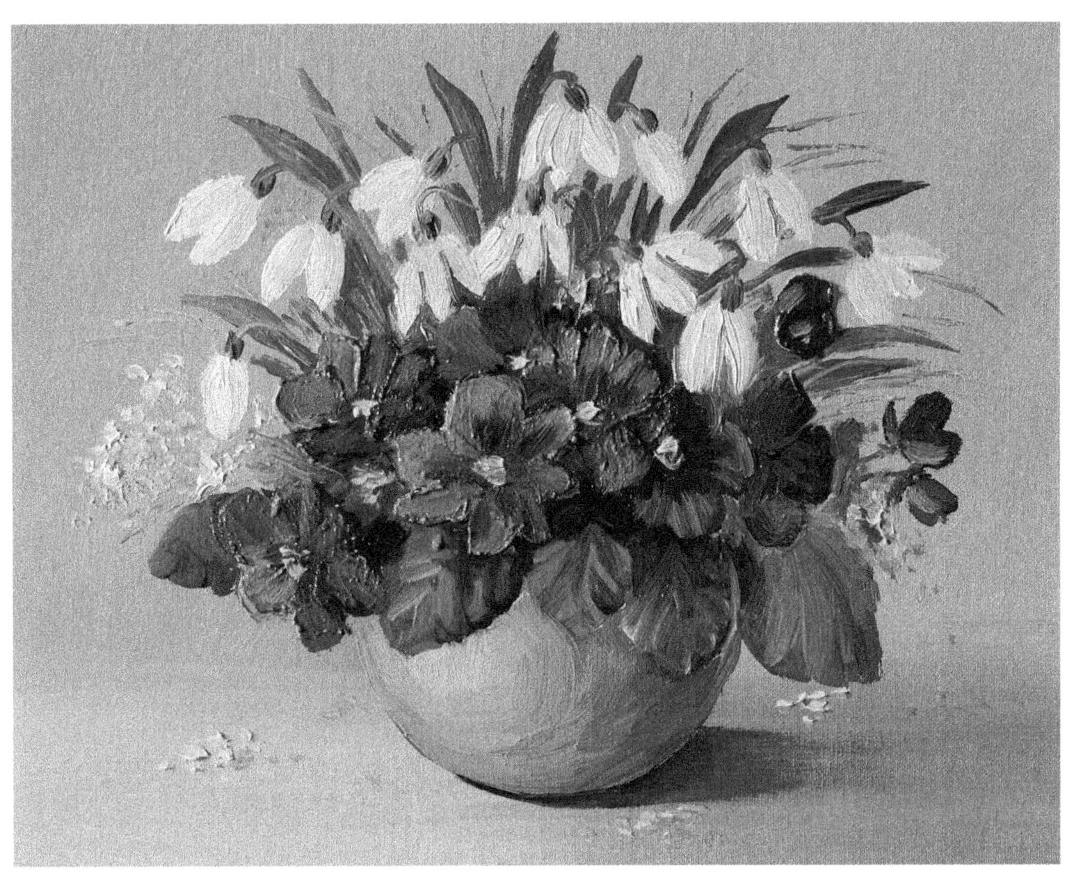

Test Images: Try out your colors here!

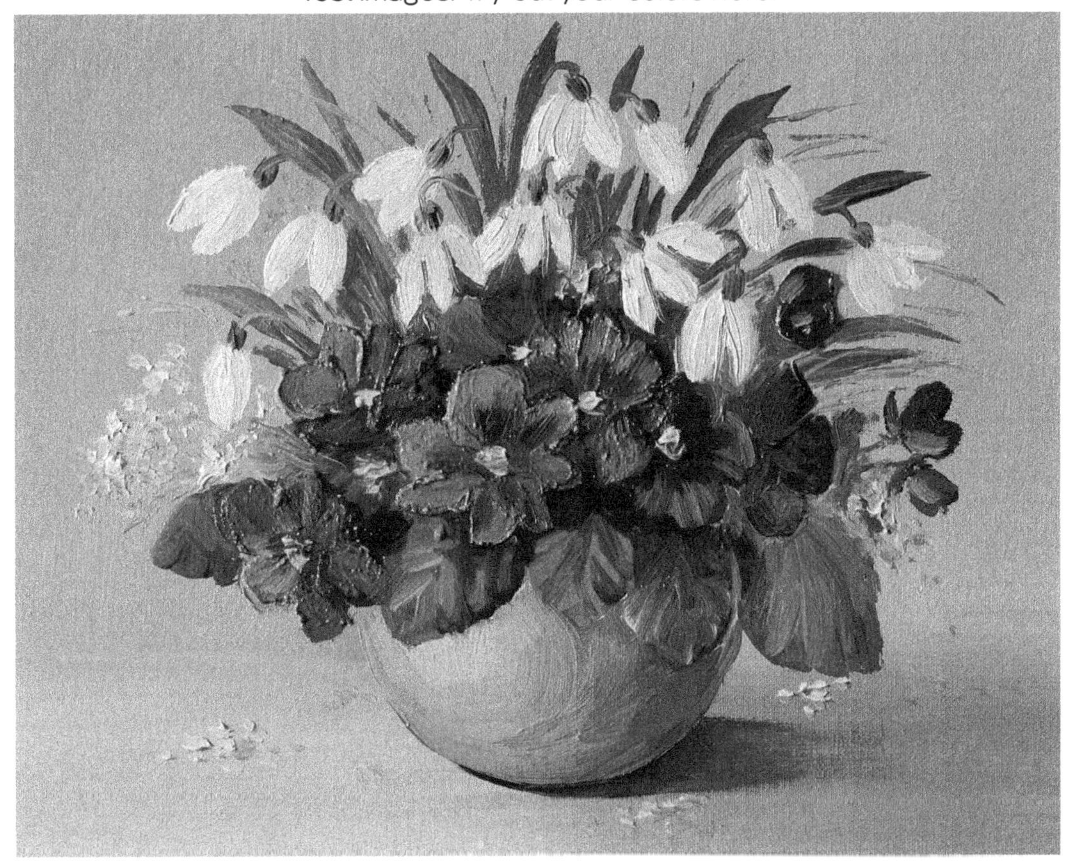

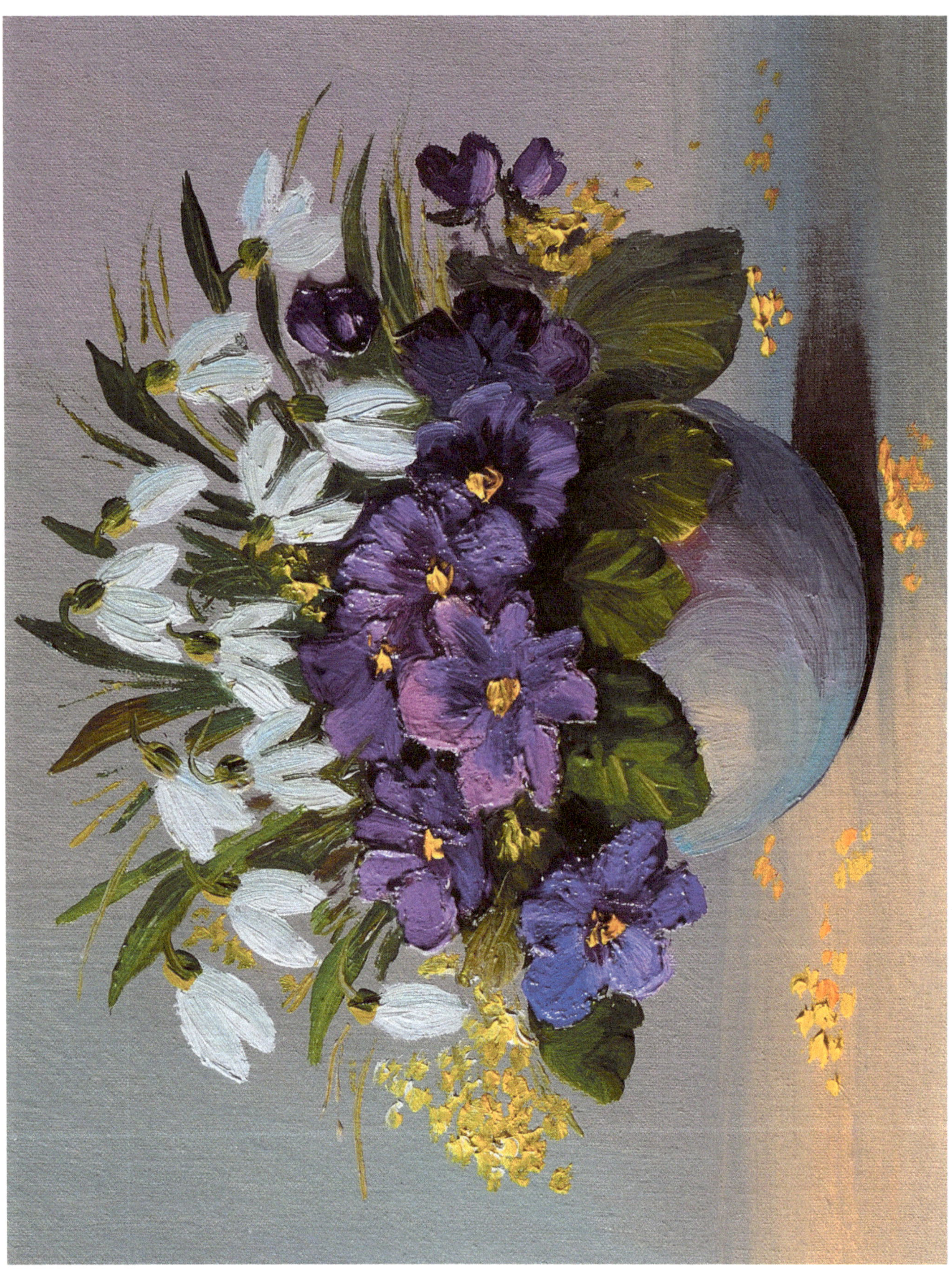

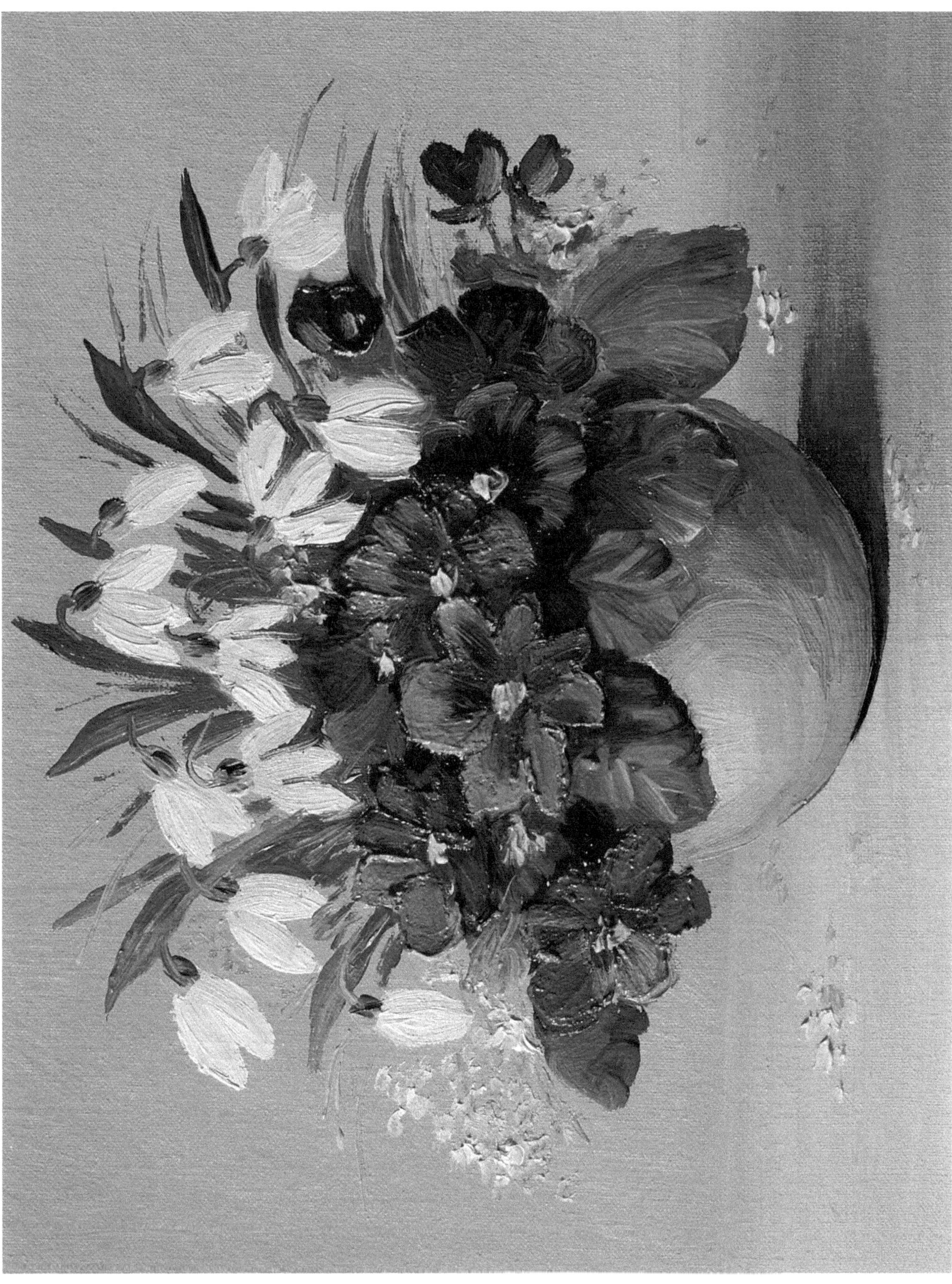

Colored By ______________________ Date ______________________

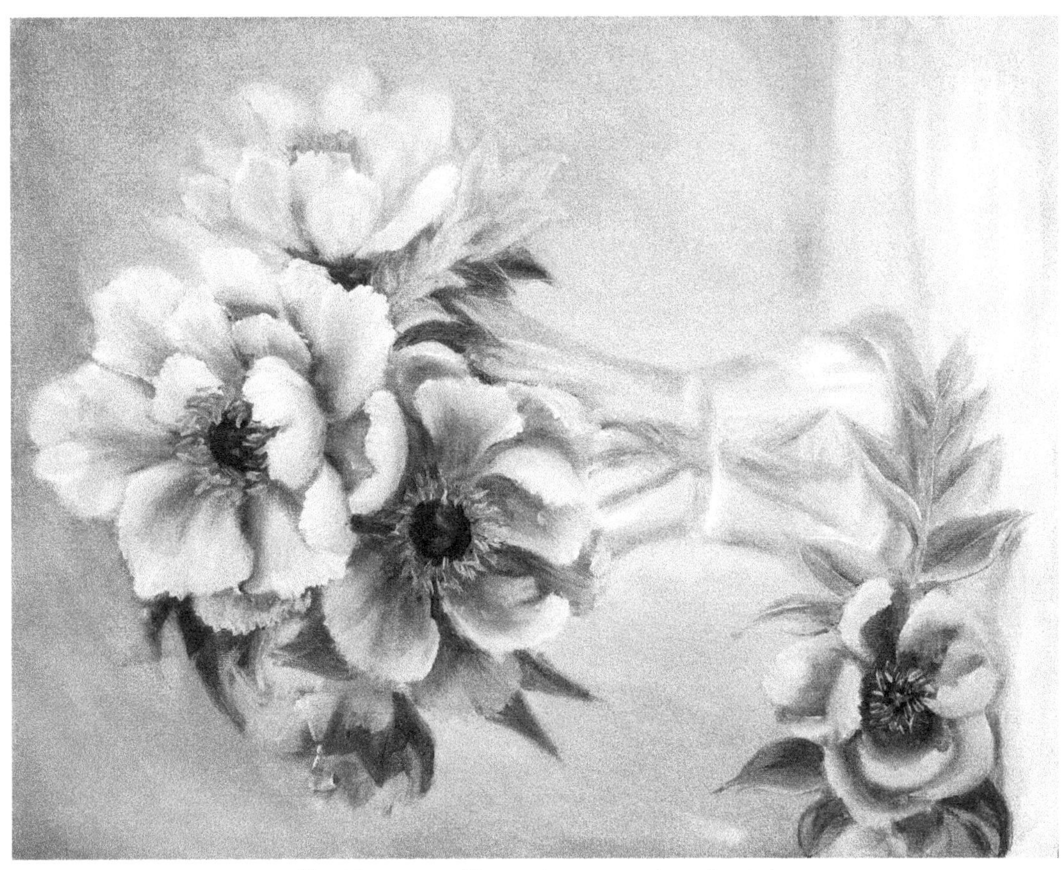

Test Images: Try out your colors here!

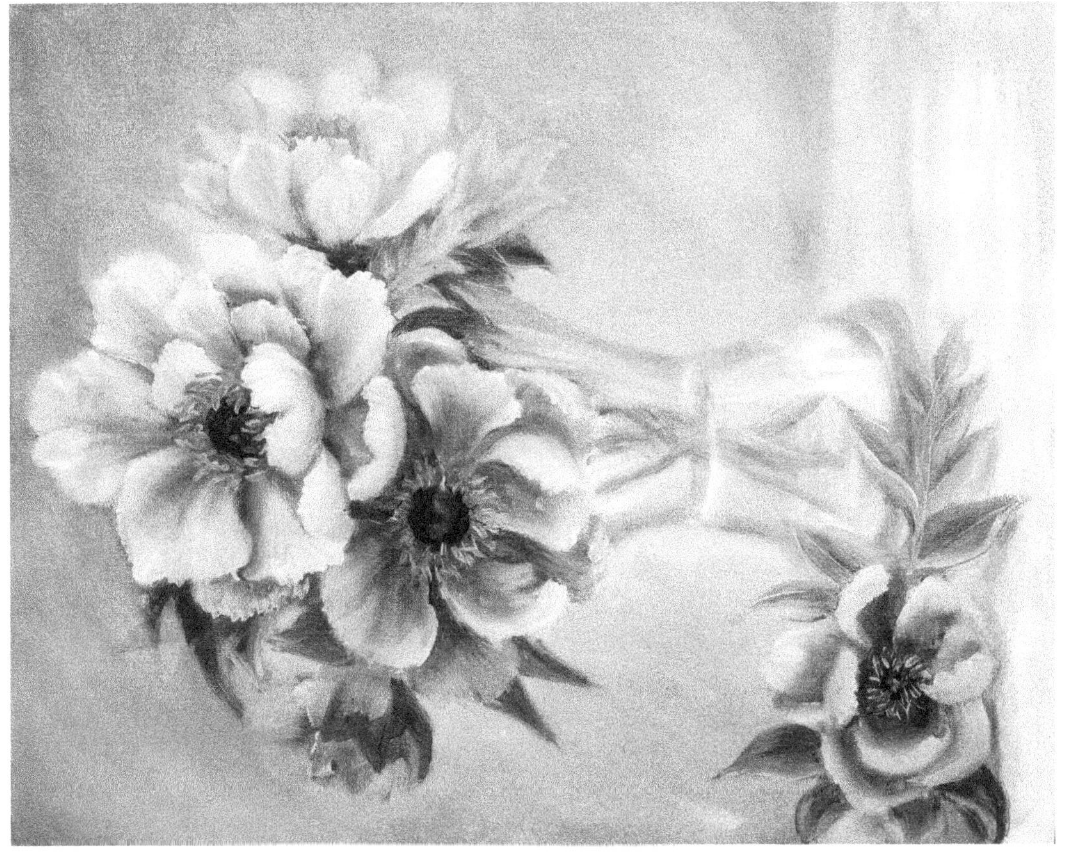

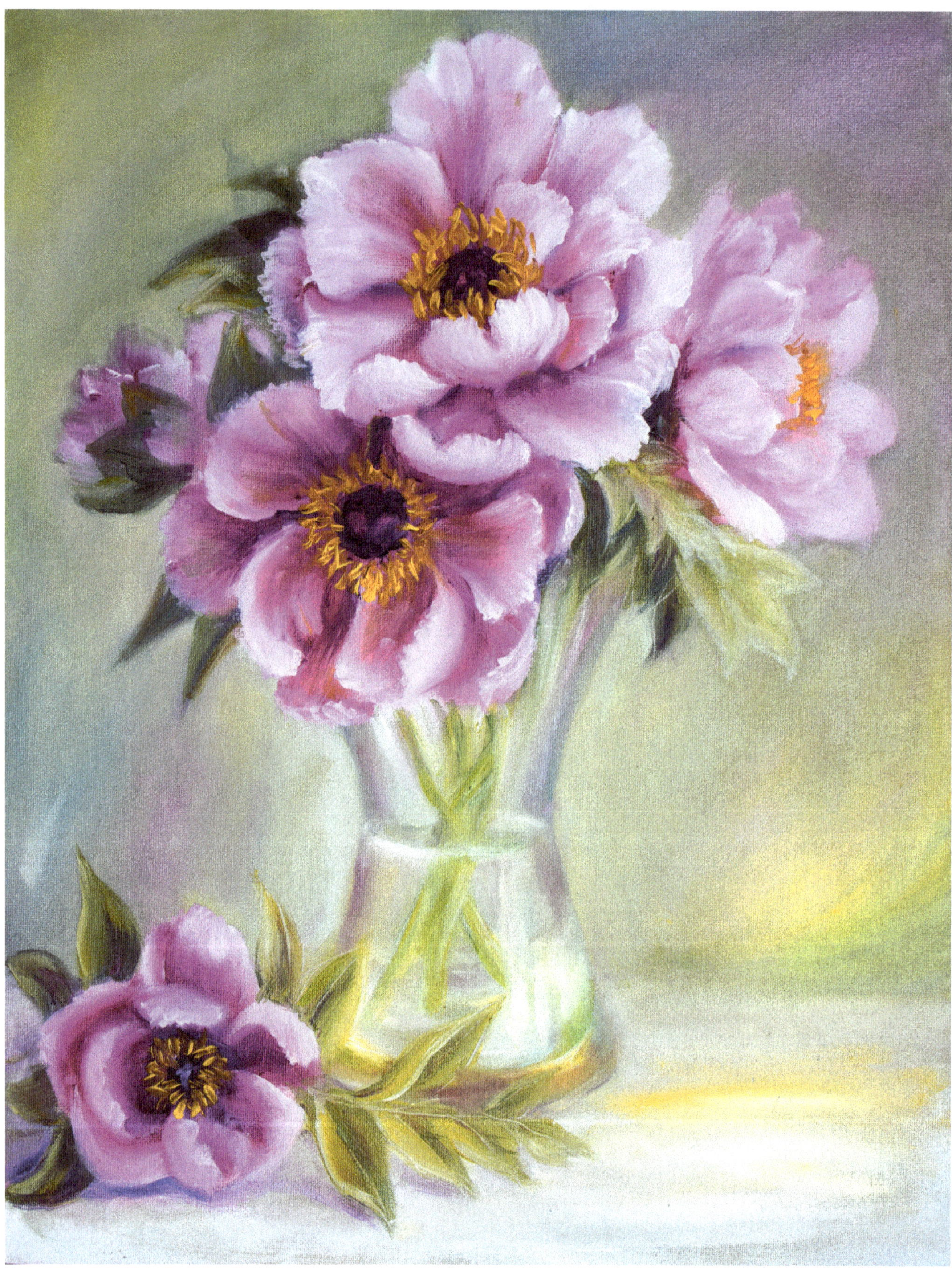

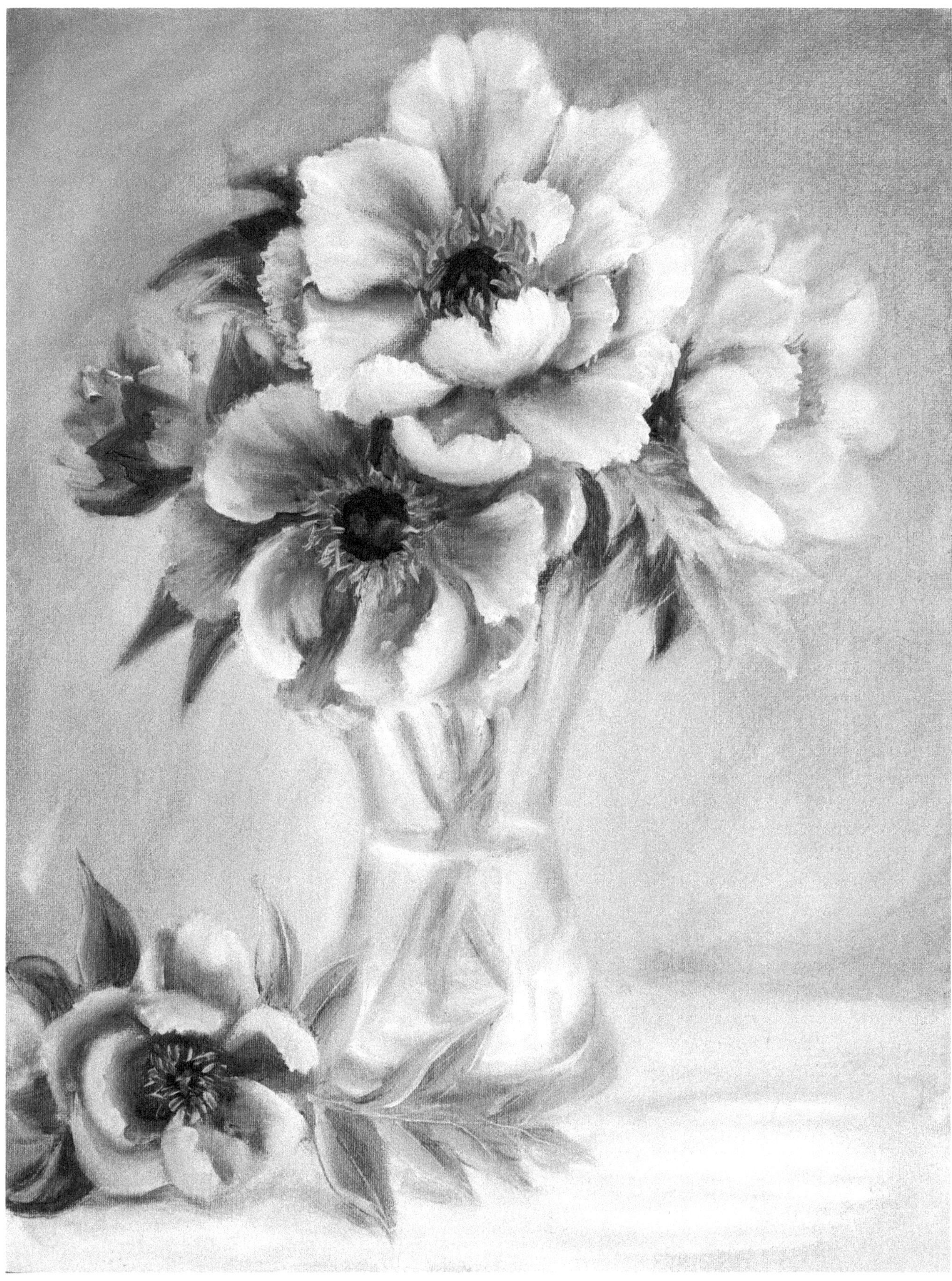

COLORED BY ____

DATE ____

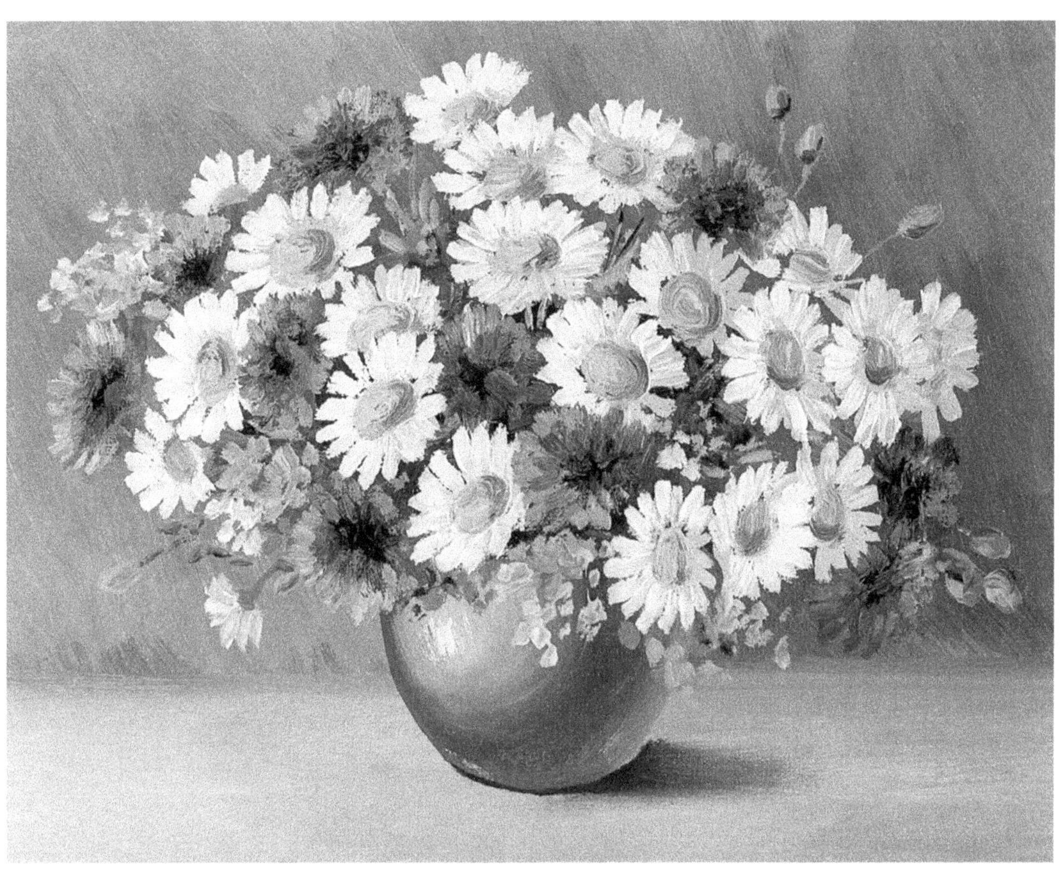

Test Images: Try out your colors here!

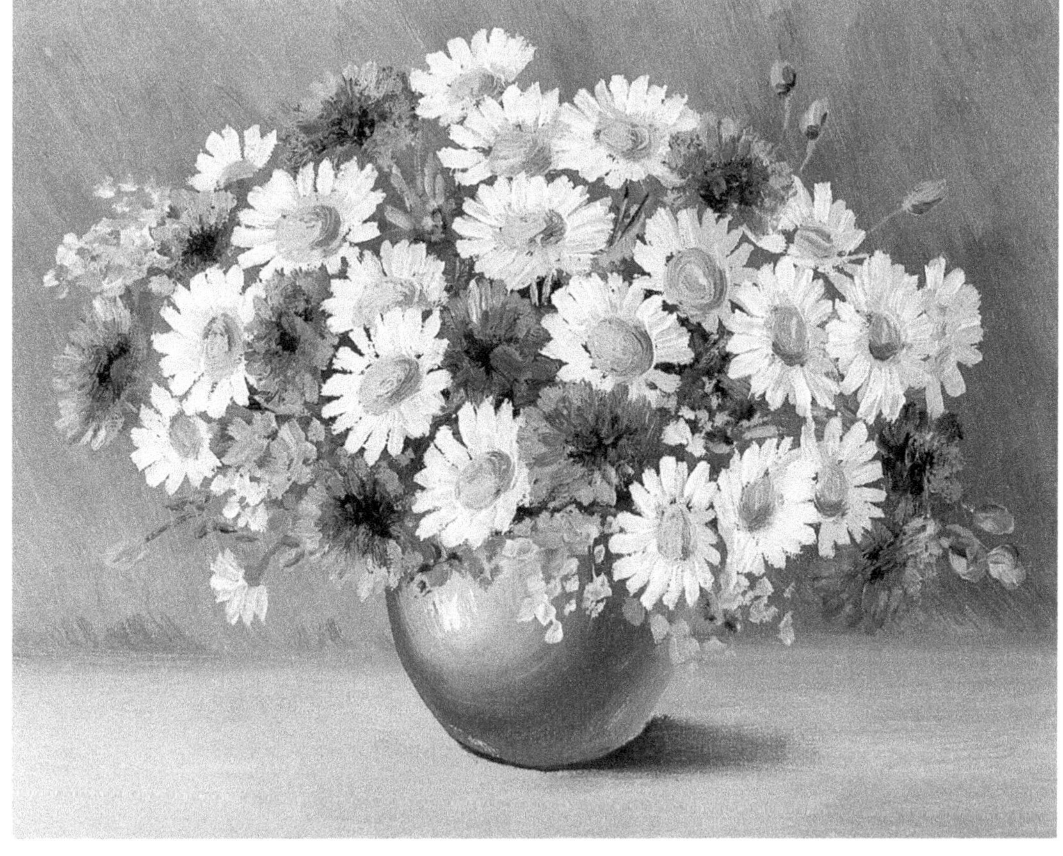

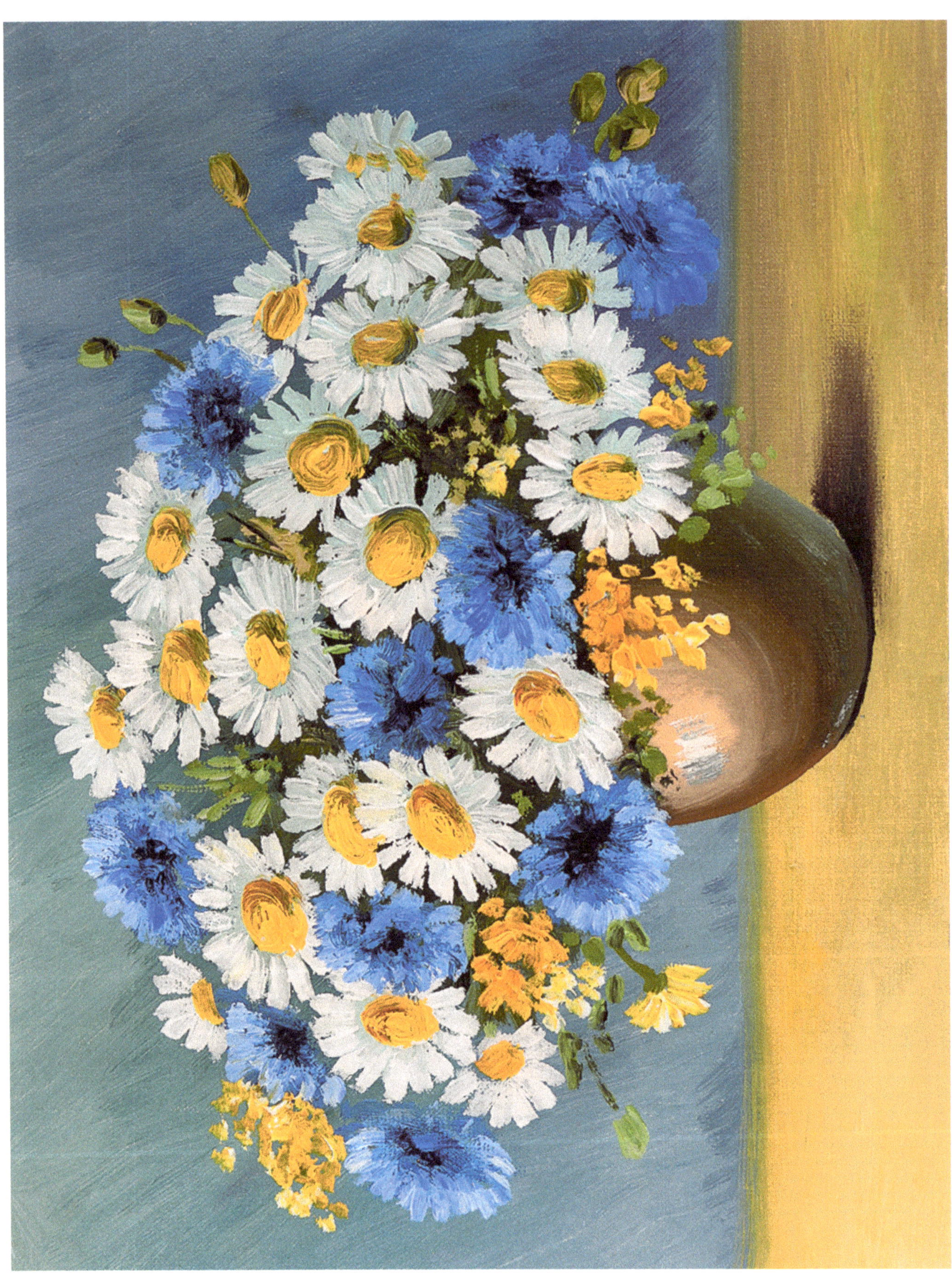

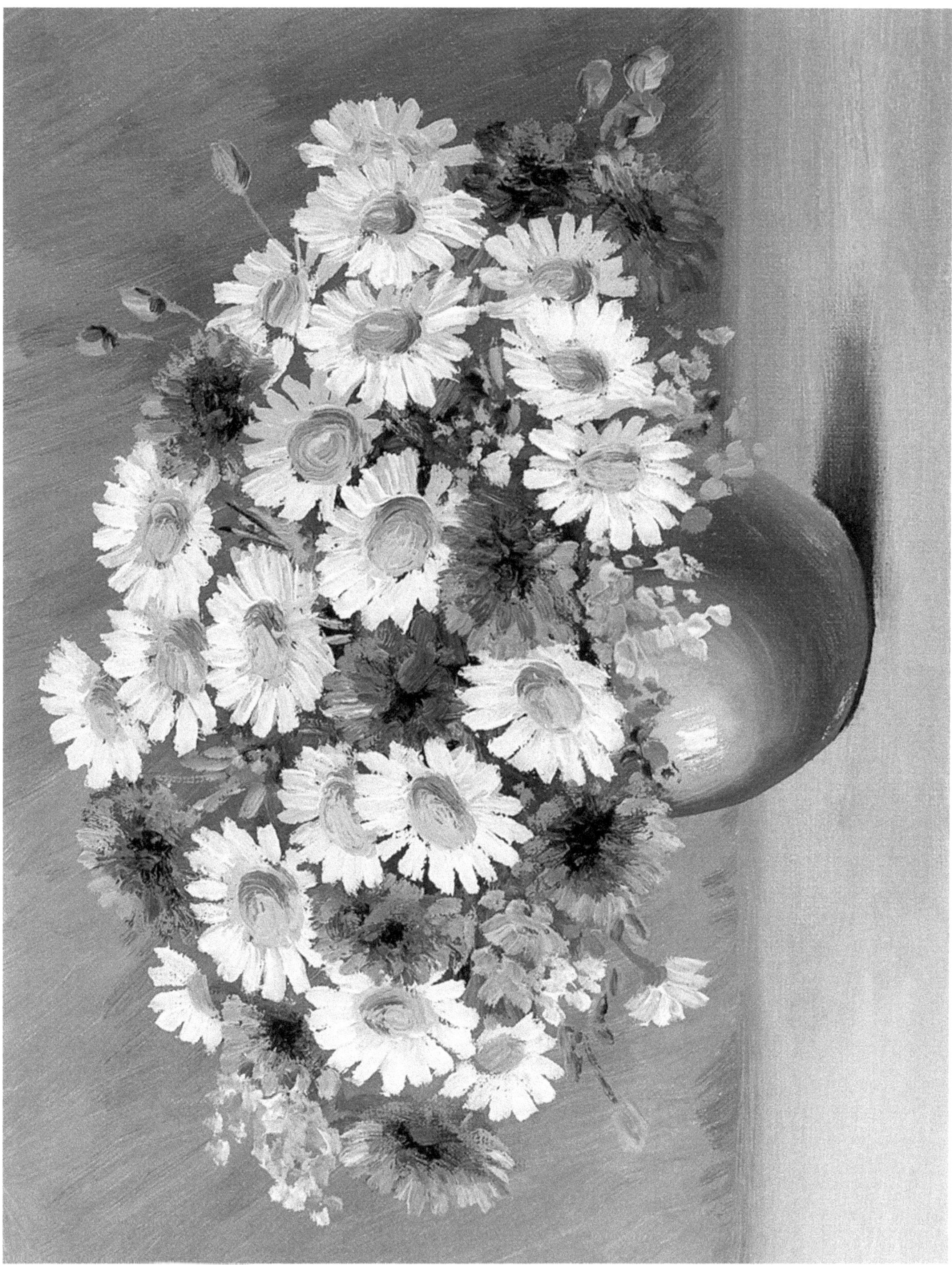

COLORED BY ______________________________ DATE ______________________

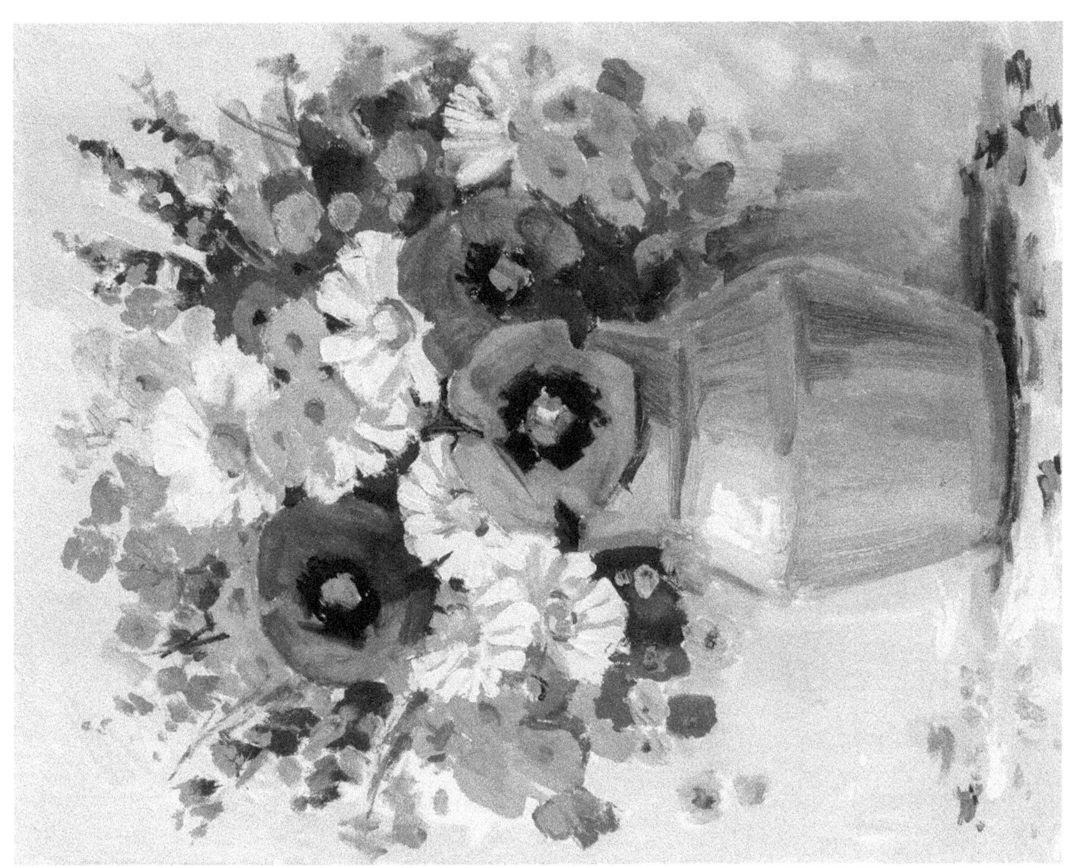

Test Images: Try out your colors here!

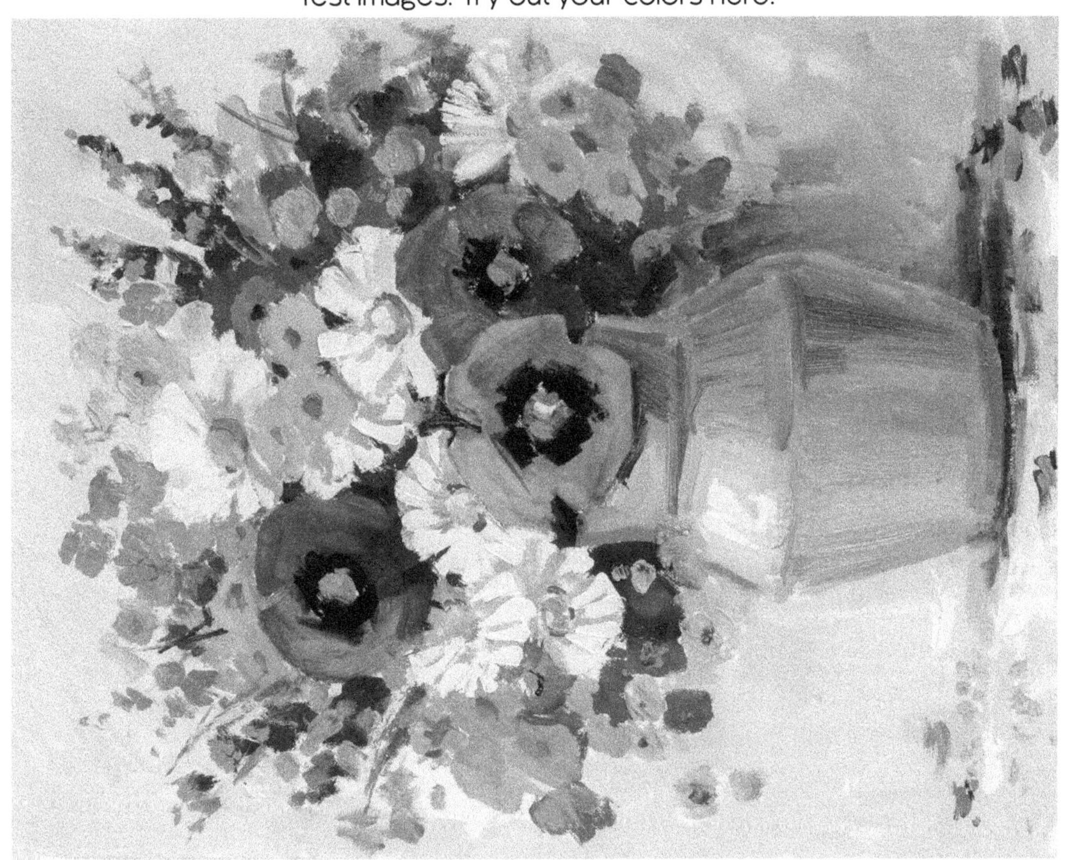

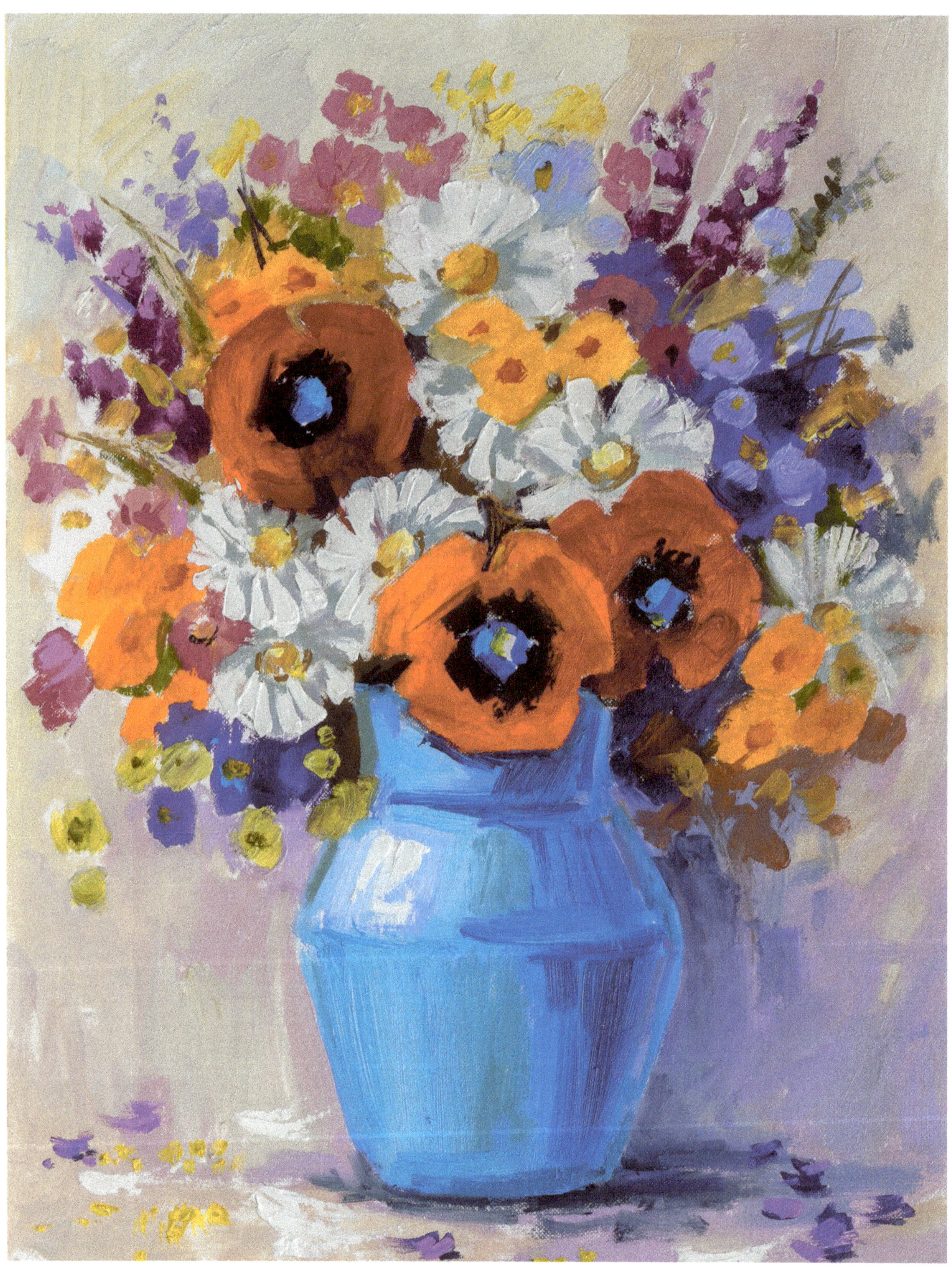

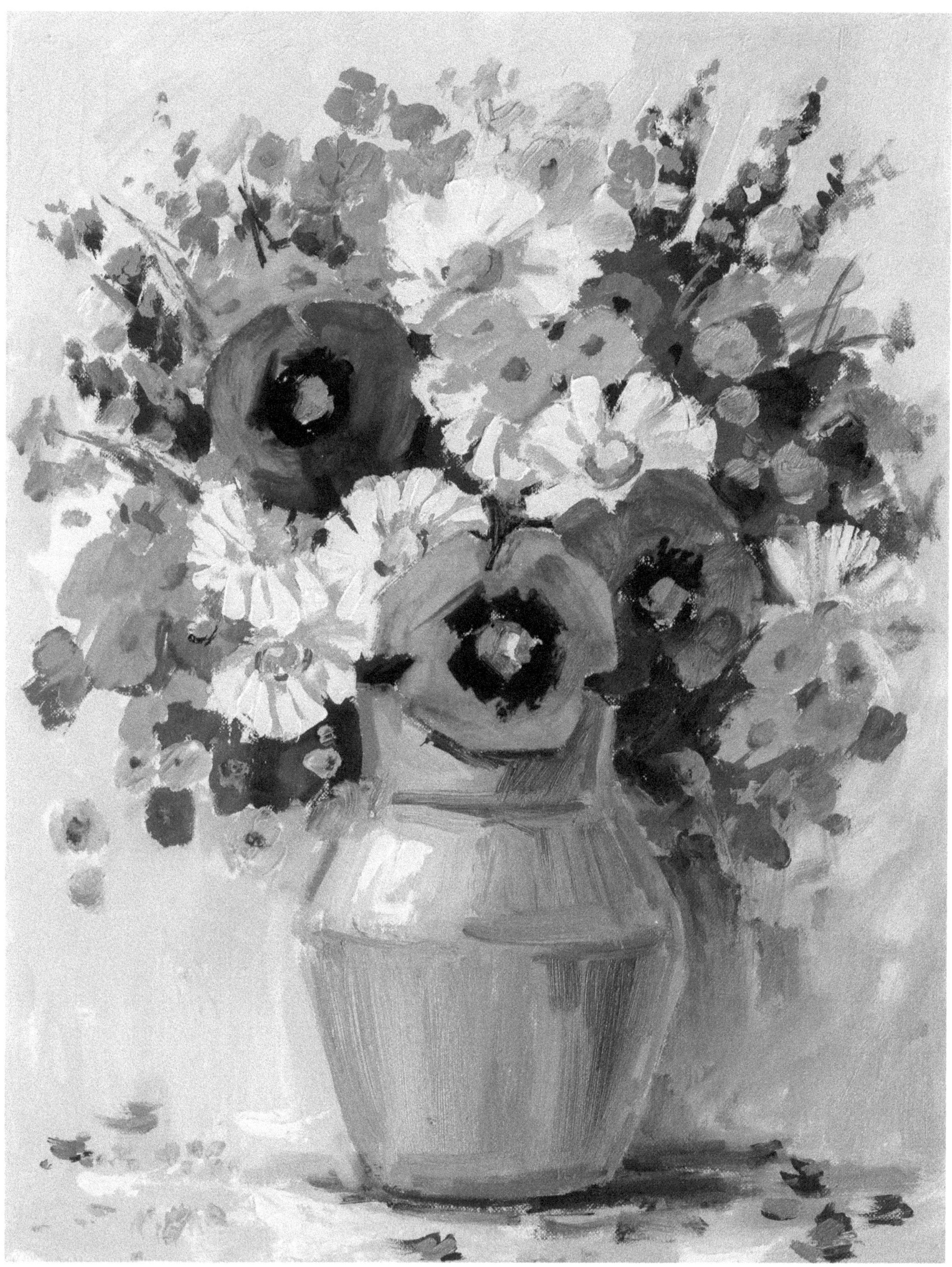

COLORED BY ____

DATE ____

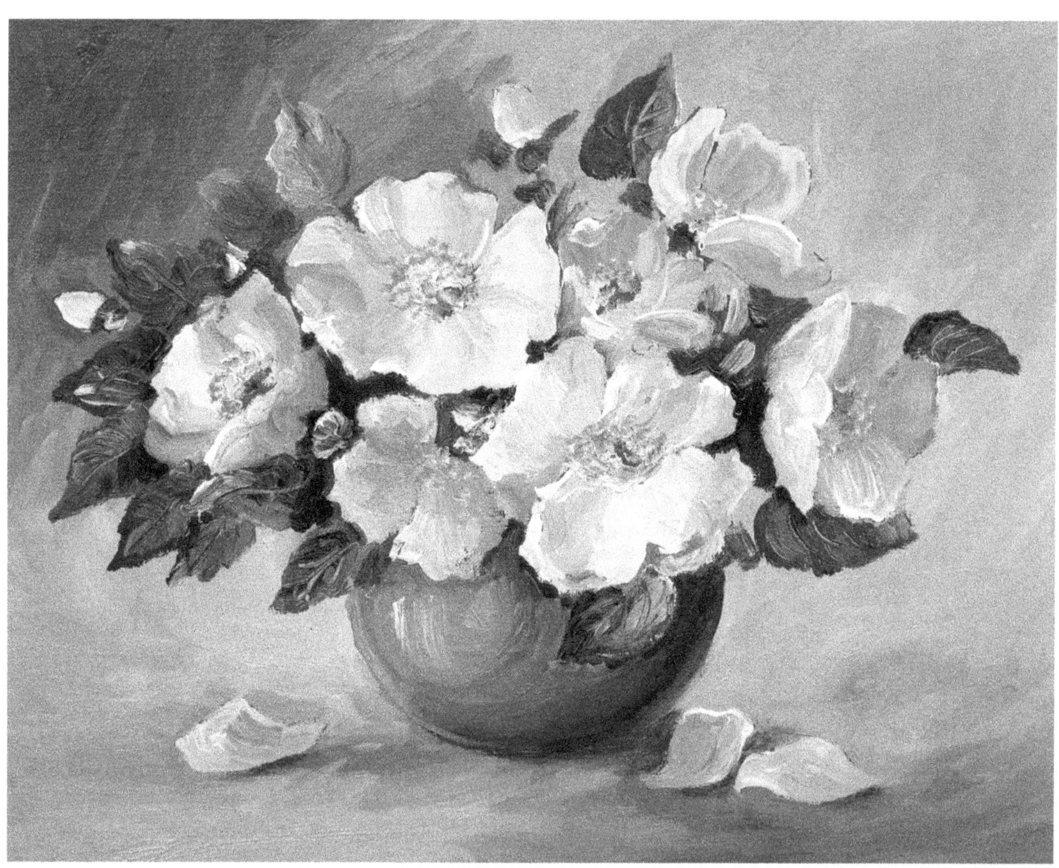

Test Images: Try out your colors here!

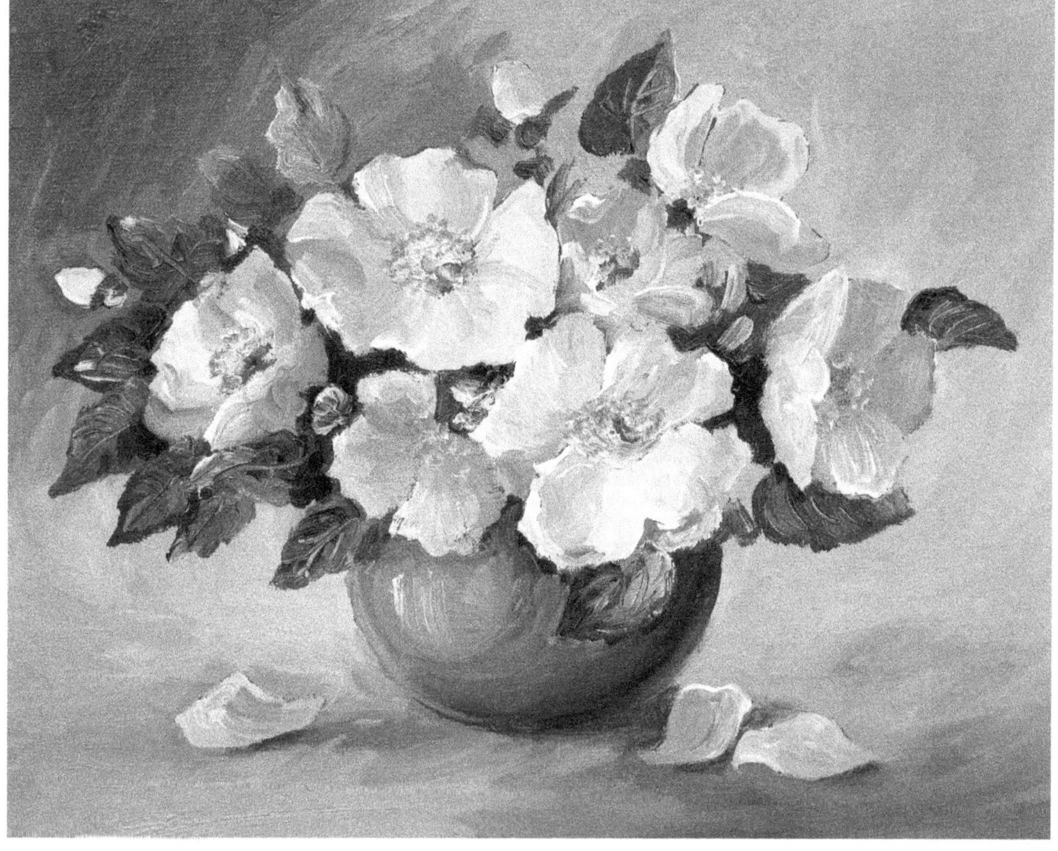

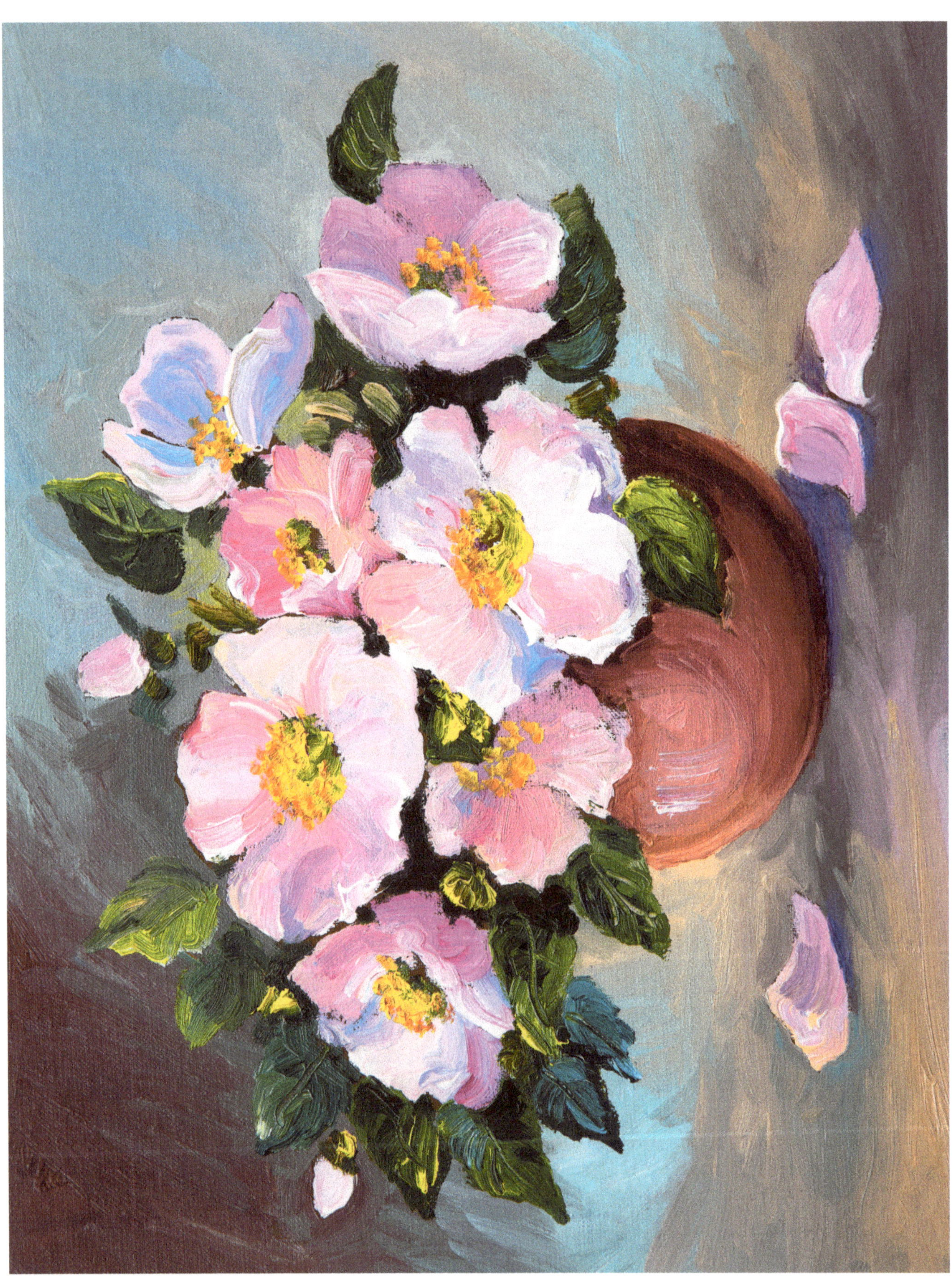

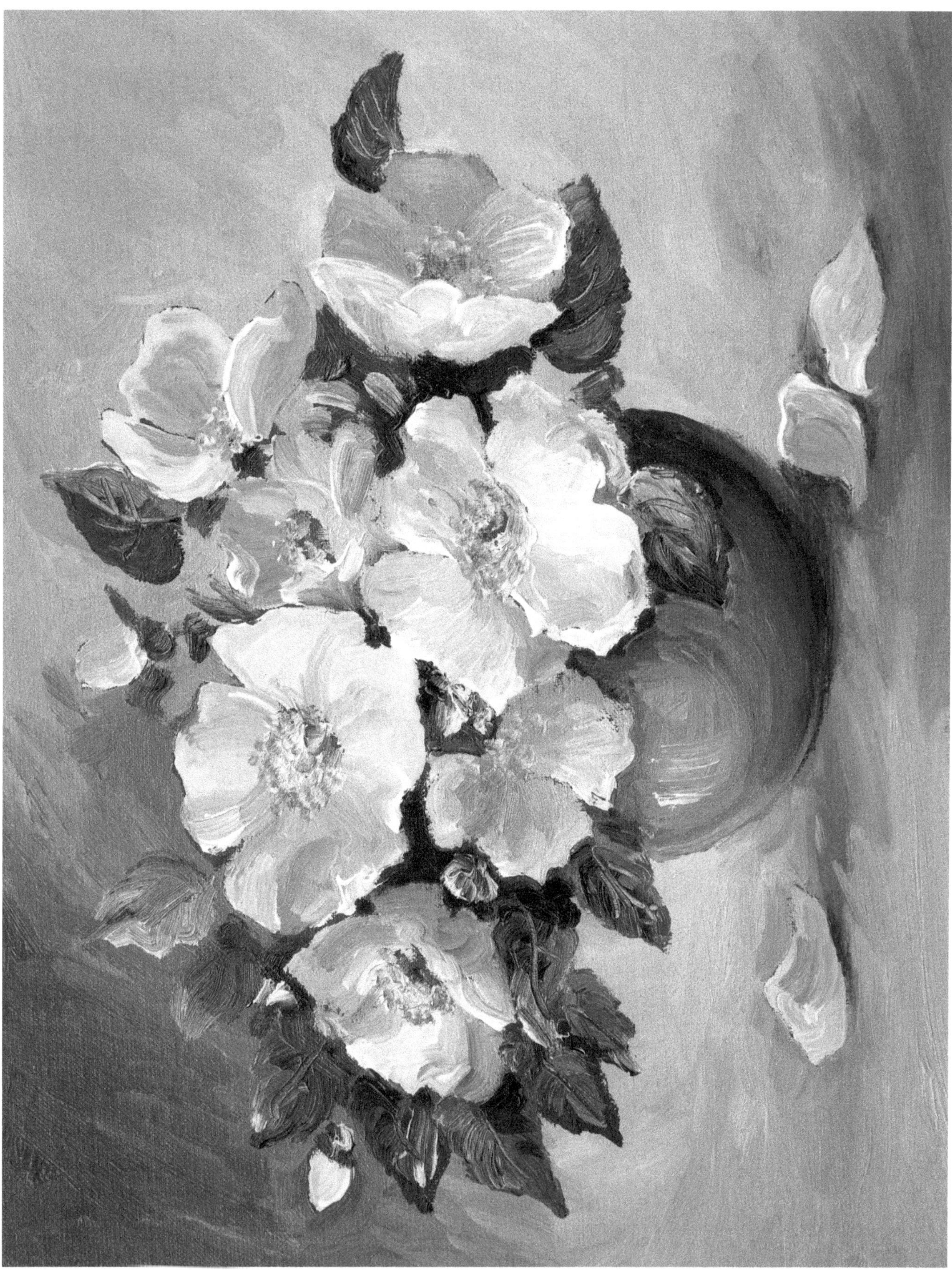

Colored By ______________________________ Date ______________________

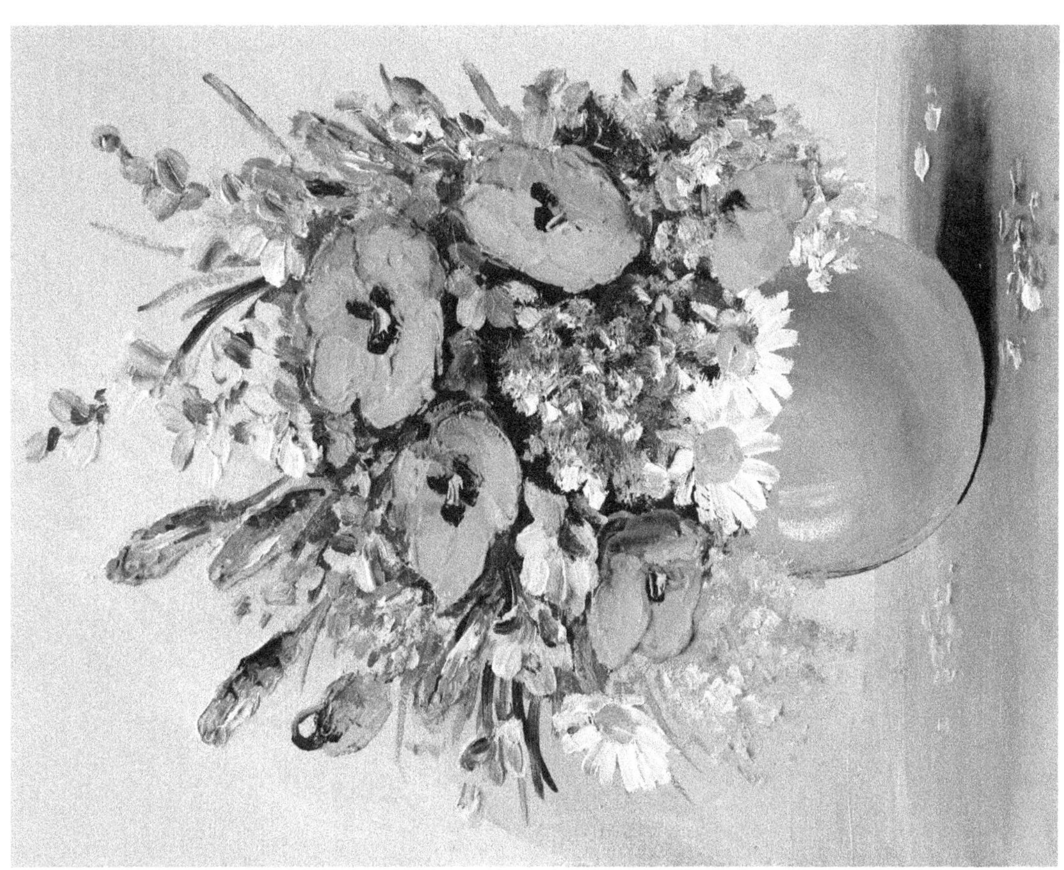

Test Images: Try out your colors here!

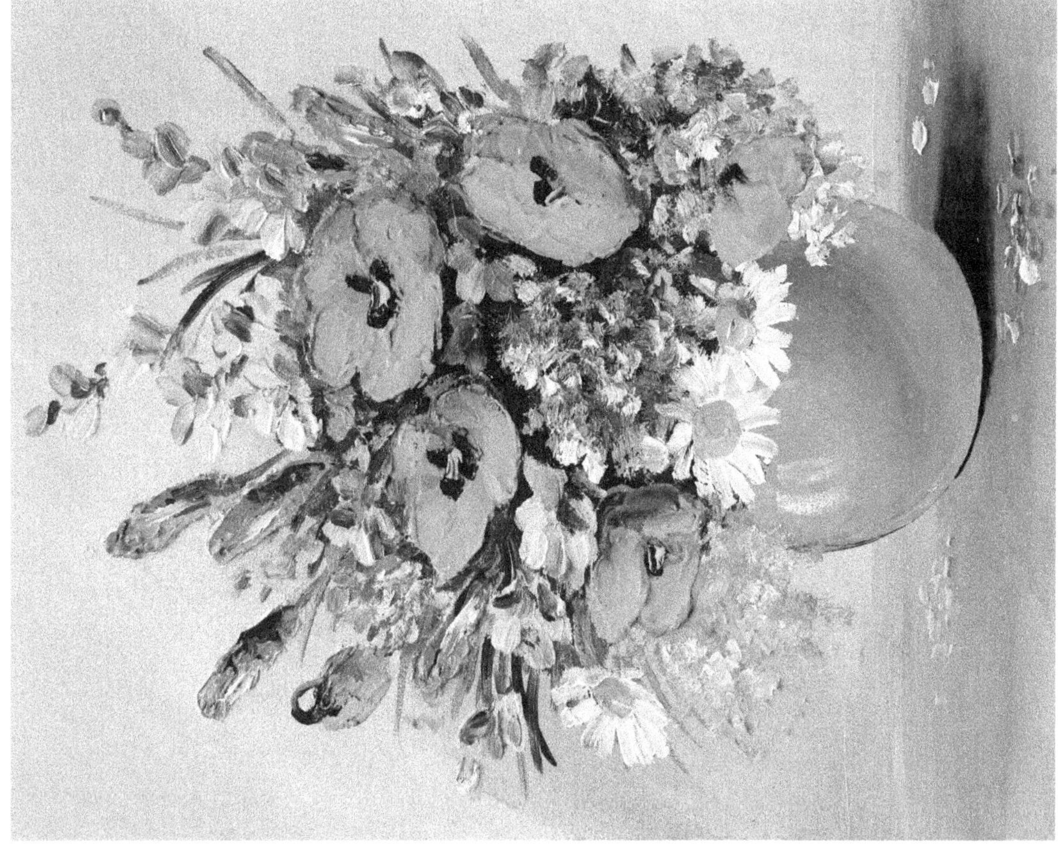

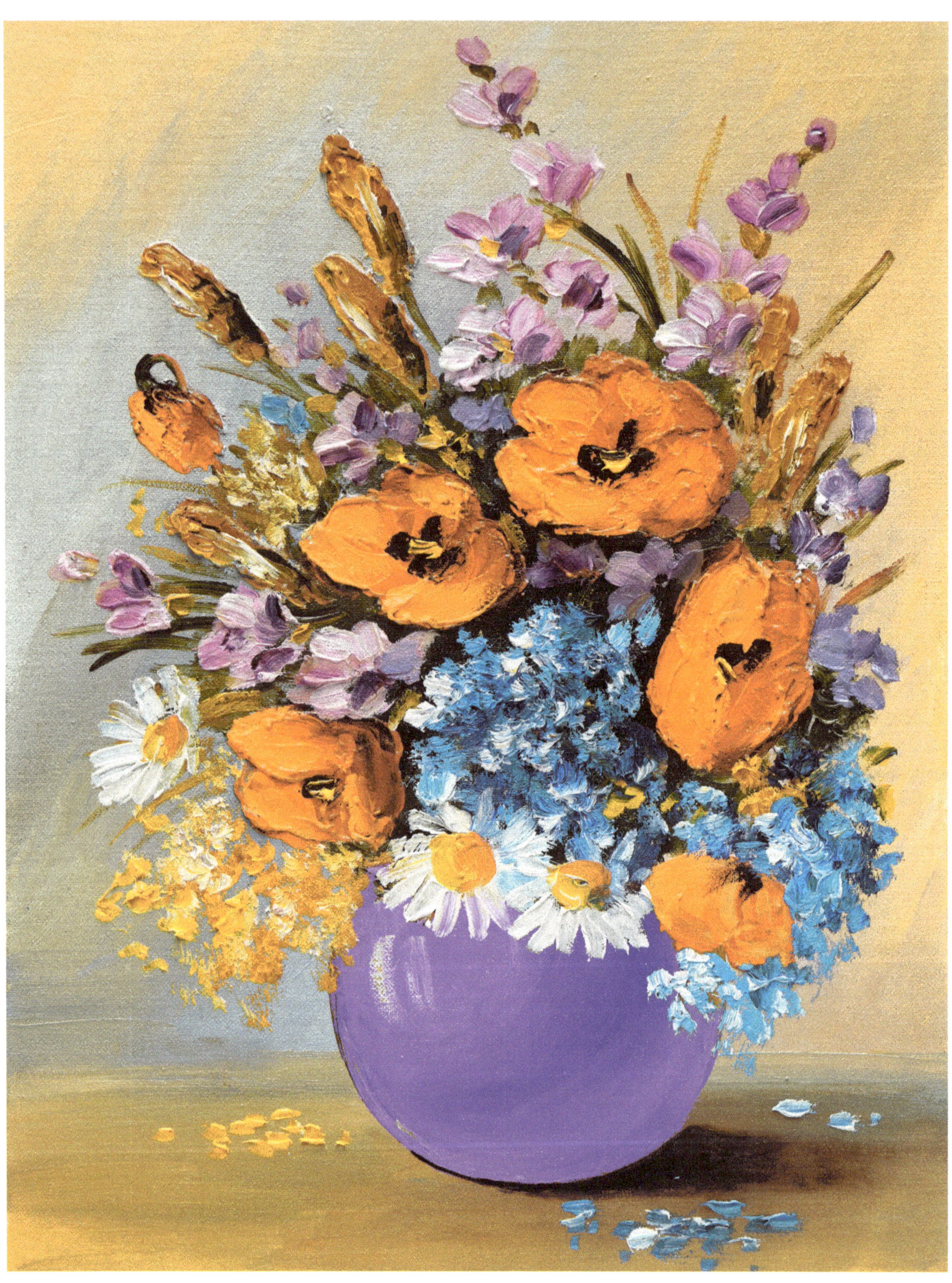

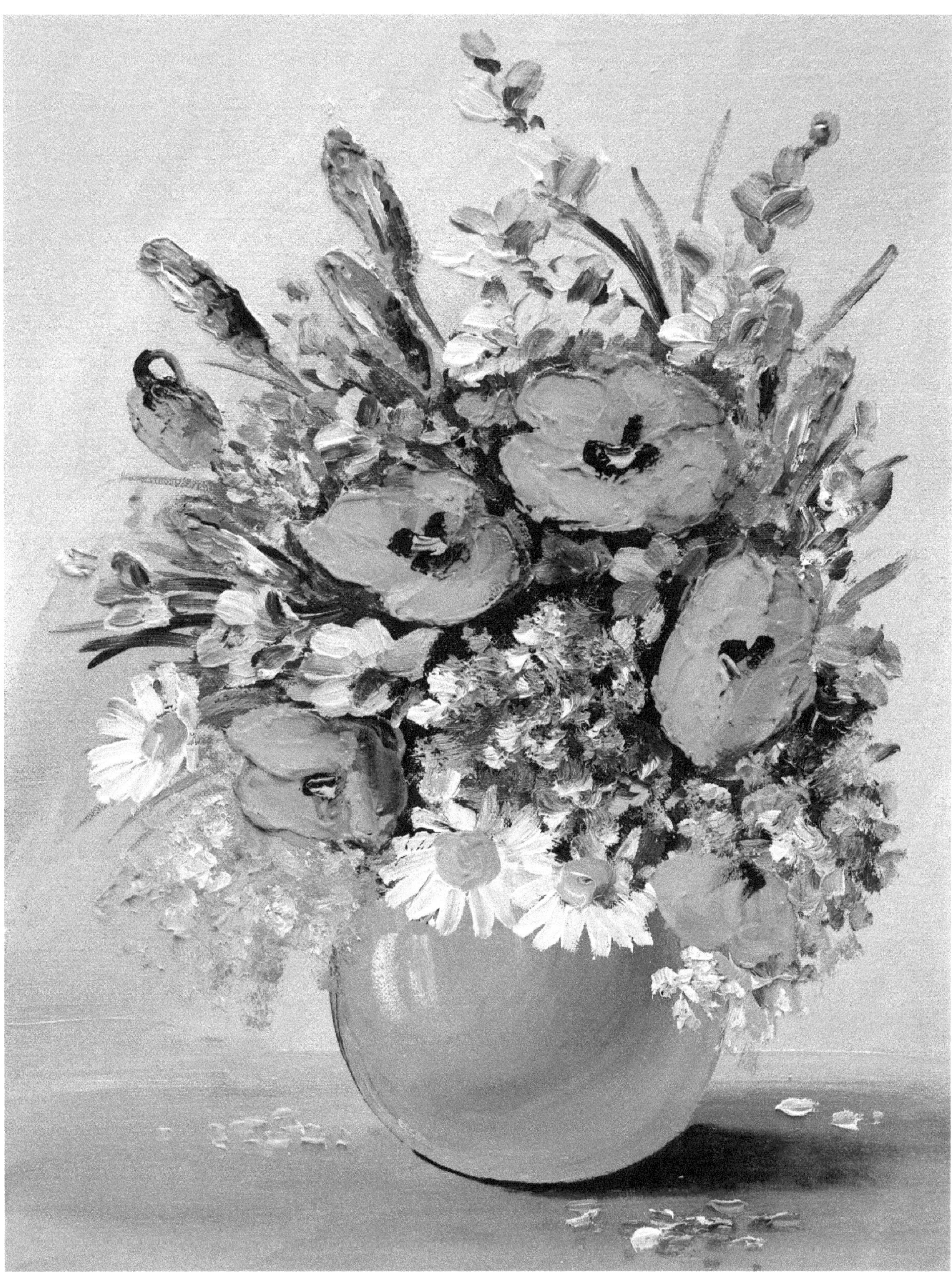

Colored By ____

Date ____

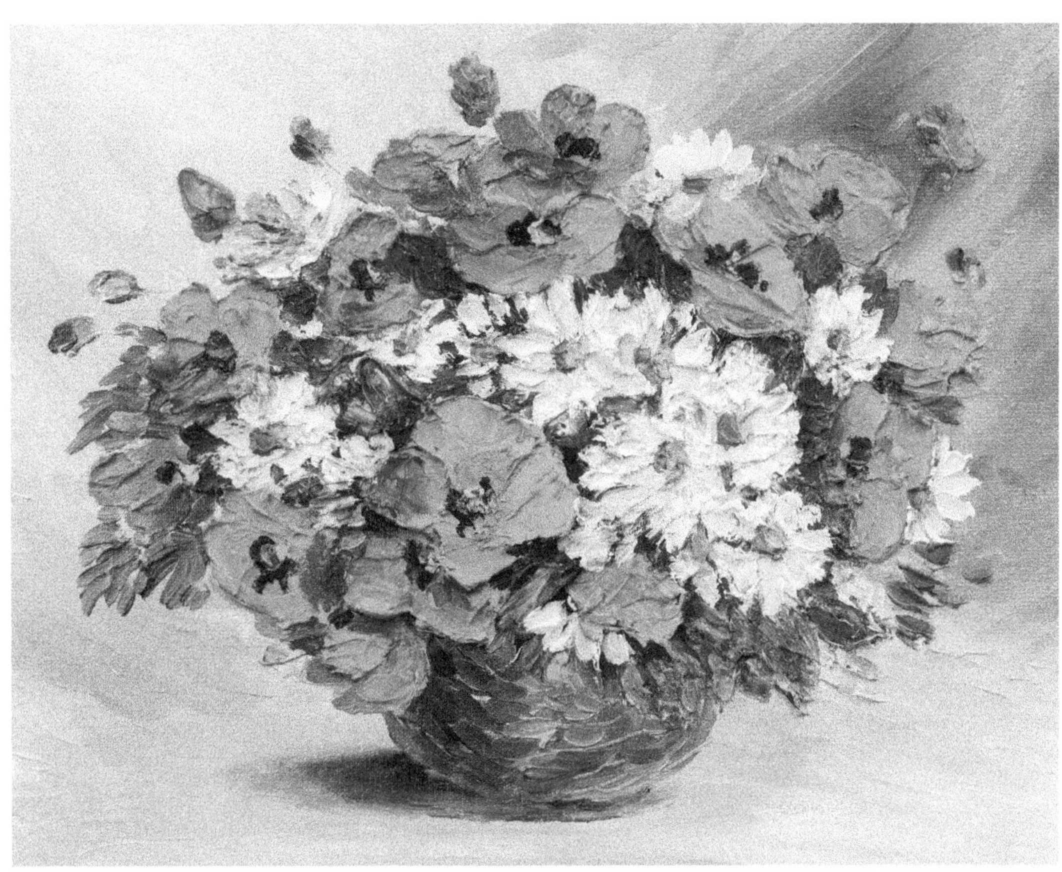

Test Images: Try out your colors here!

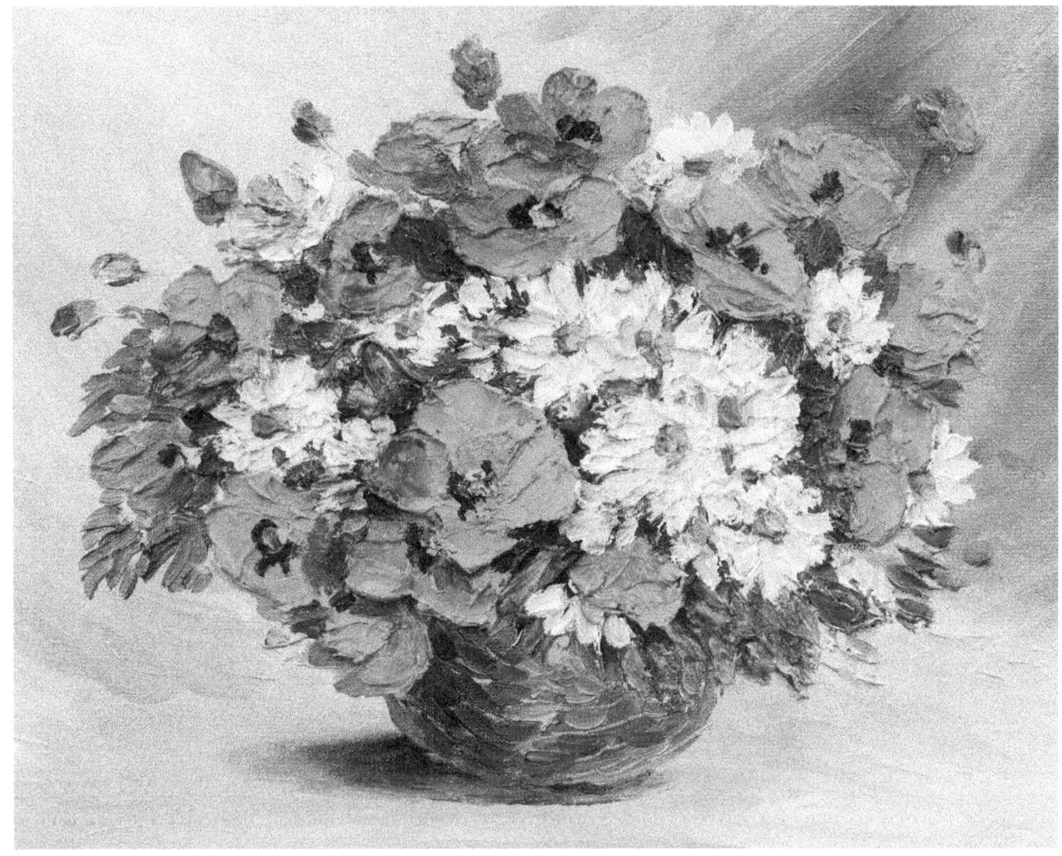

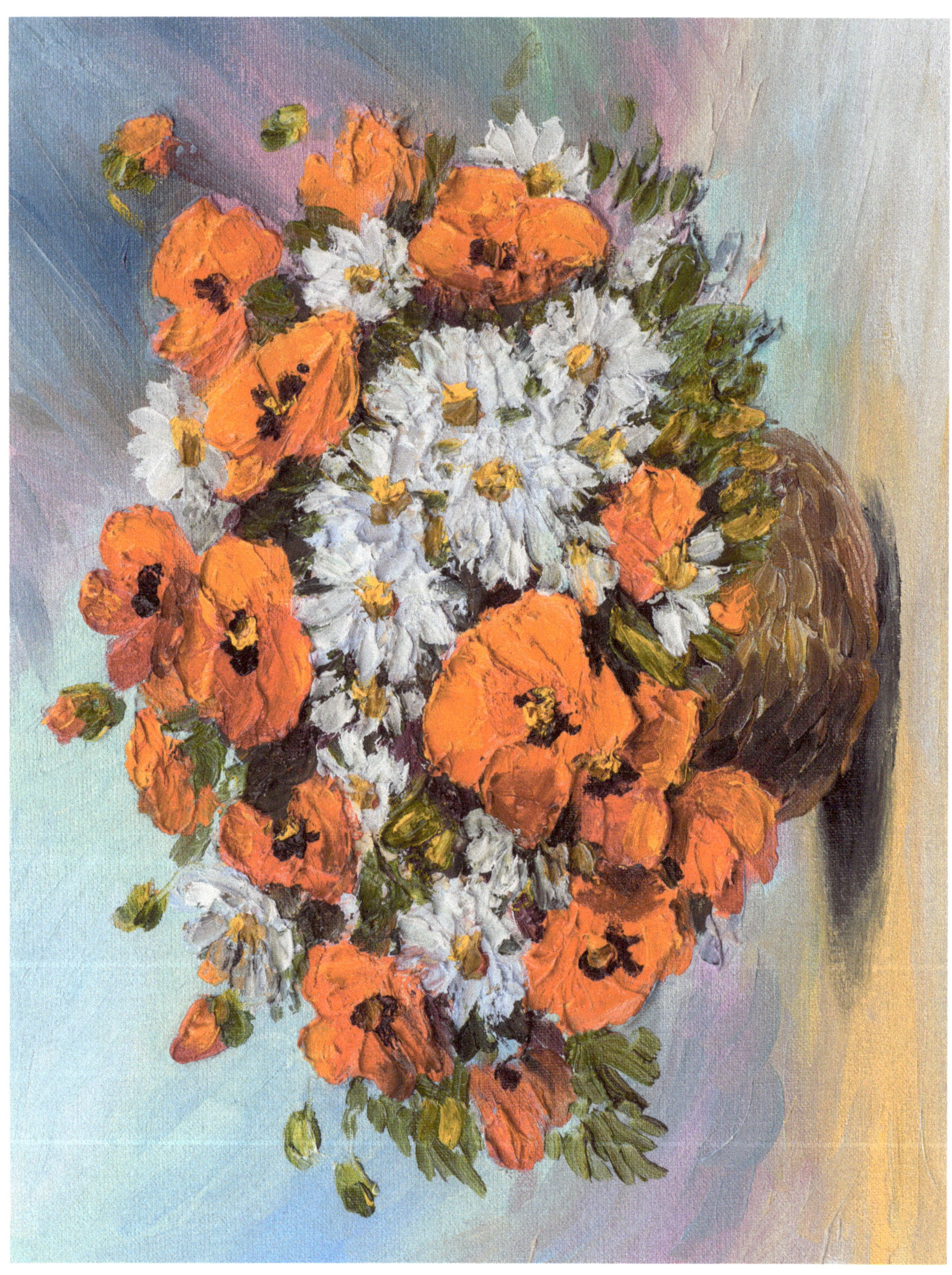

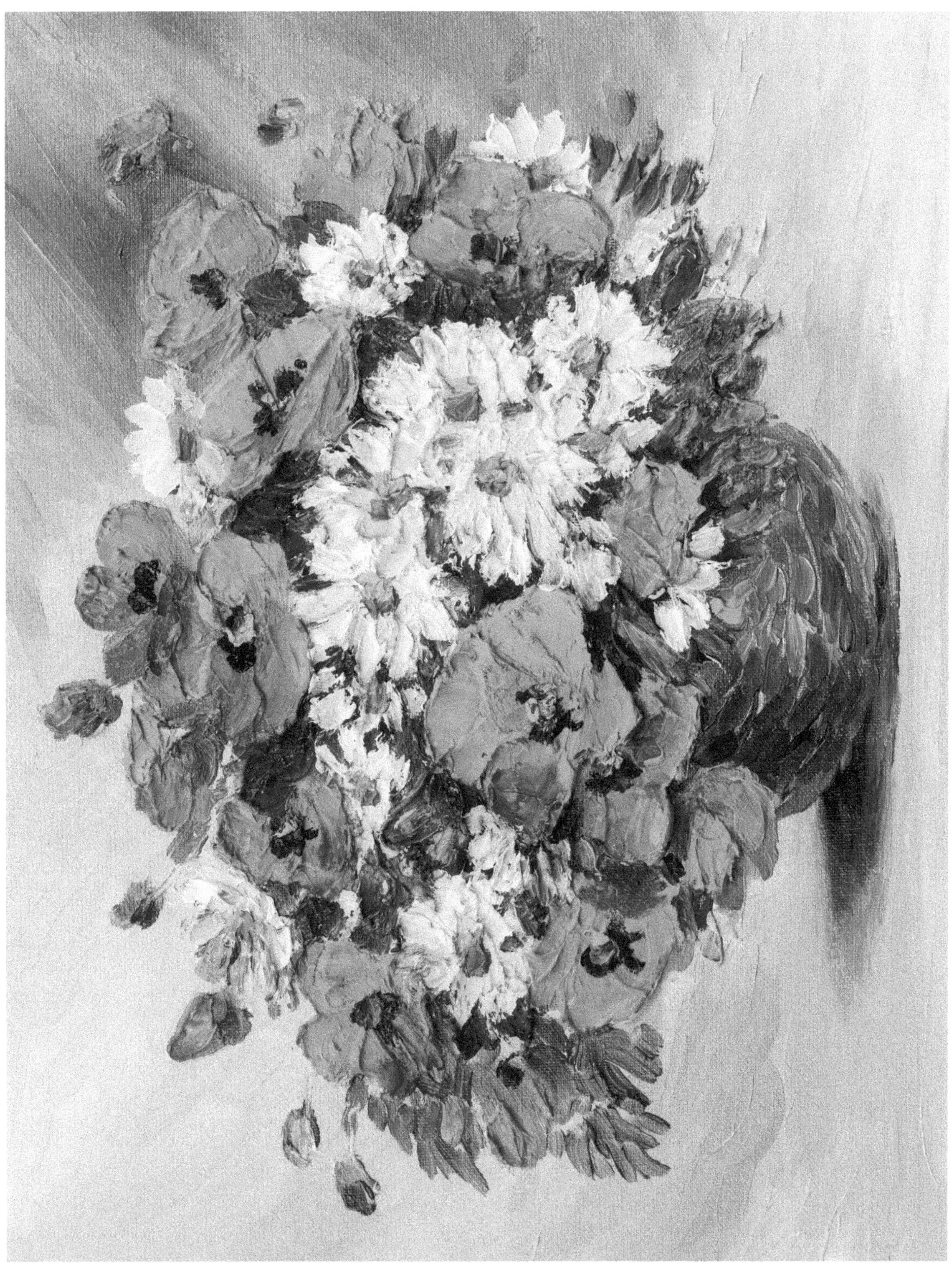

Colored By ______________________________ Date ______________________

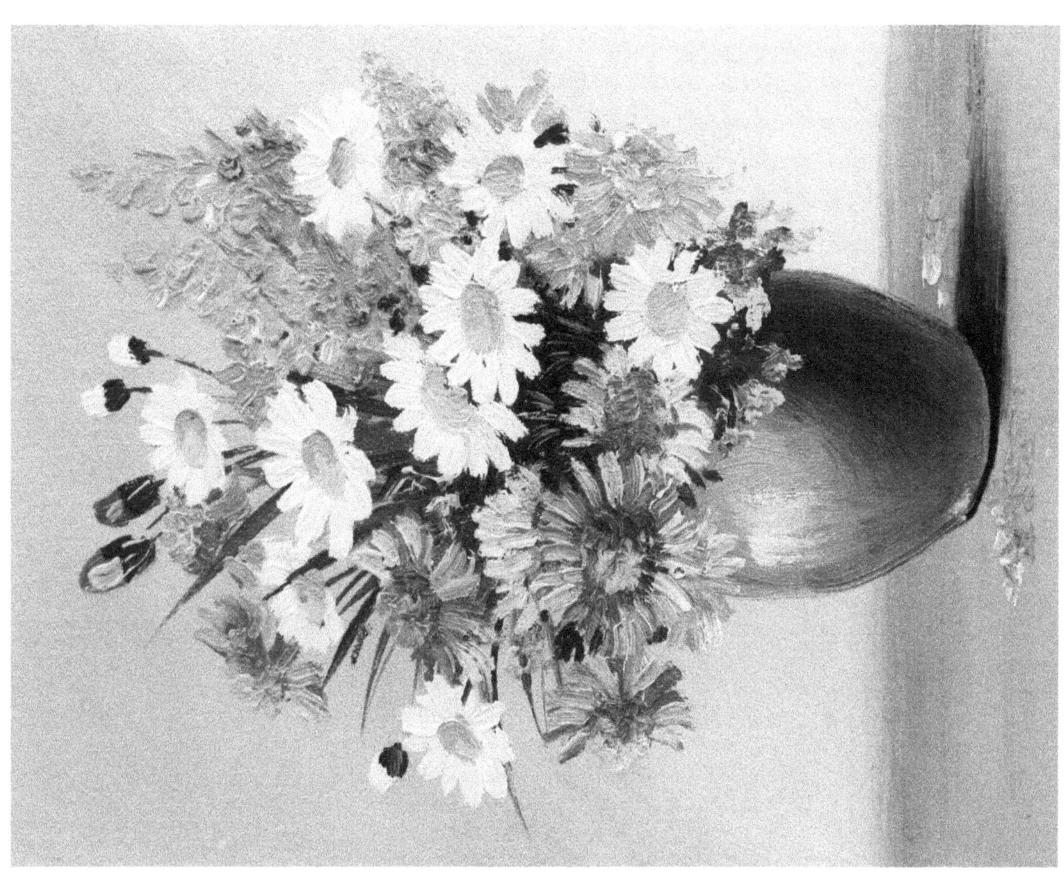

Test Images: Try out your colors here!

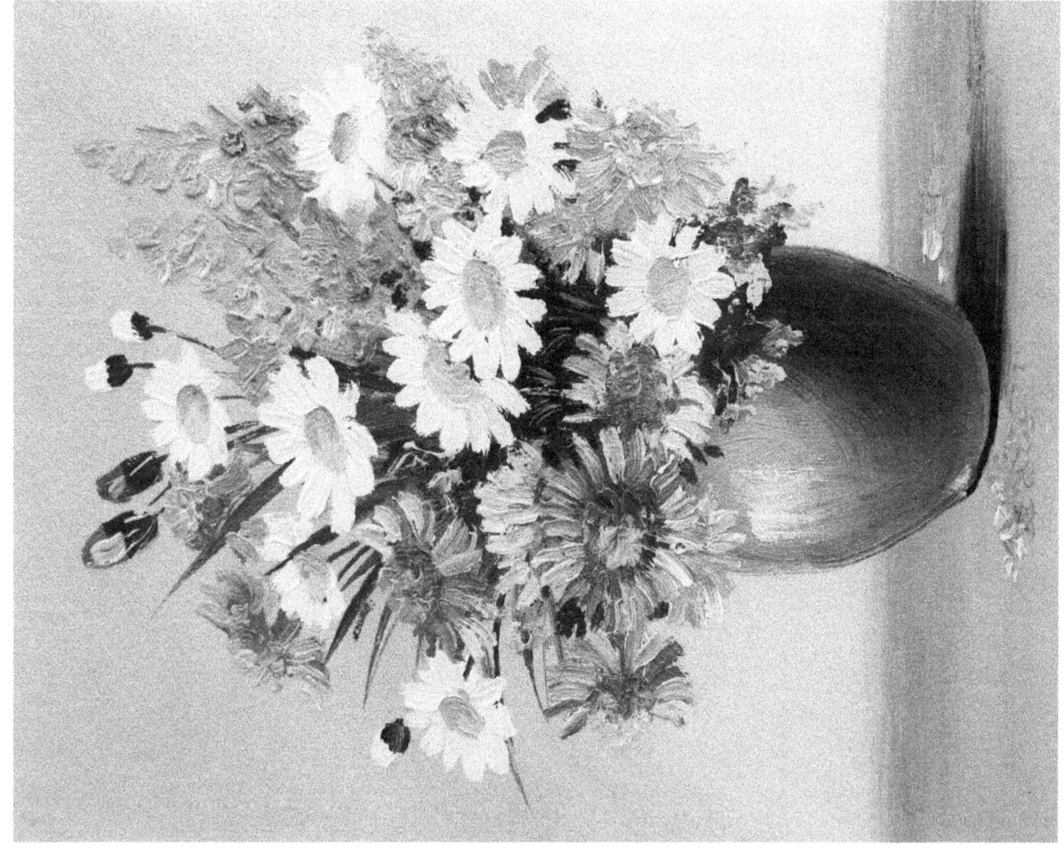

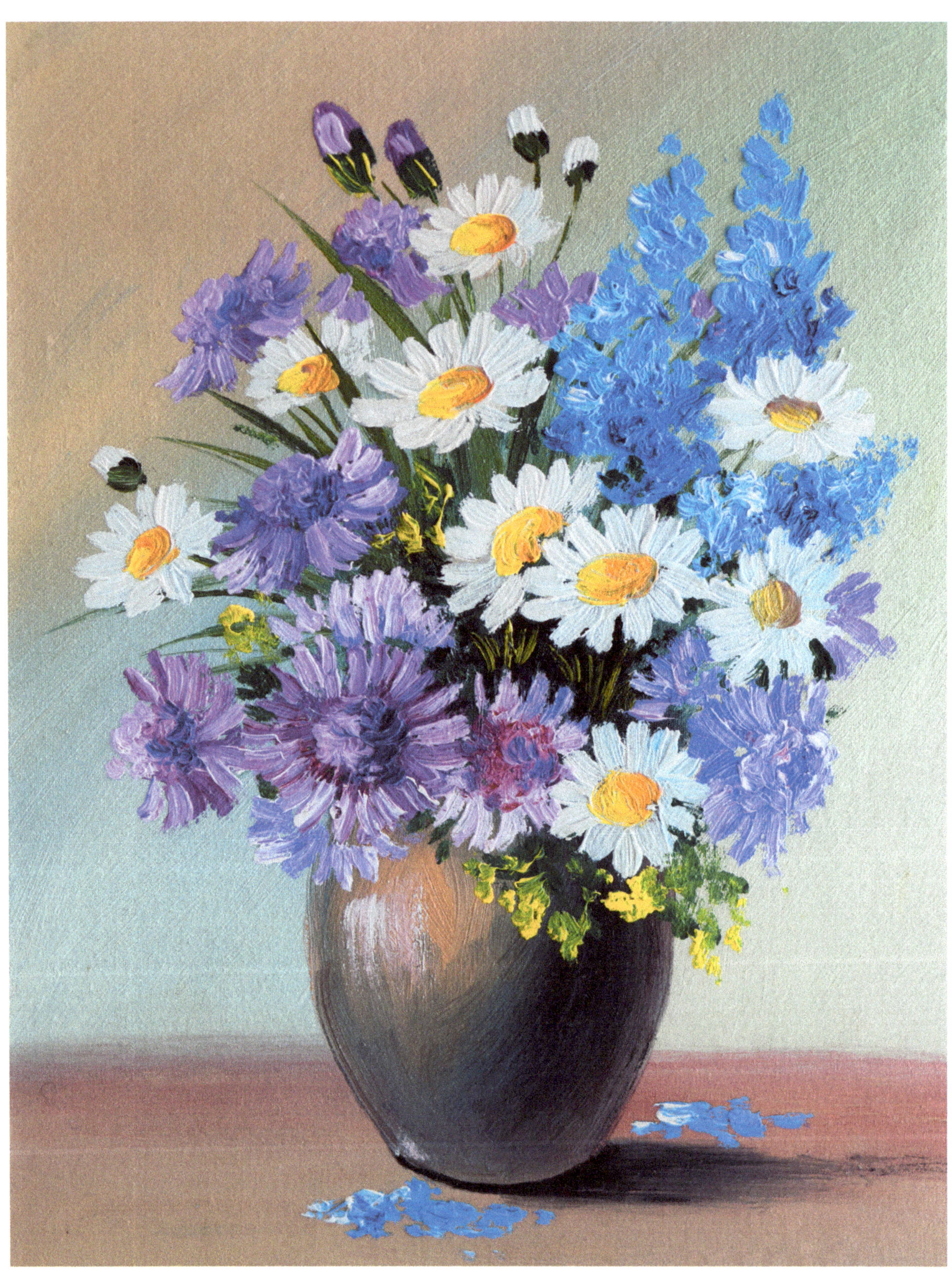

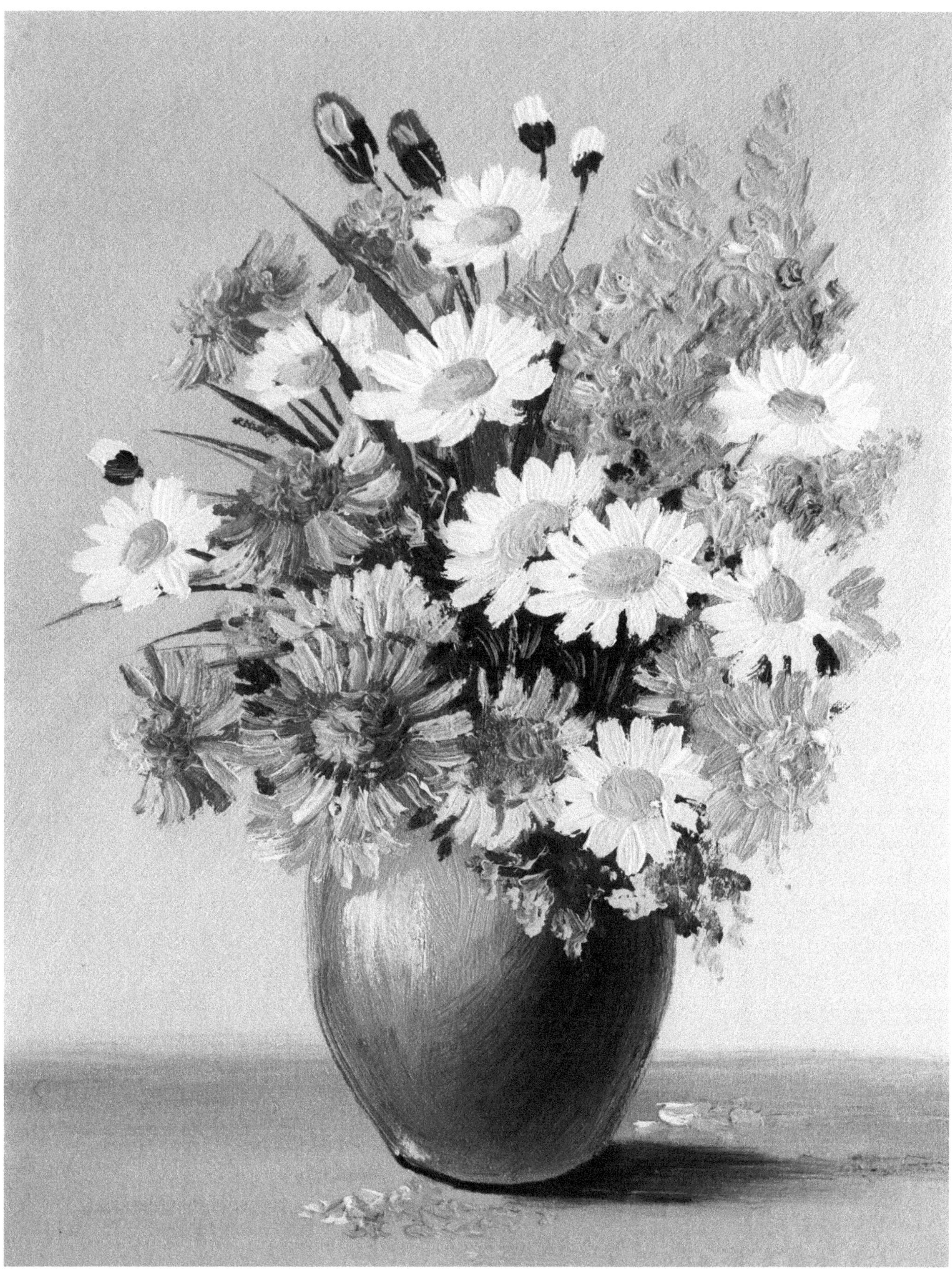

Colored By ____

Date ____

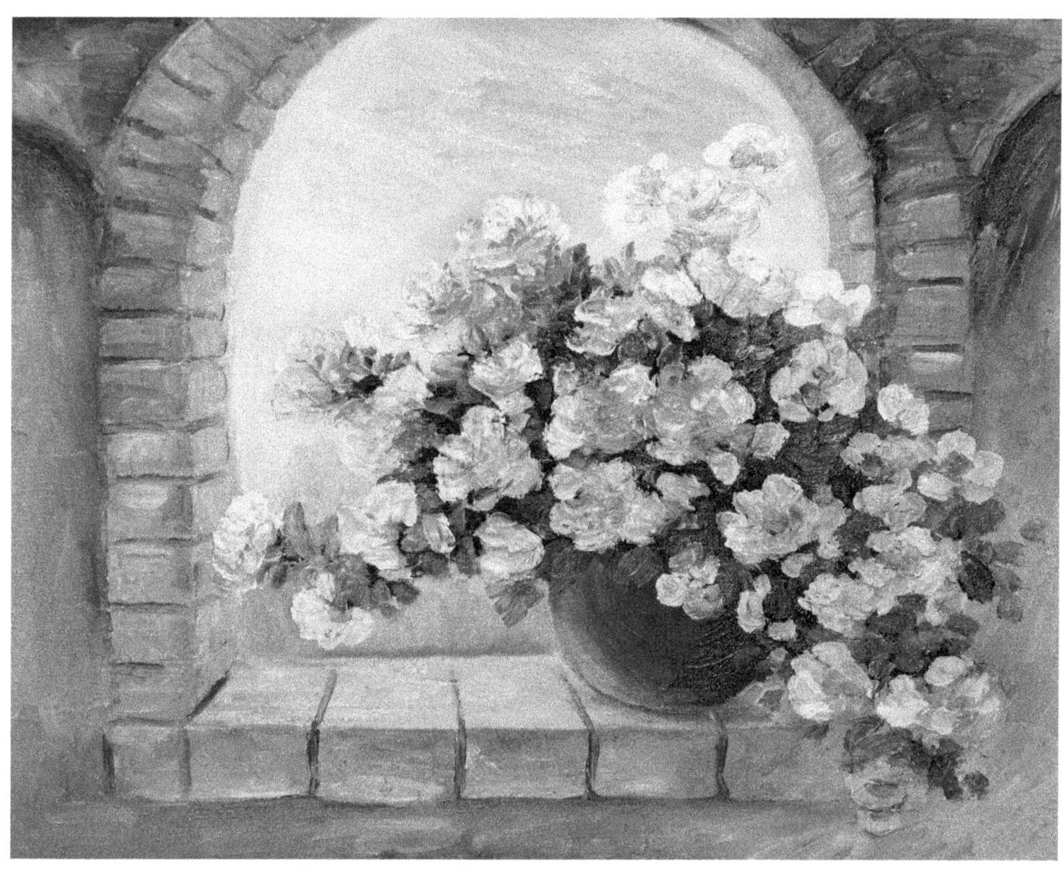

Test Images: Try out your colors here!

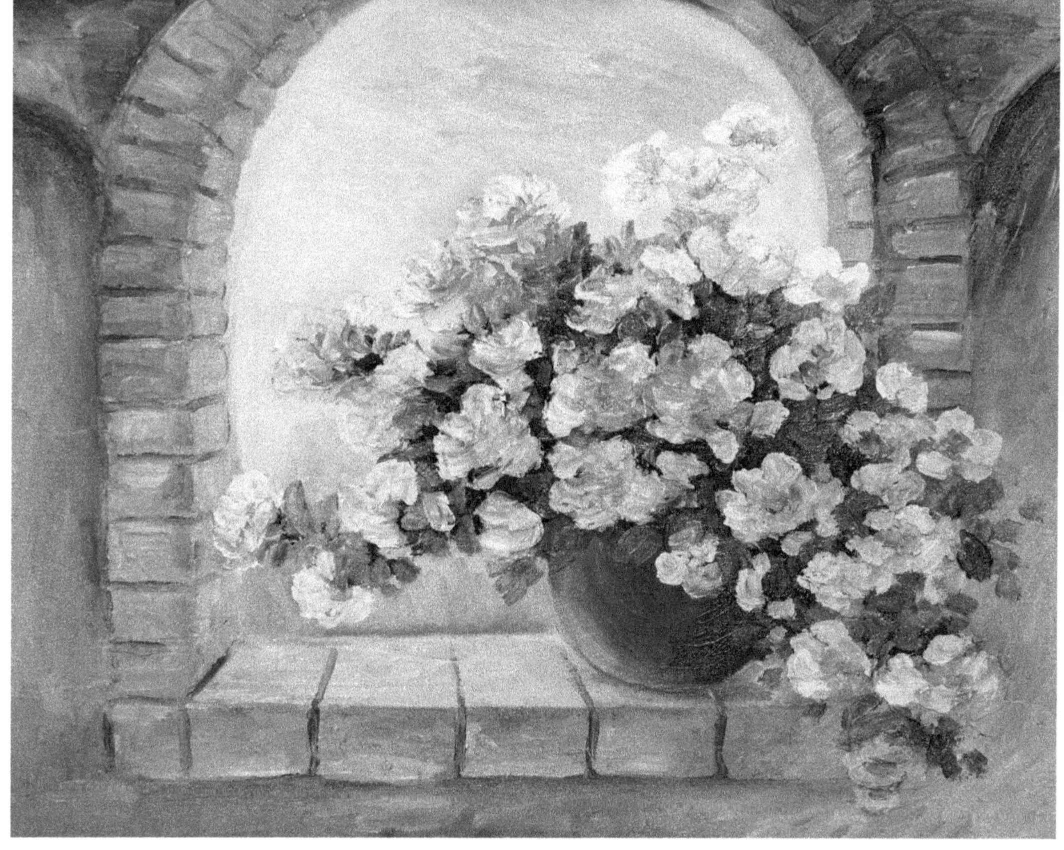

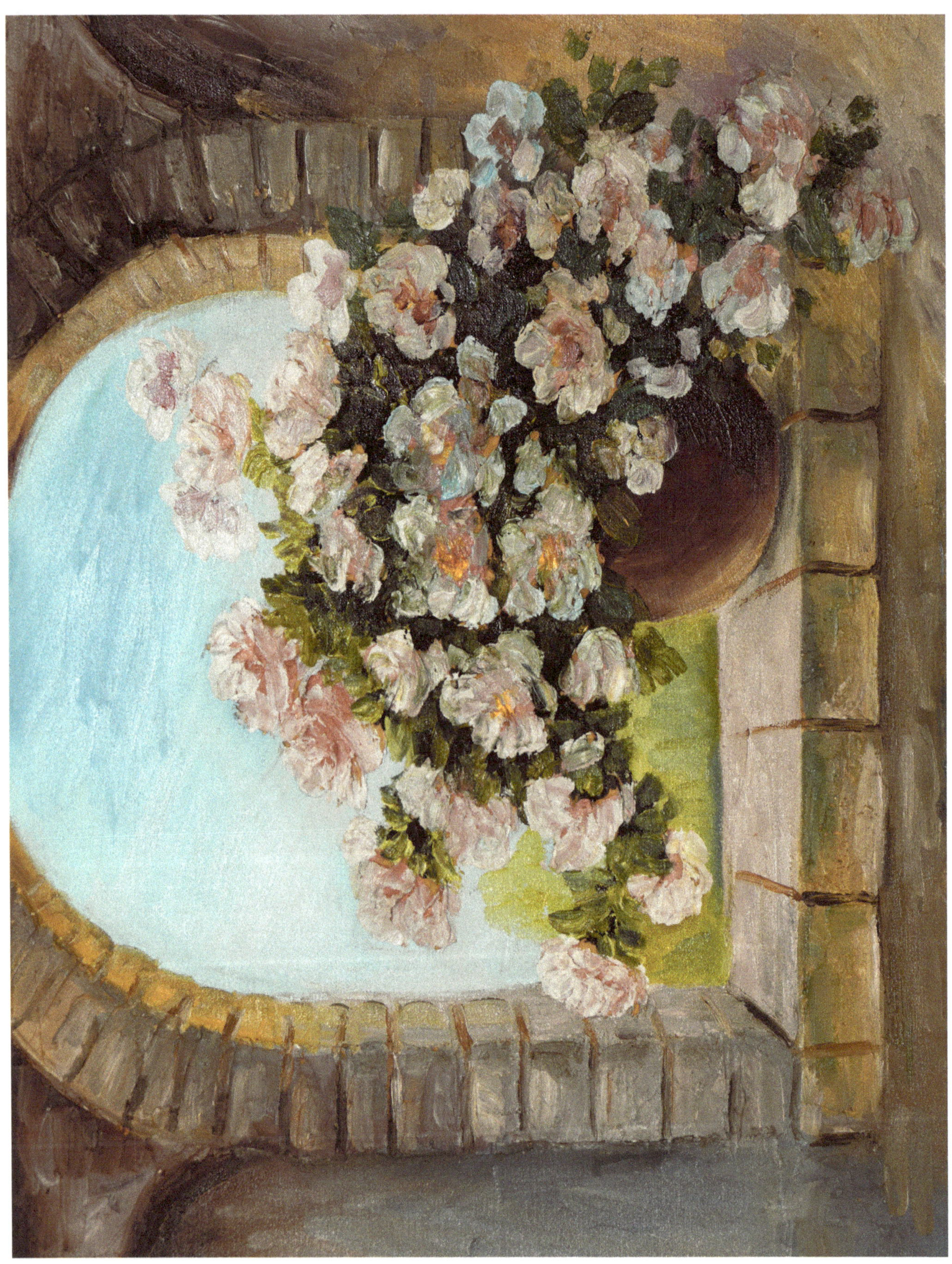

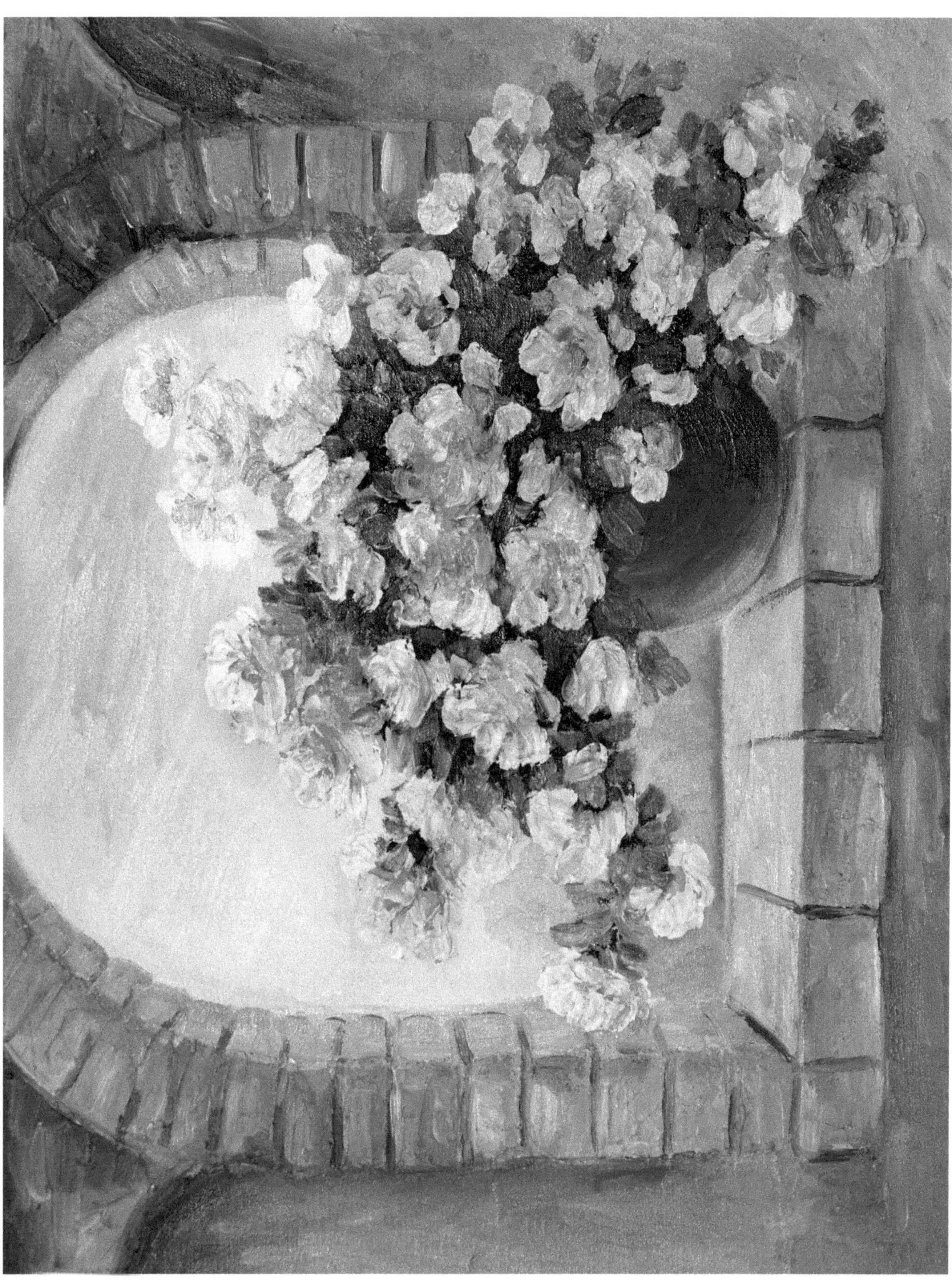

COLORED BY ______________________________ DATE ______________________

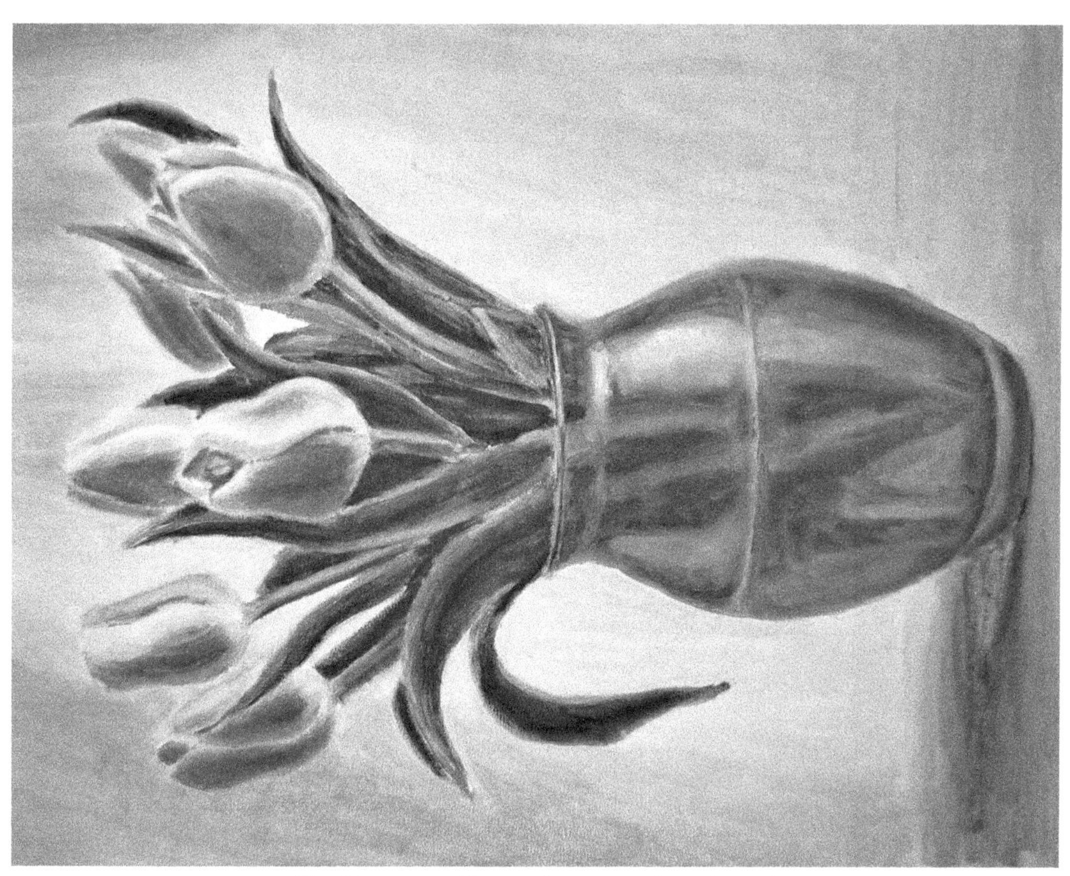

Test Images: Try out your colors here!

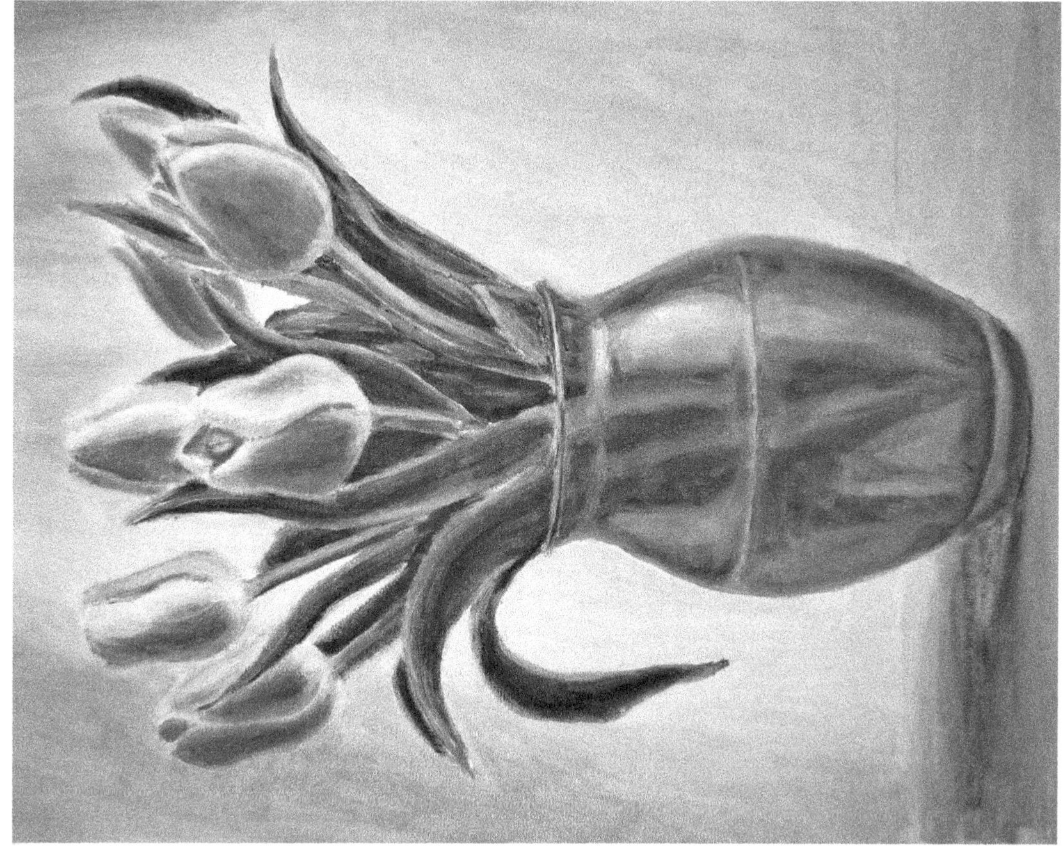

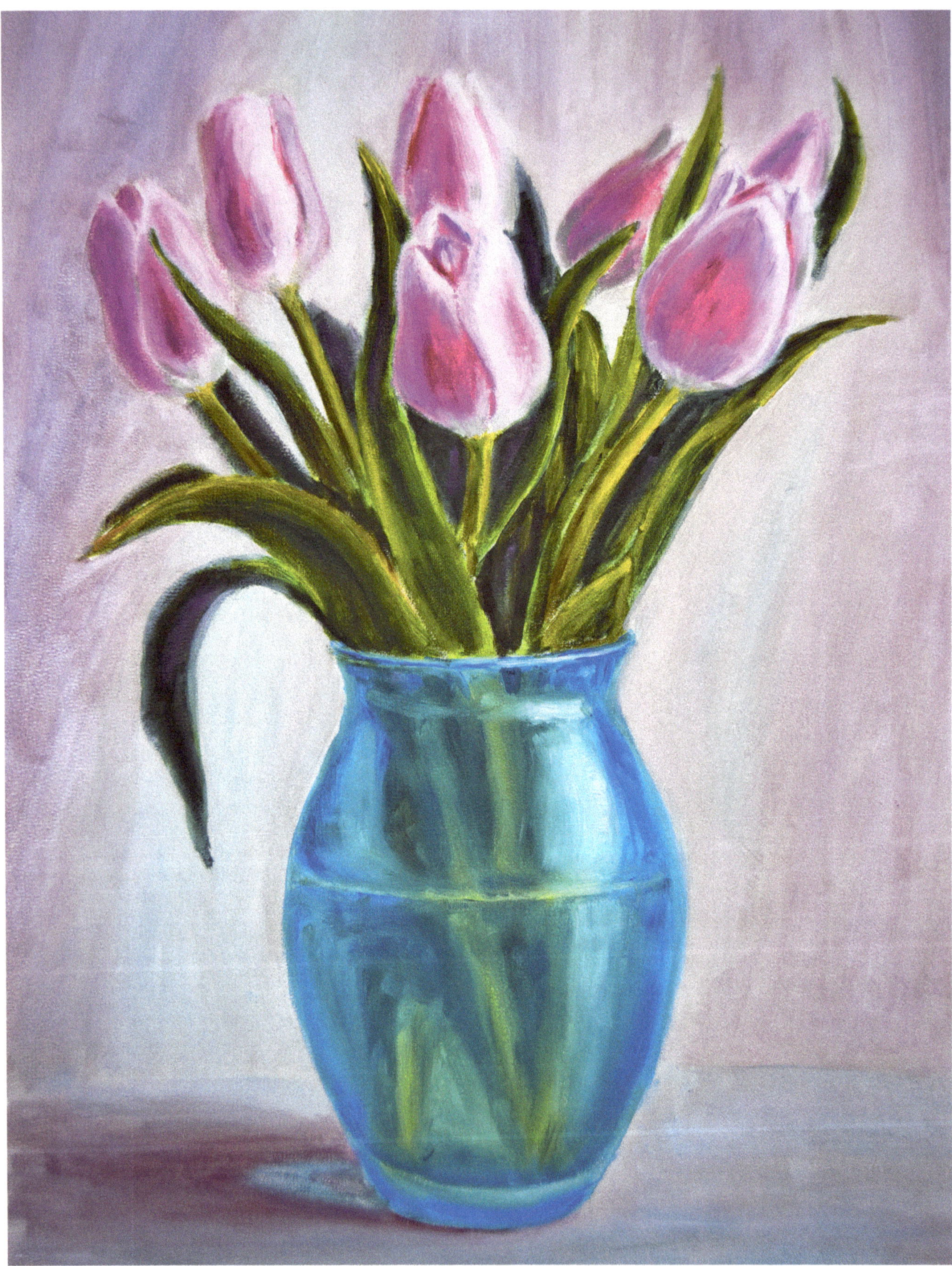

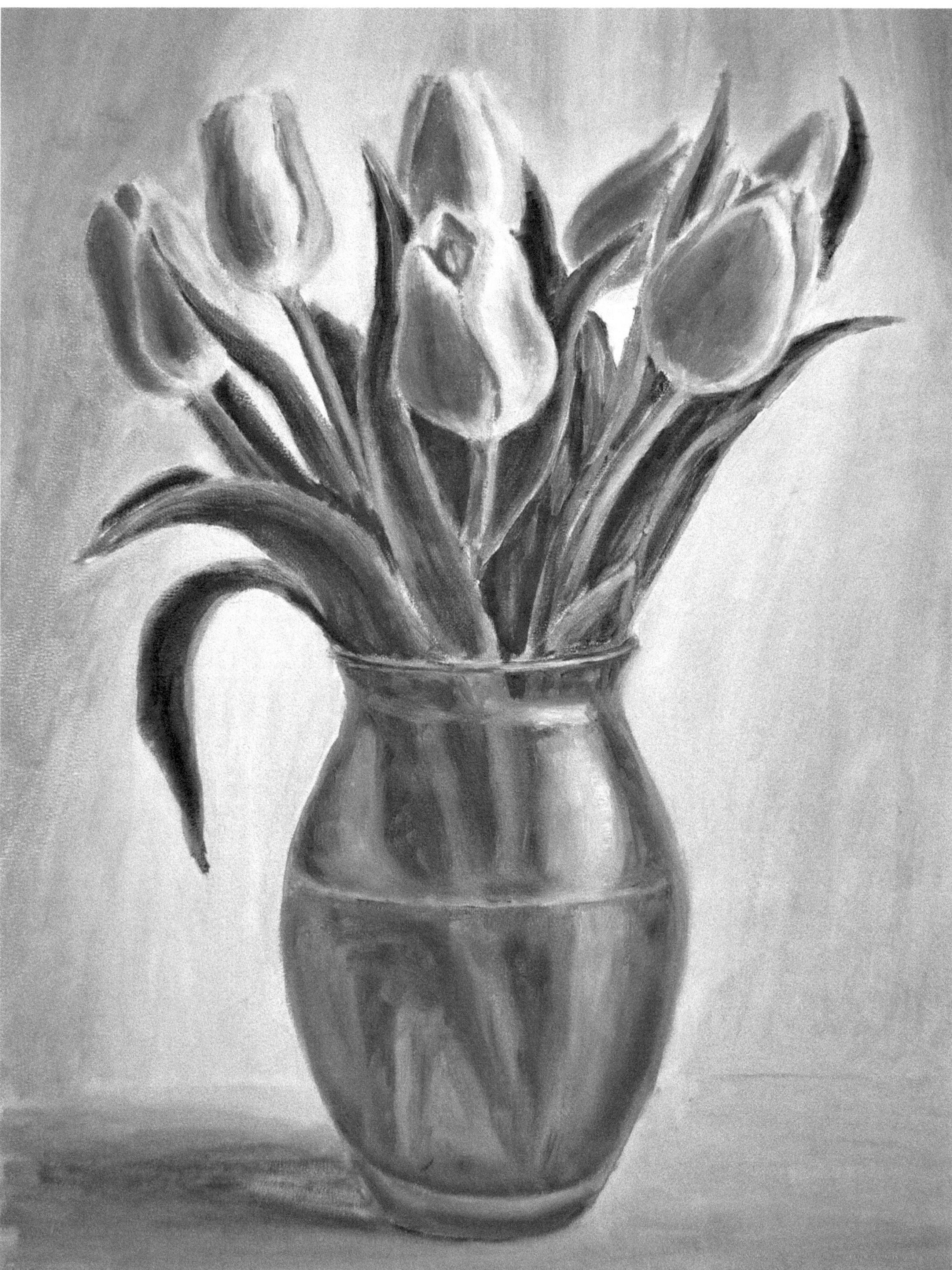

Colored By ____

Date ____

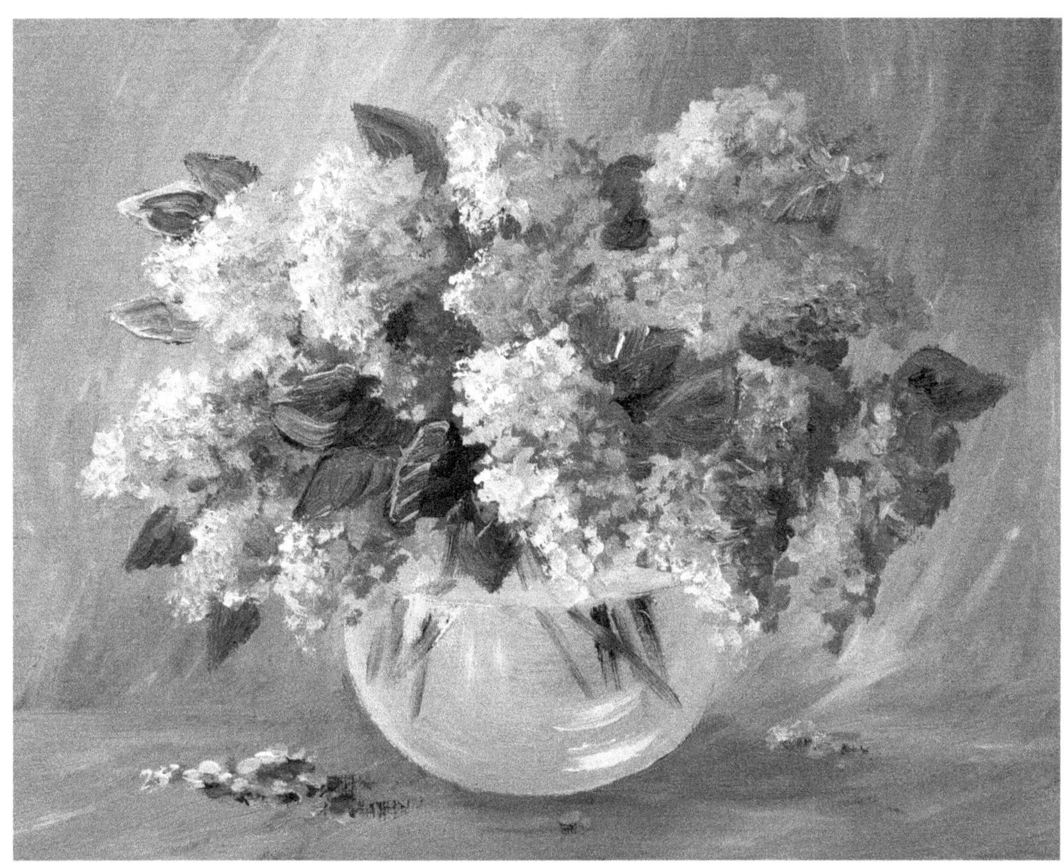

Test Images: Try out your colors here!

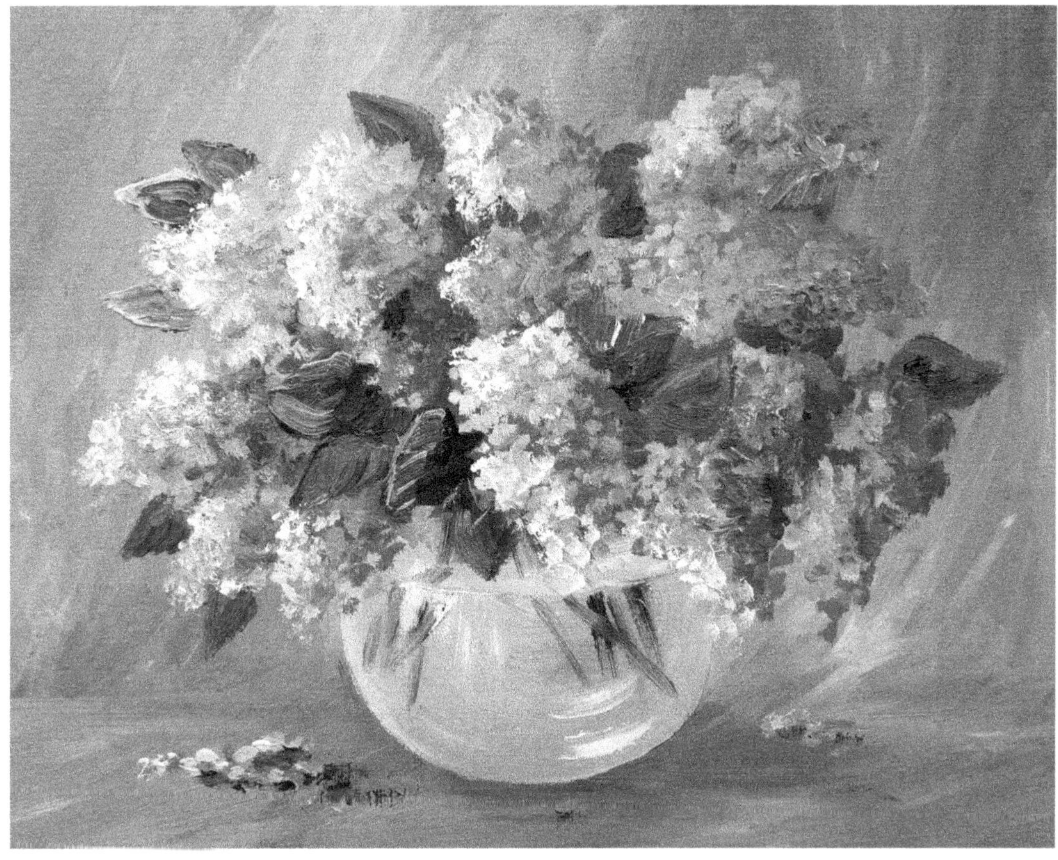

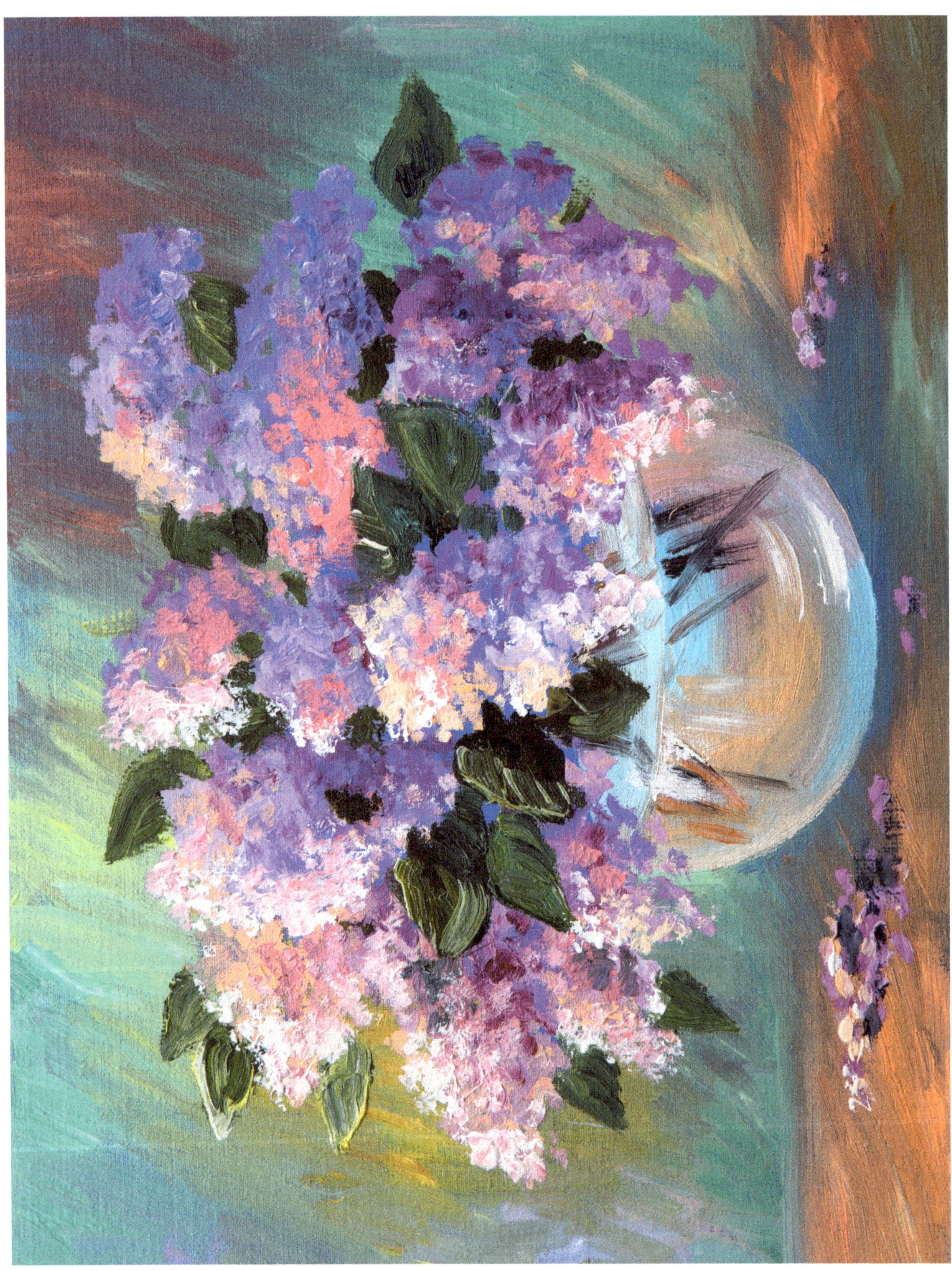

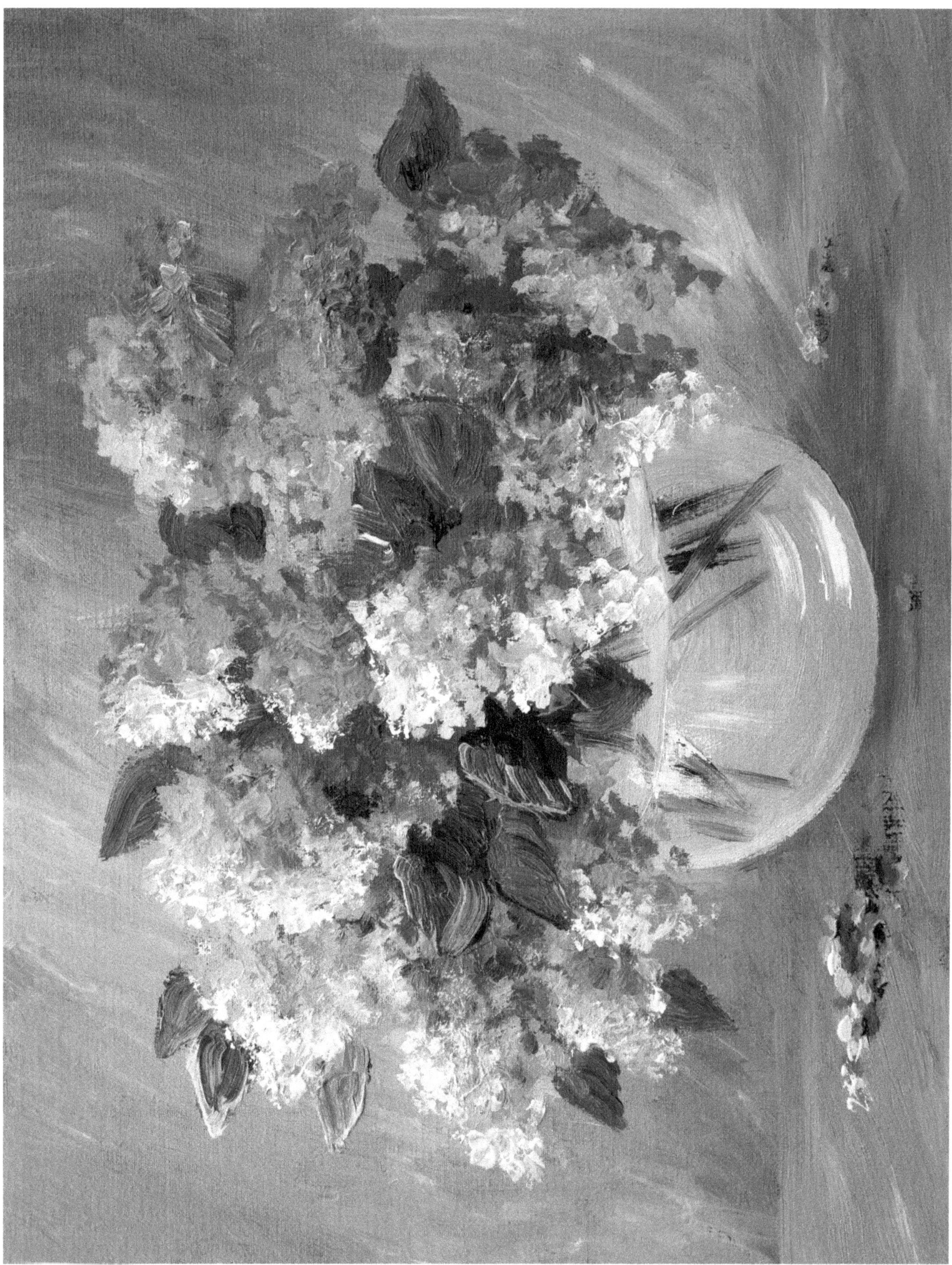

Colored By ______________________________ Date ______________________

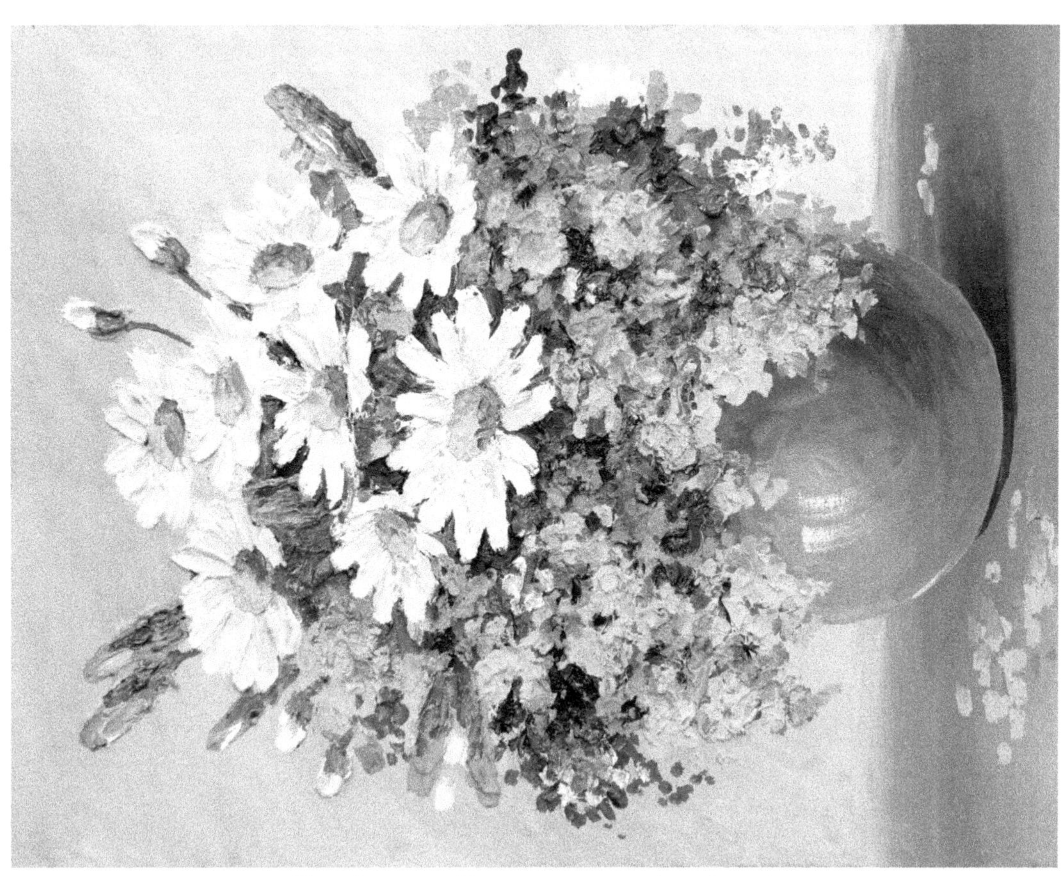

Test Images: Try out your colors here!

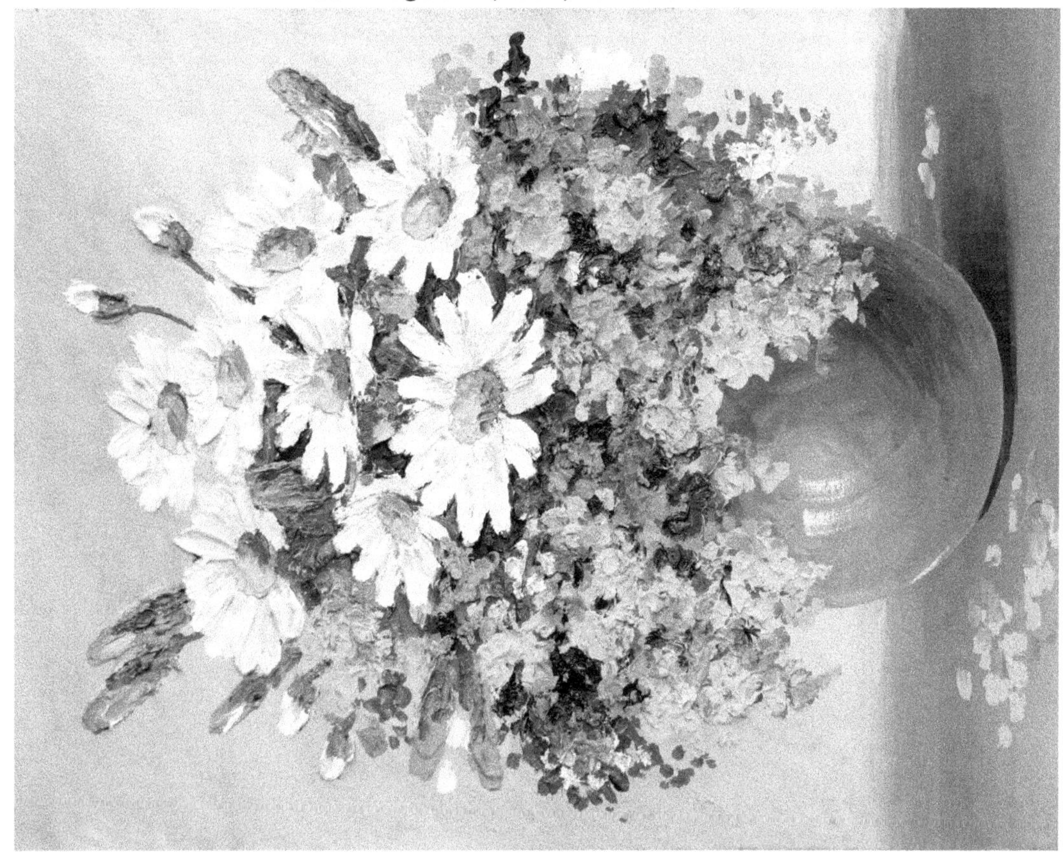

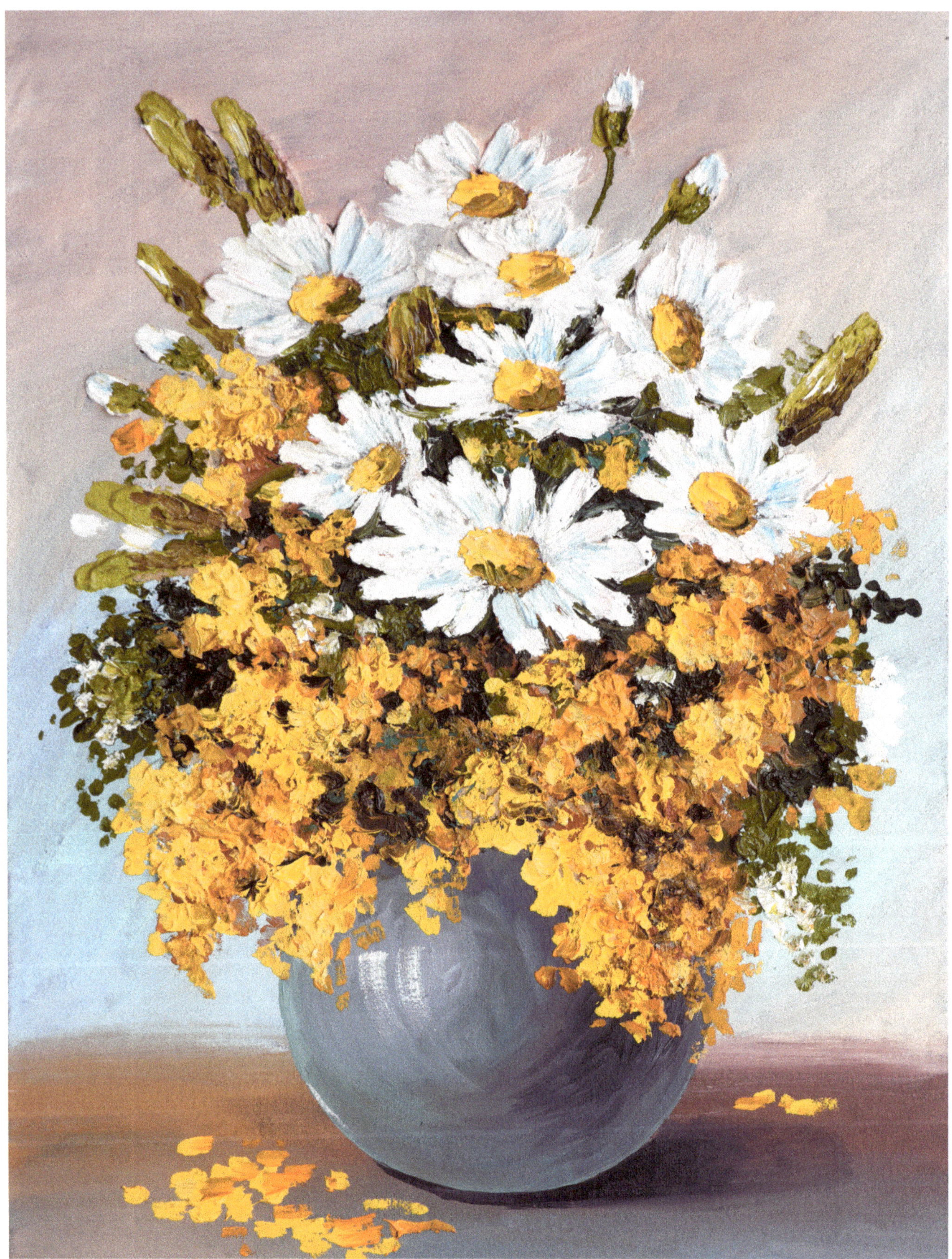

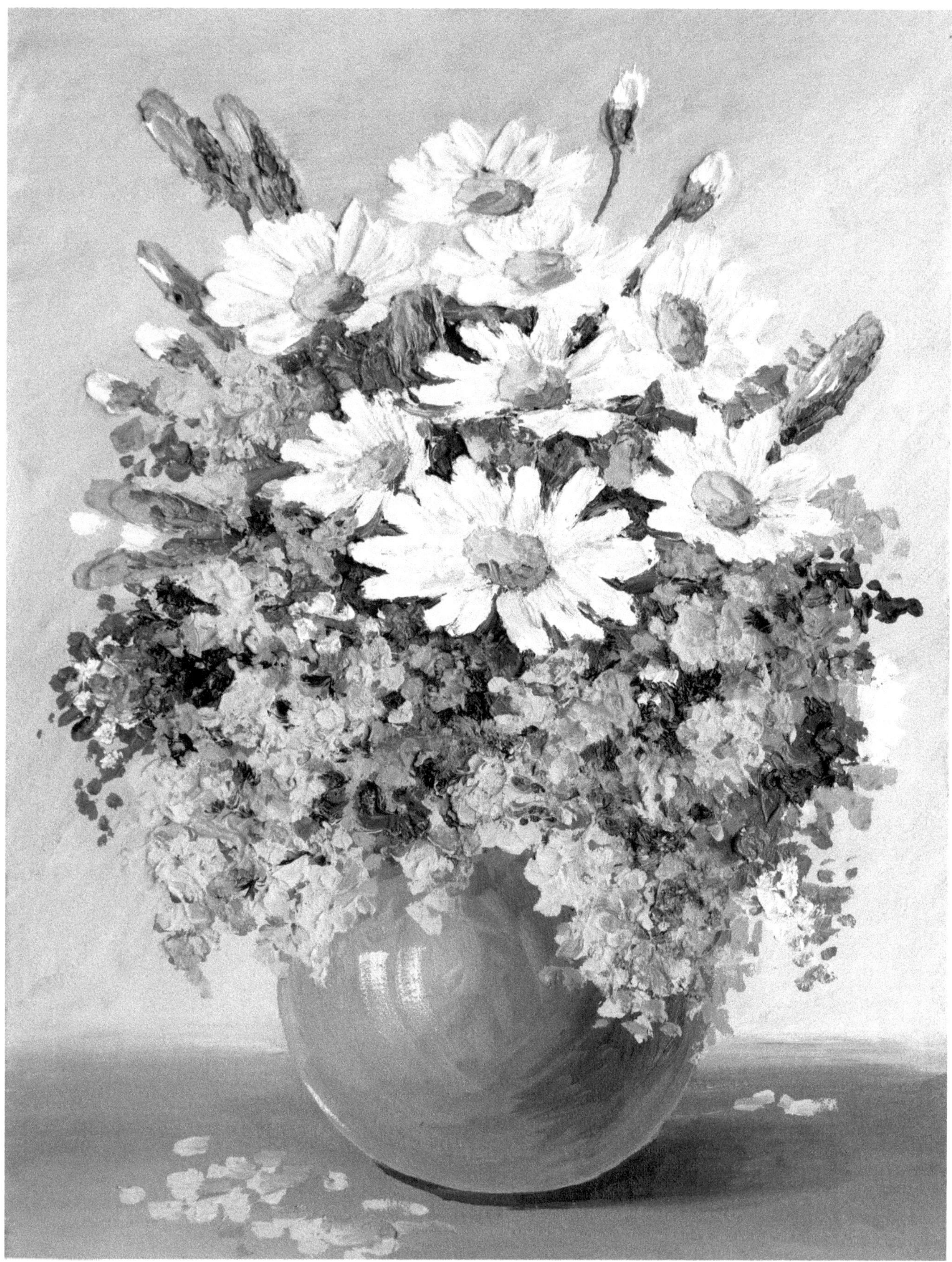

Colored By ____

Date ____

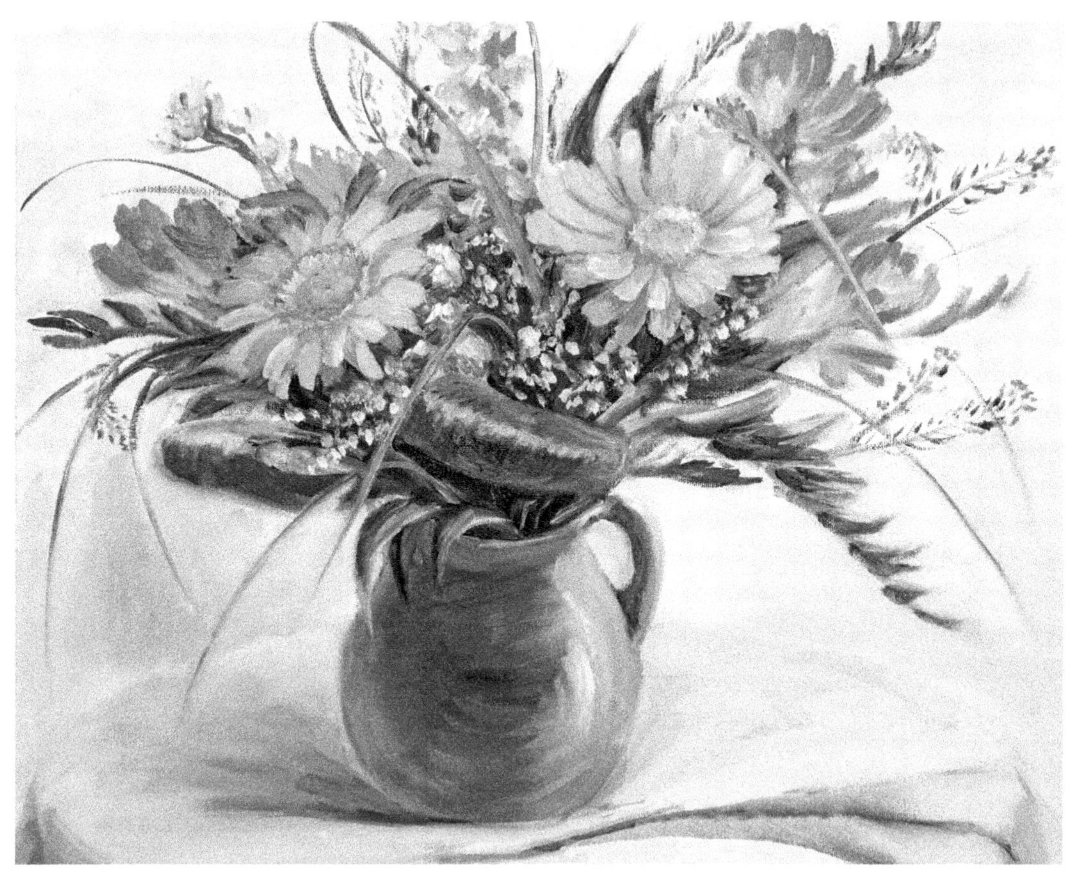

Test Images: Try out your colors here!

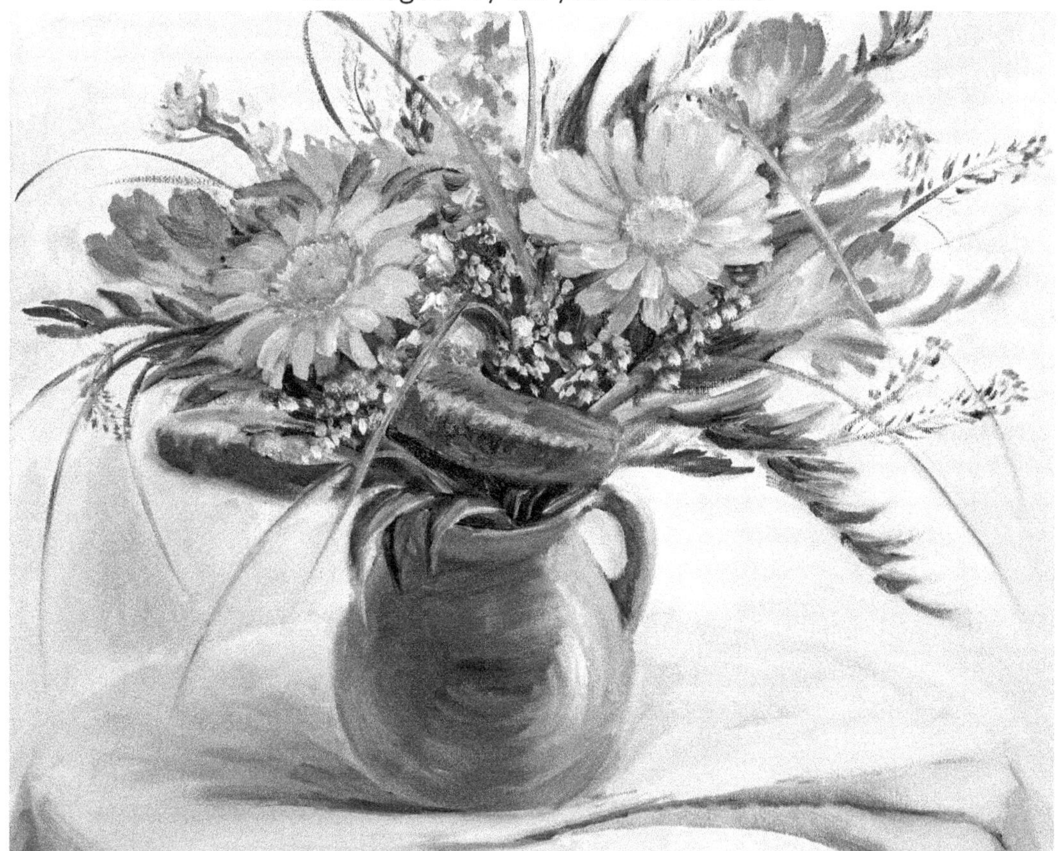

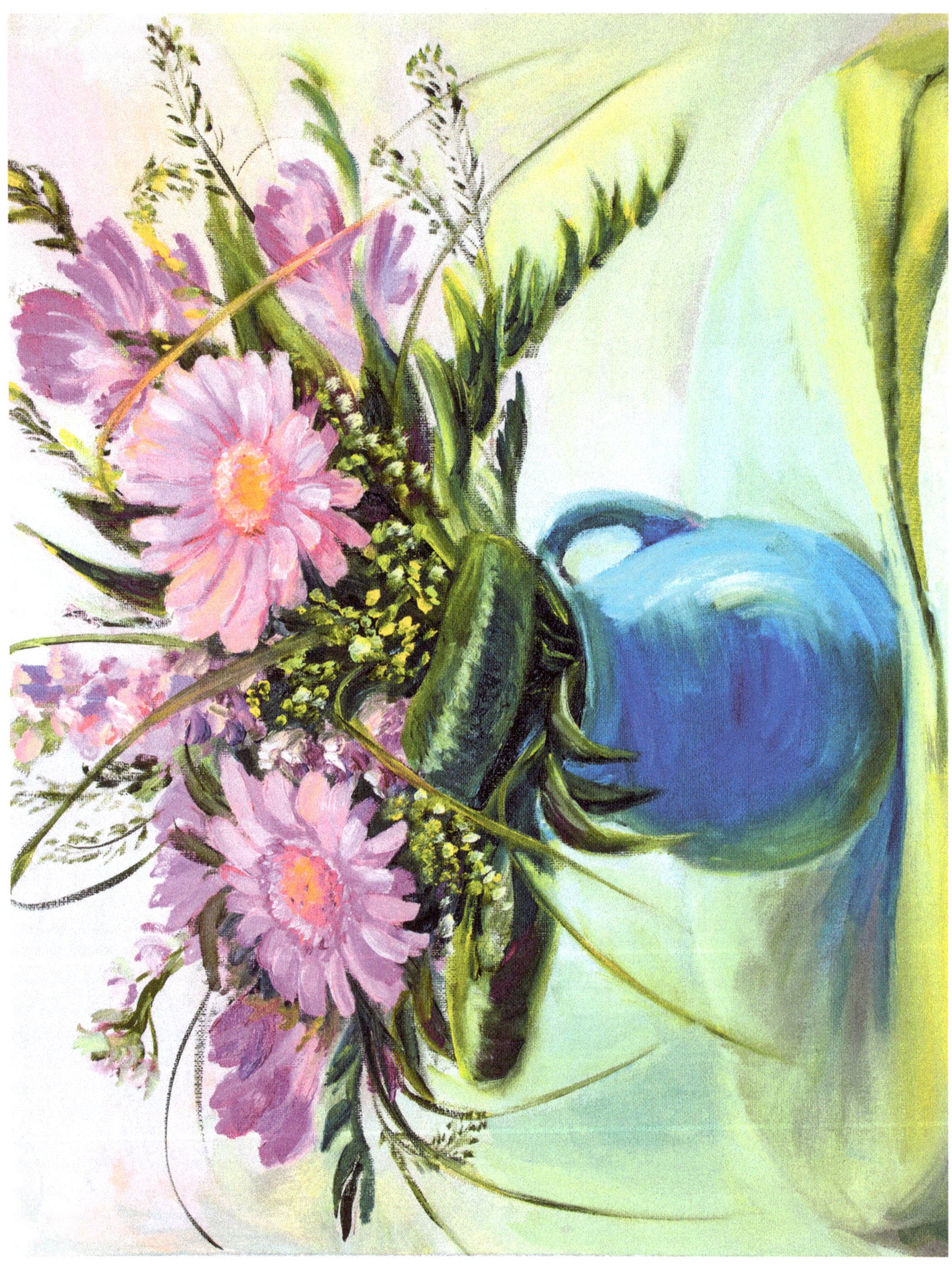

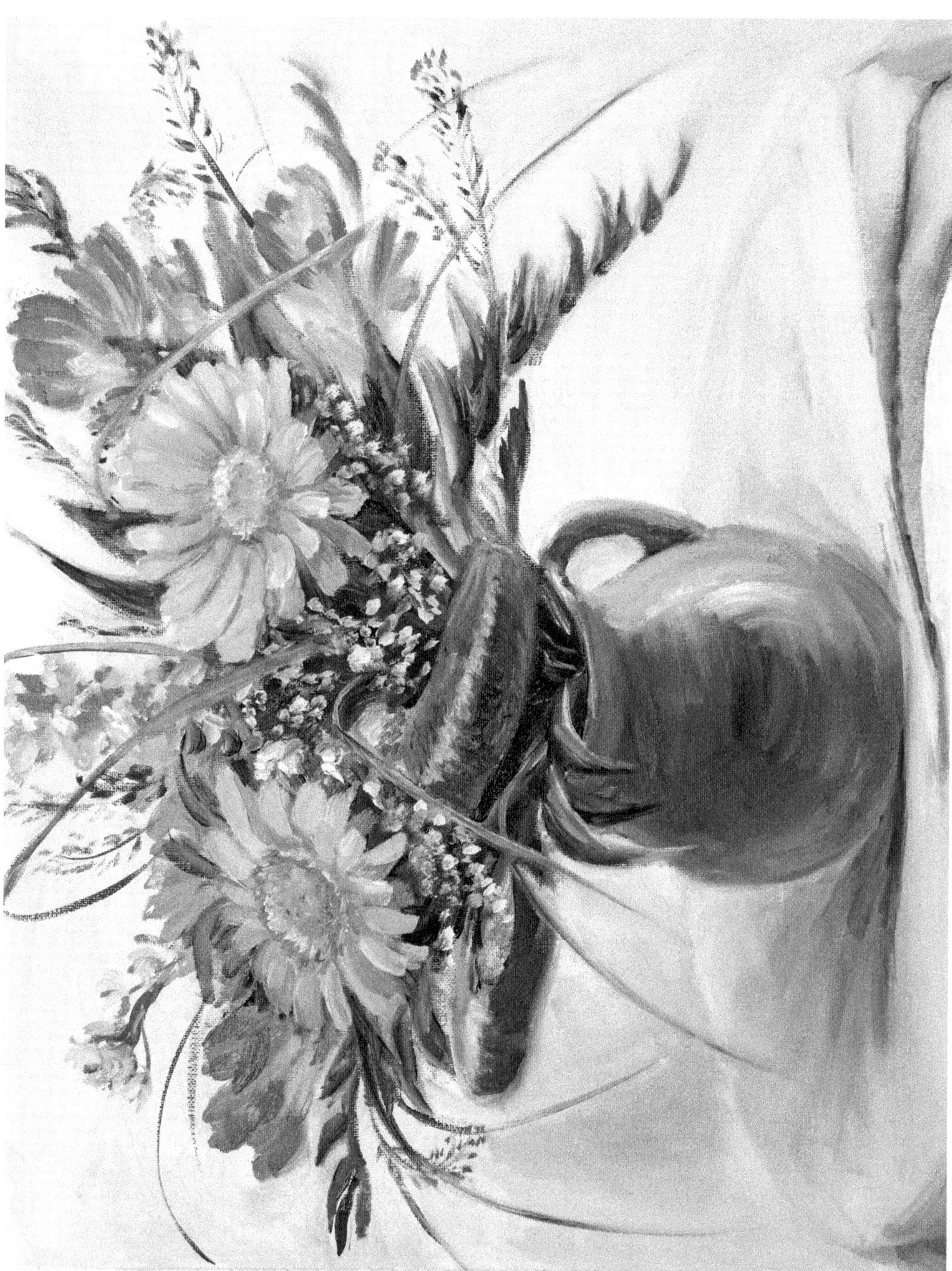

Colored By ______________________________ Date ______________________

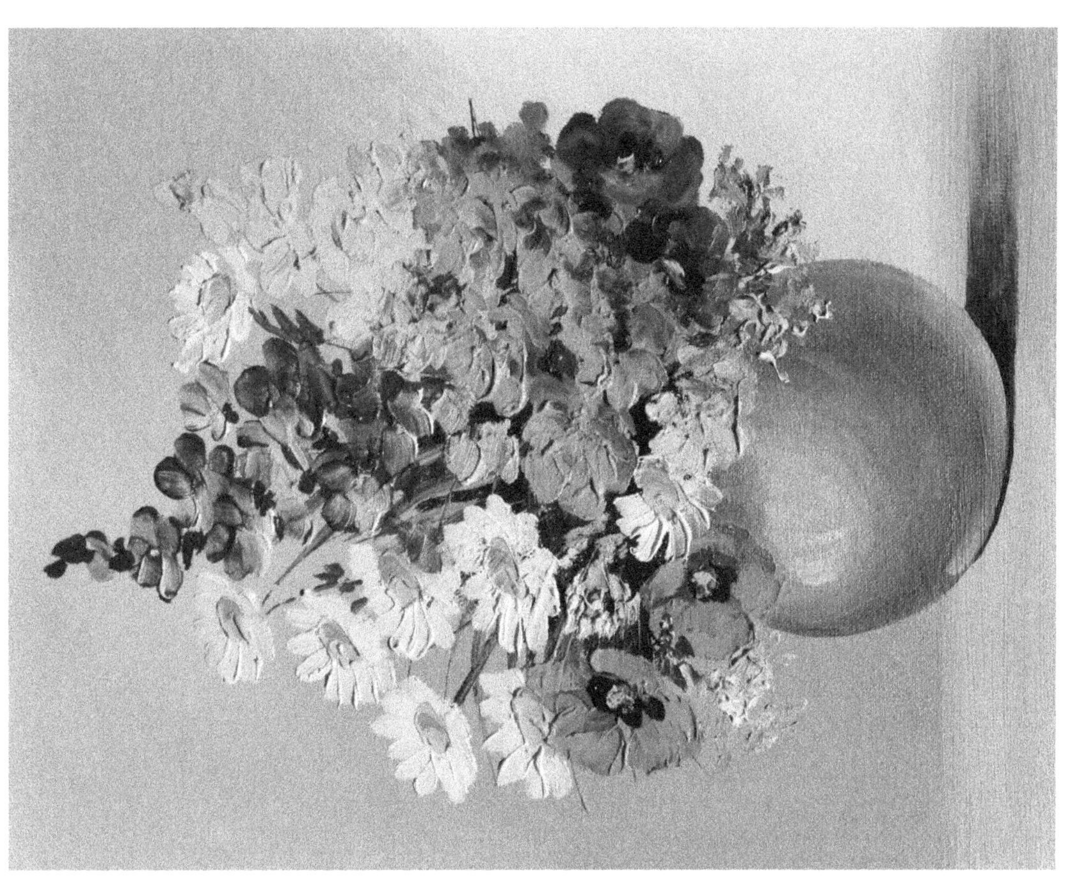

Test Images: Try out your colors here!

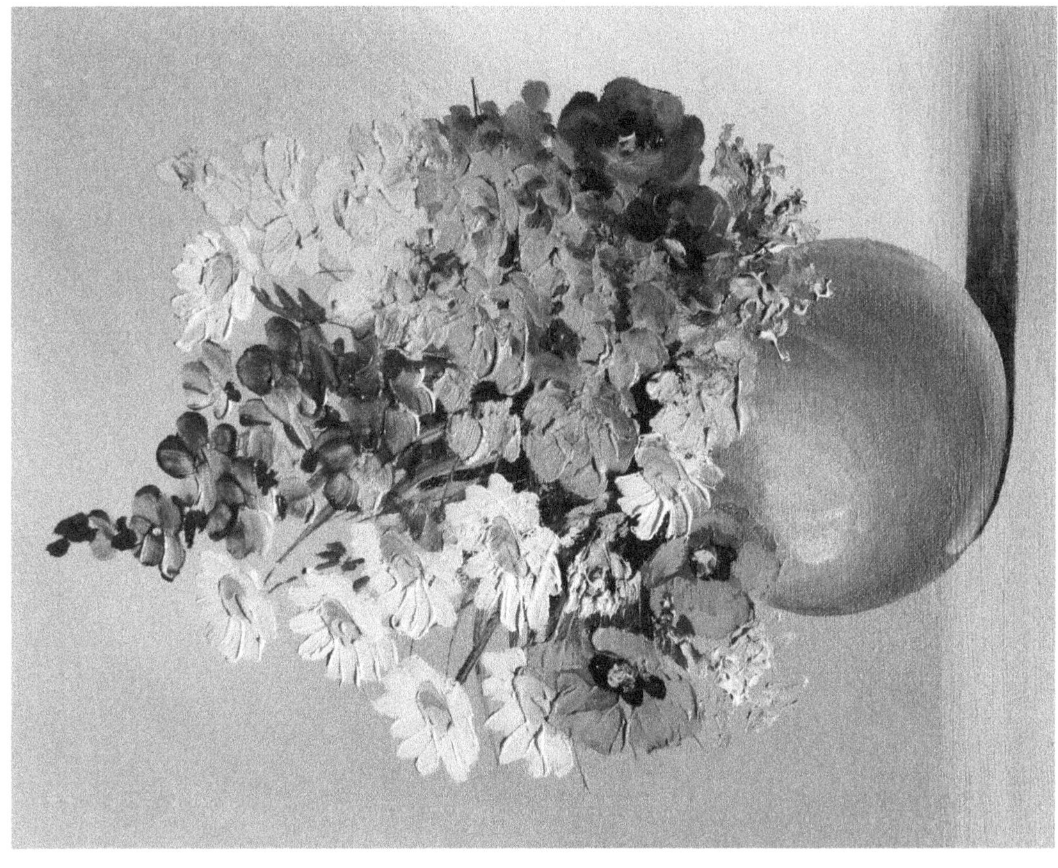

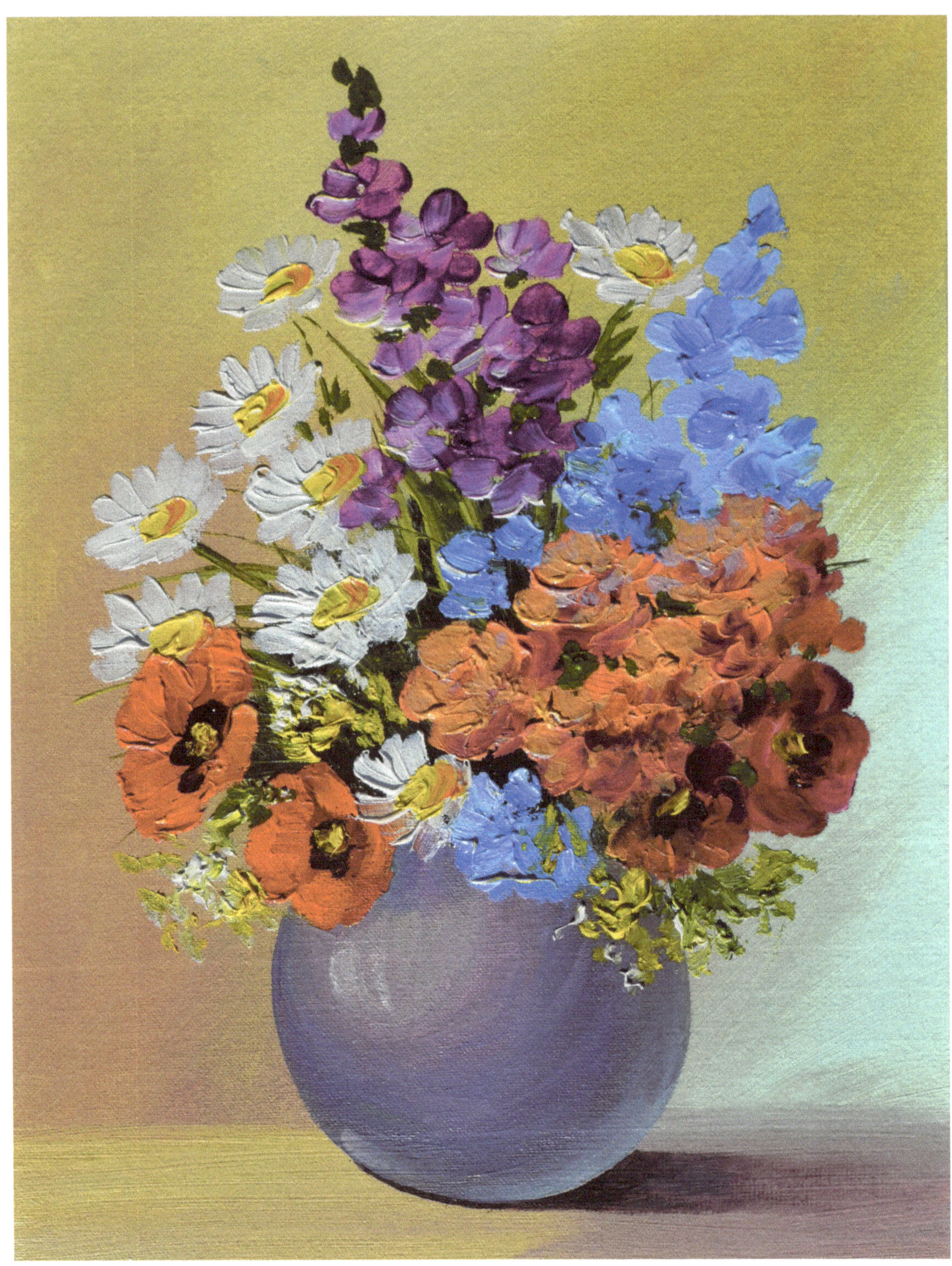

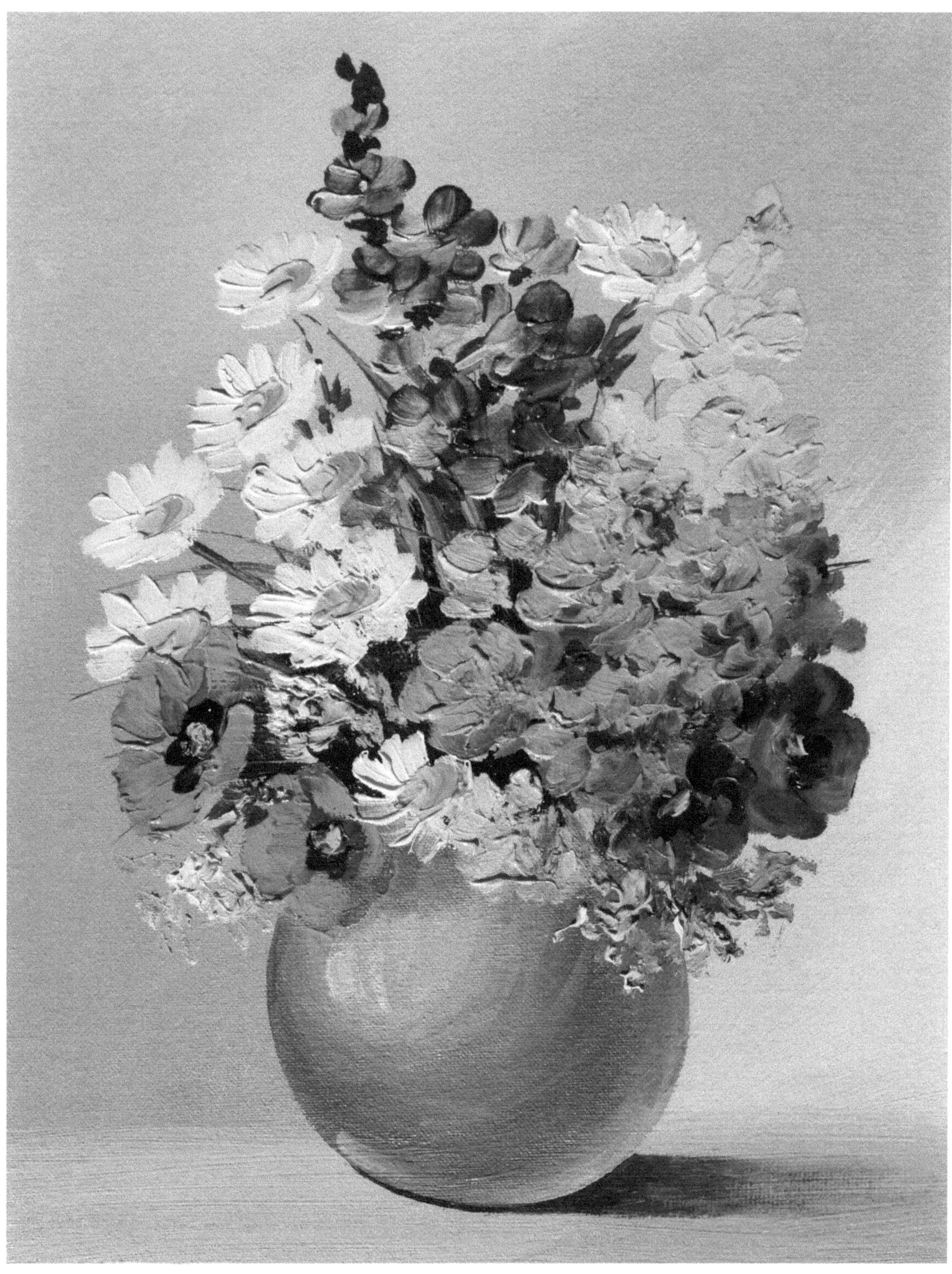

Colored By ____

Date ____

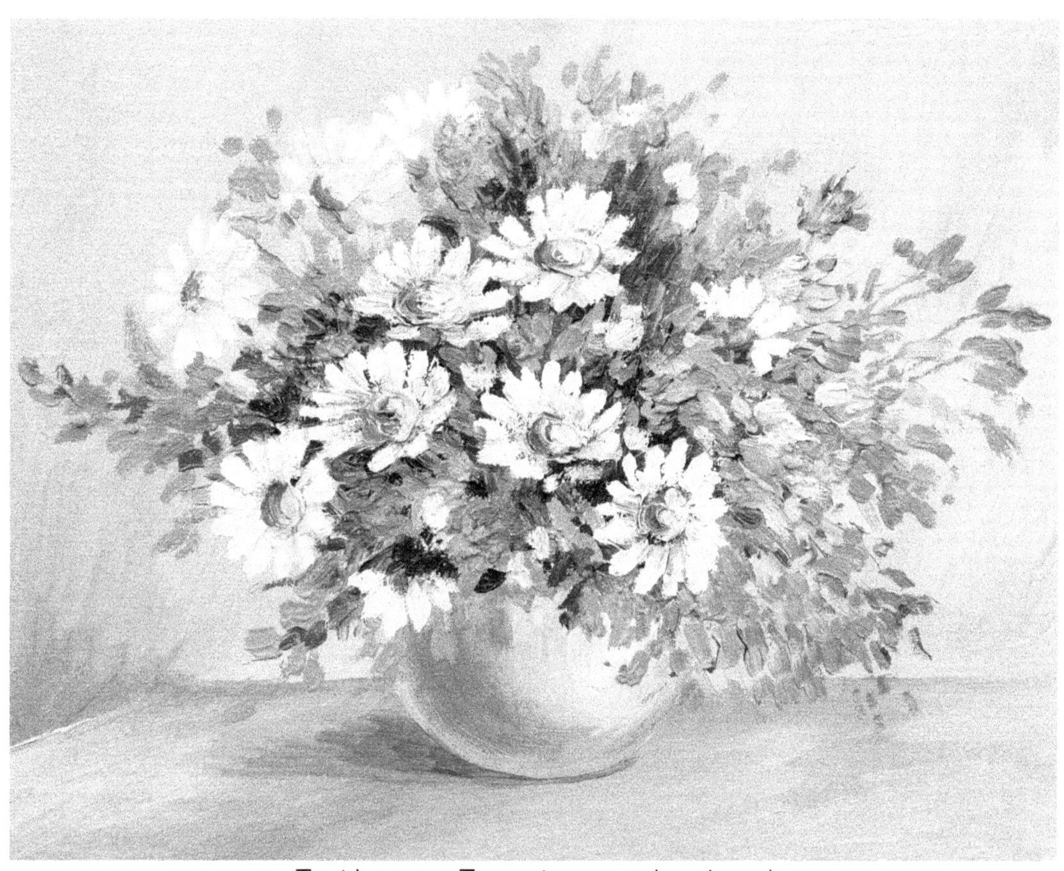

Test Images: Try out your colors here!

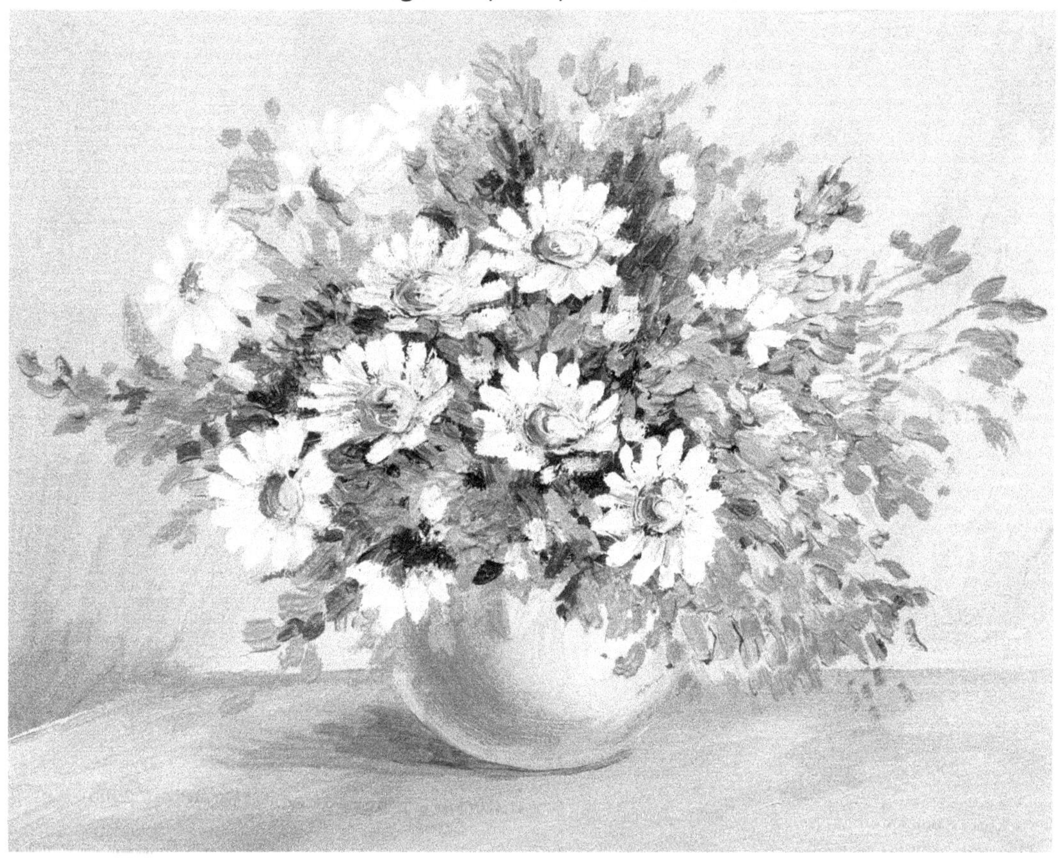

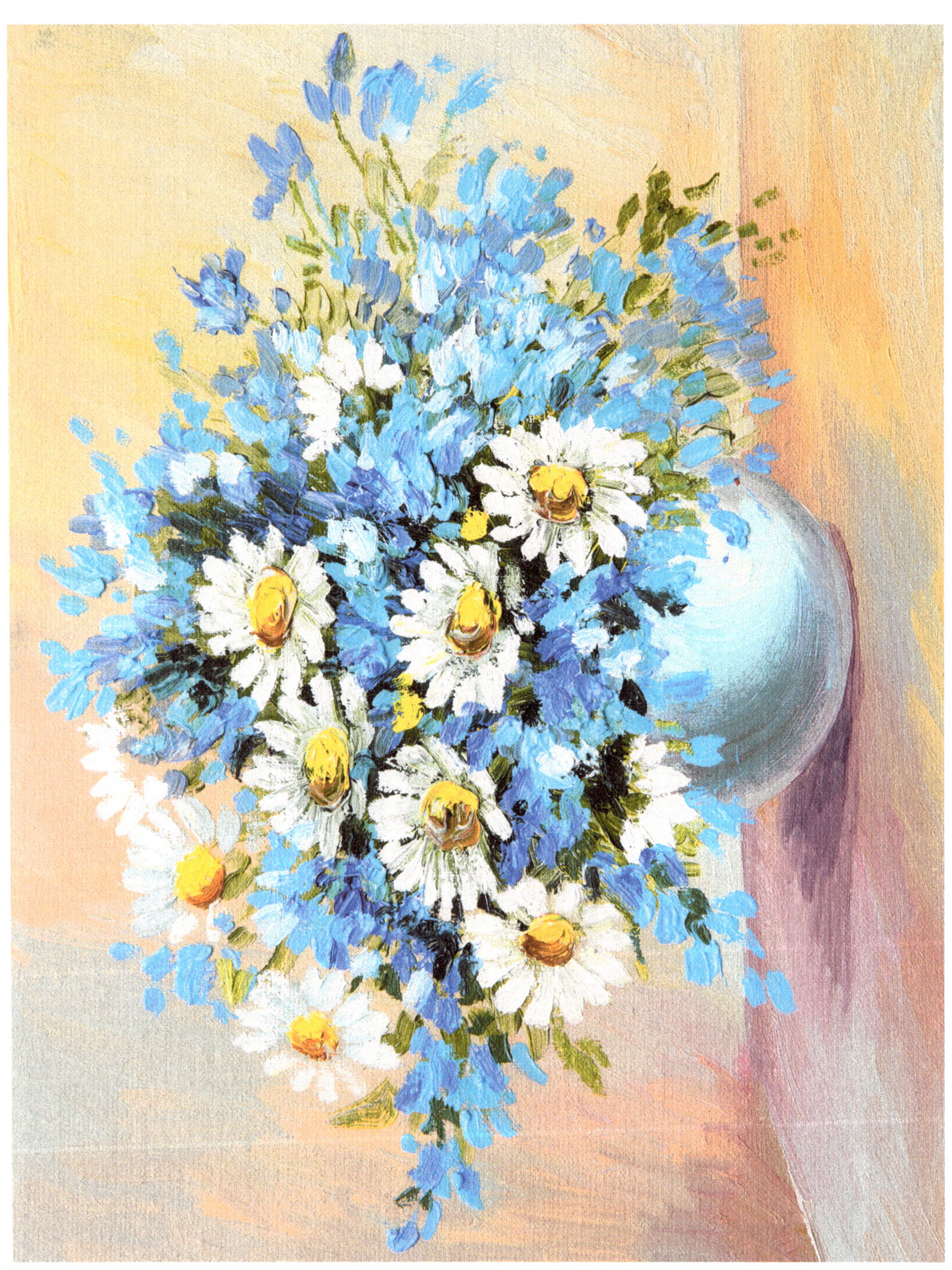

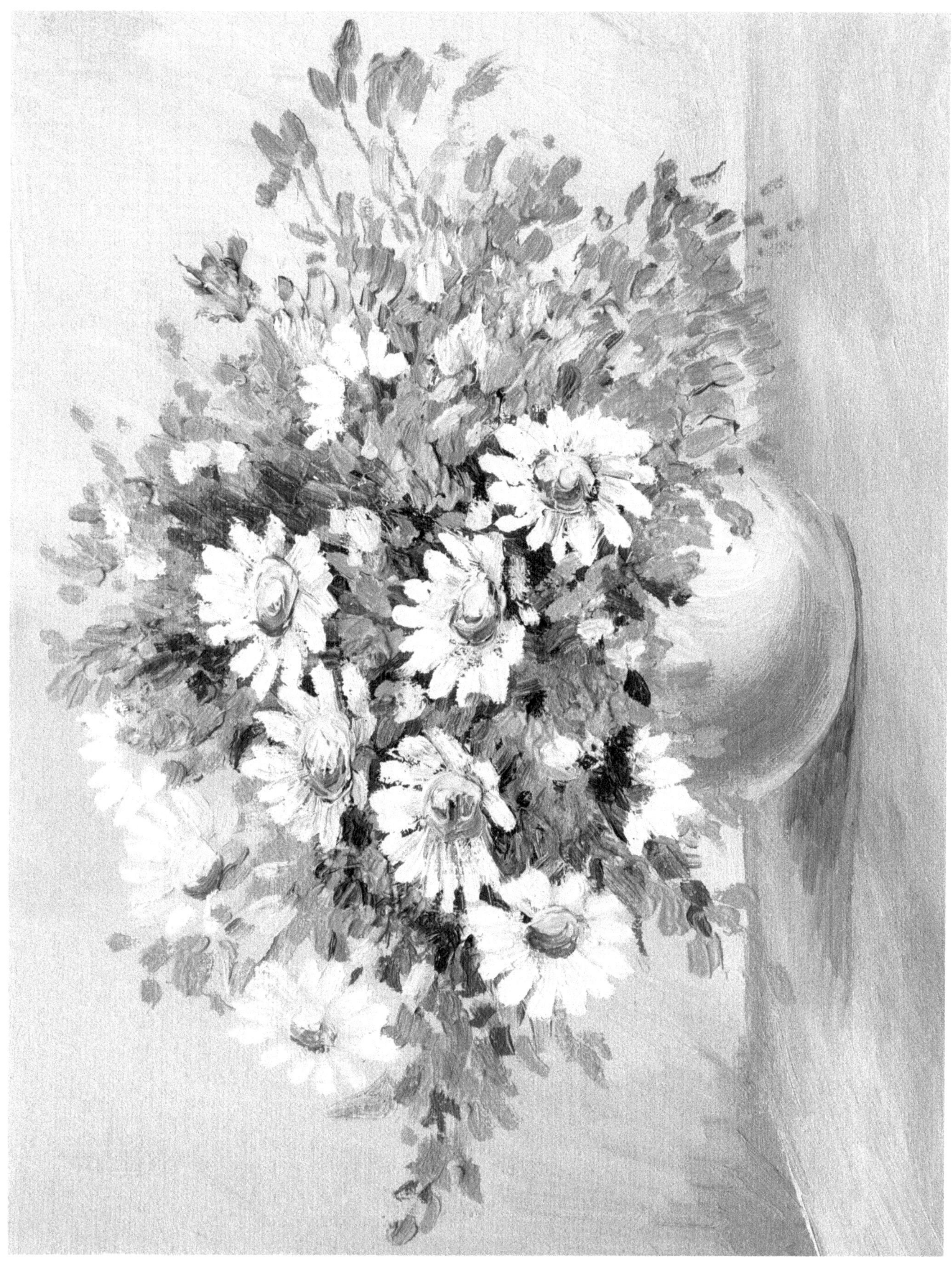

Colored By ______________________ Date ______________________

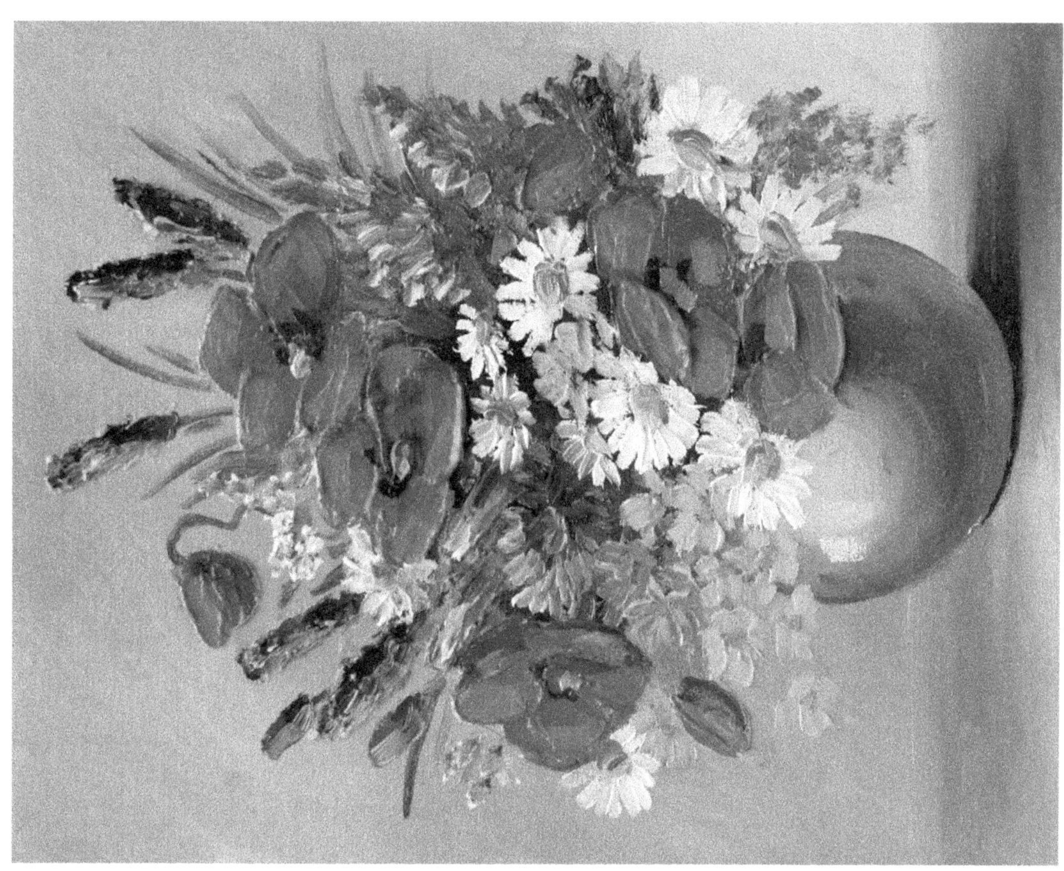

Test Images: Try out your colors here!

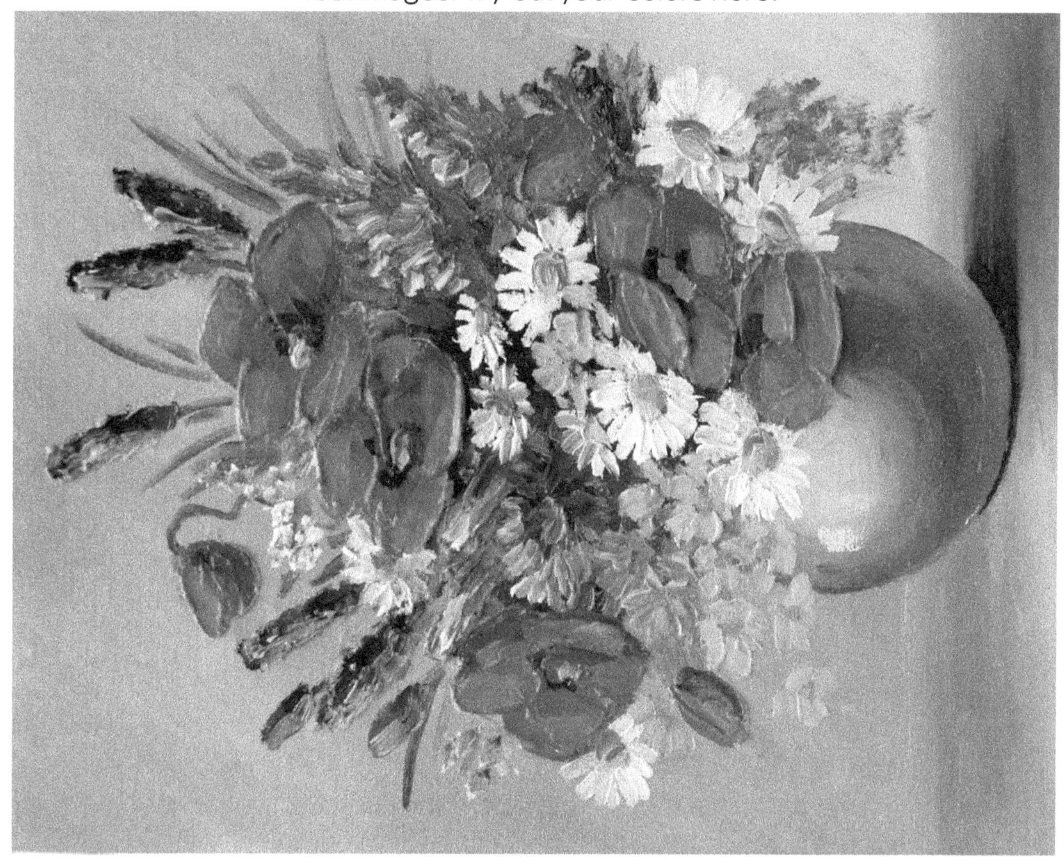

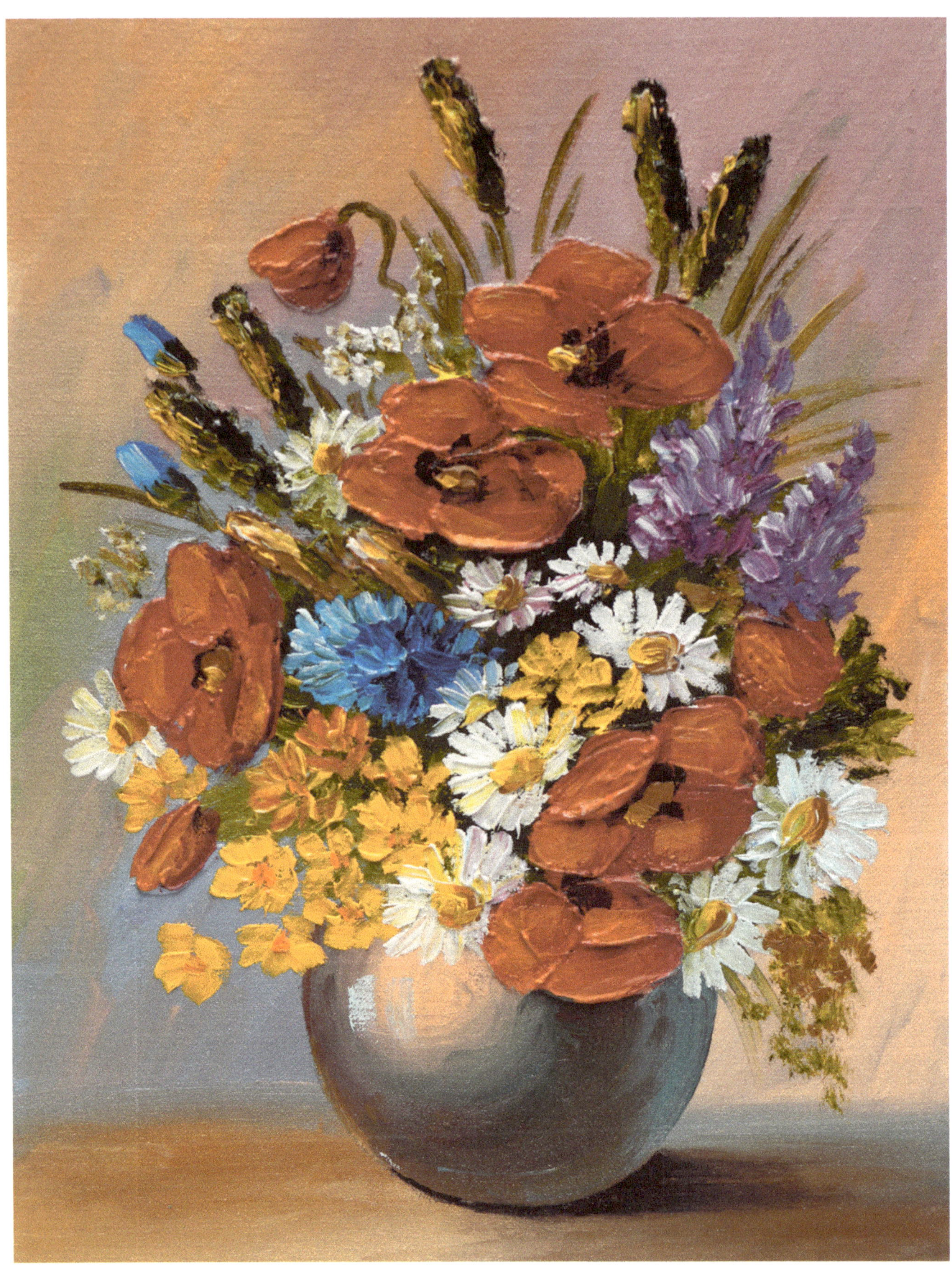

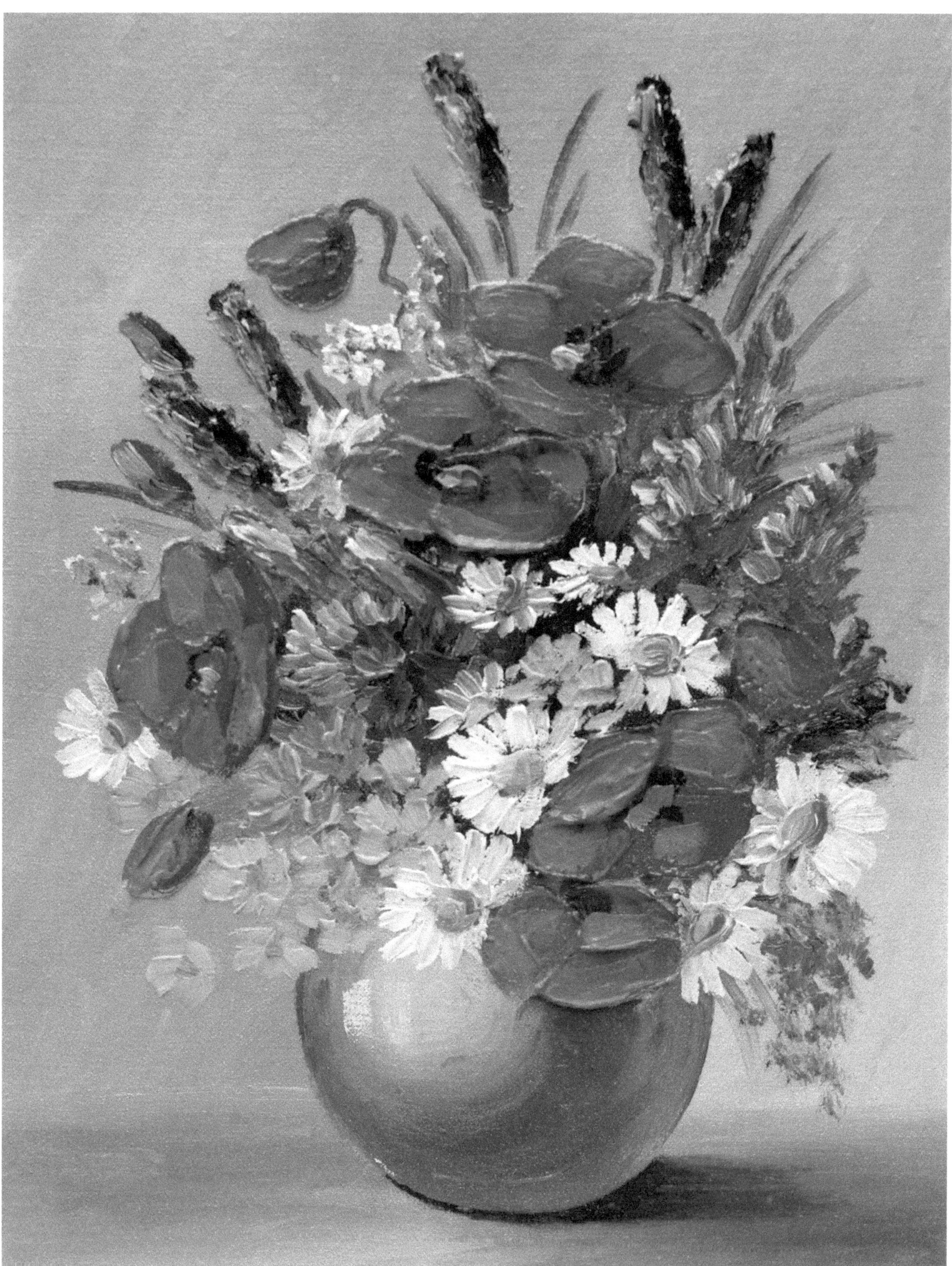

COLORED BY ____

DATE ____

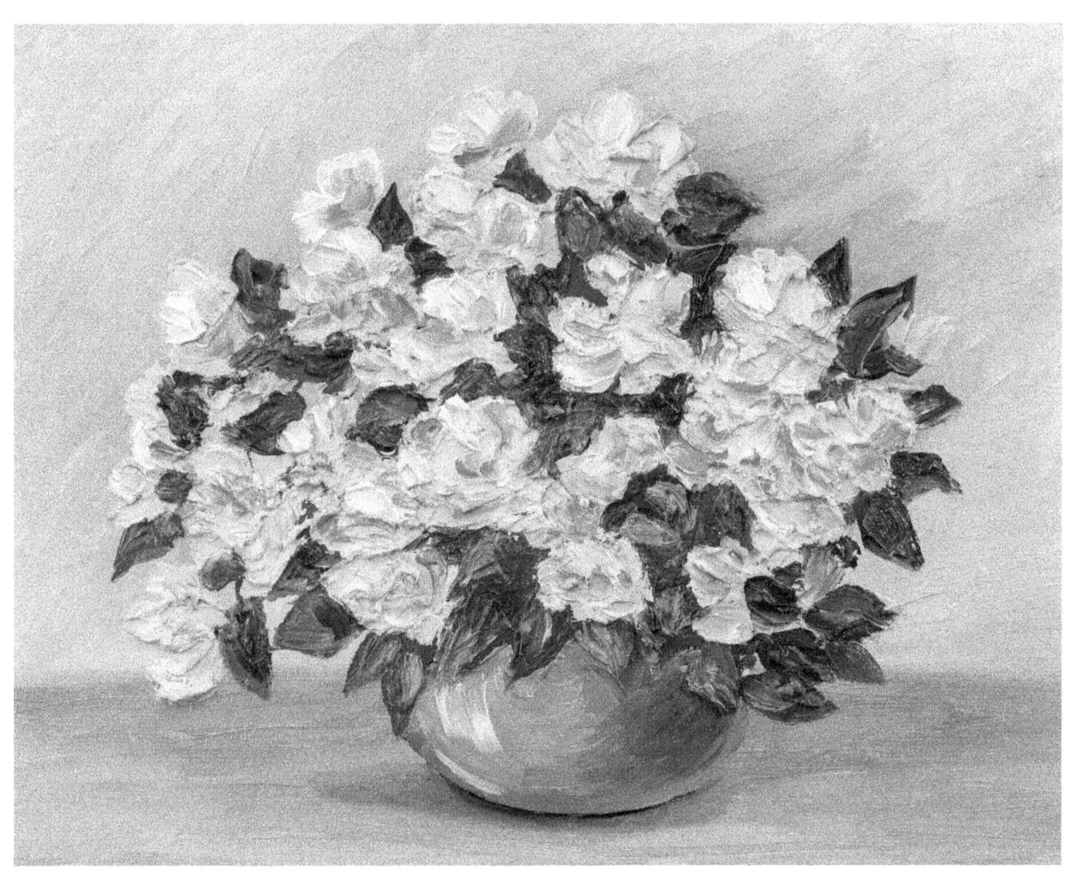

Test Images: Try out your colors here!

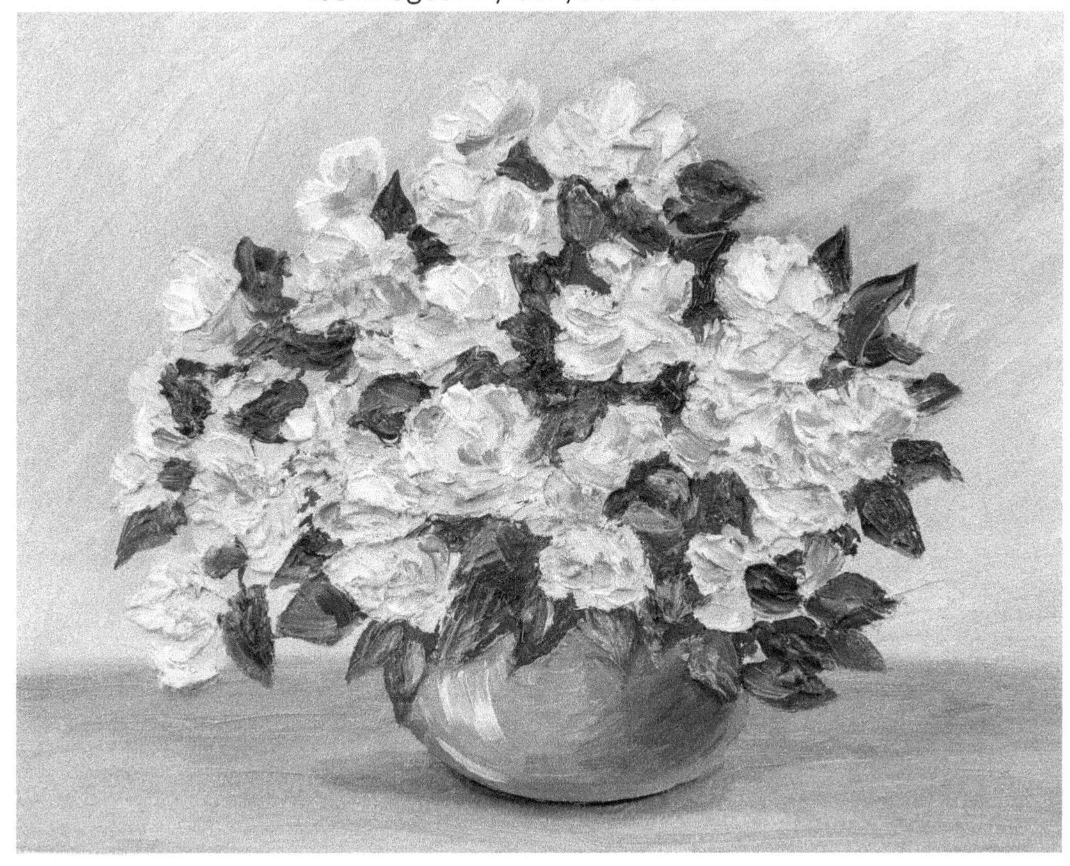

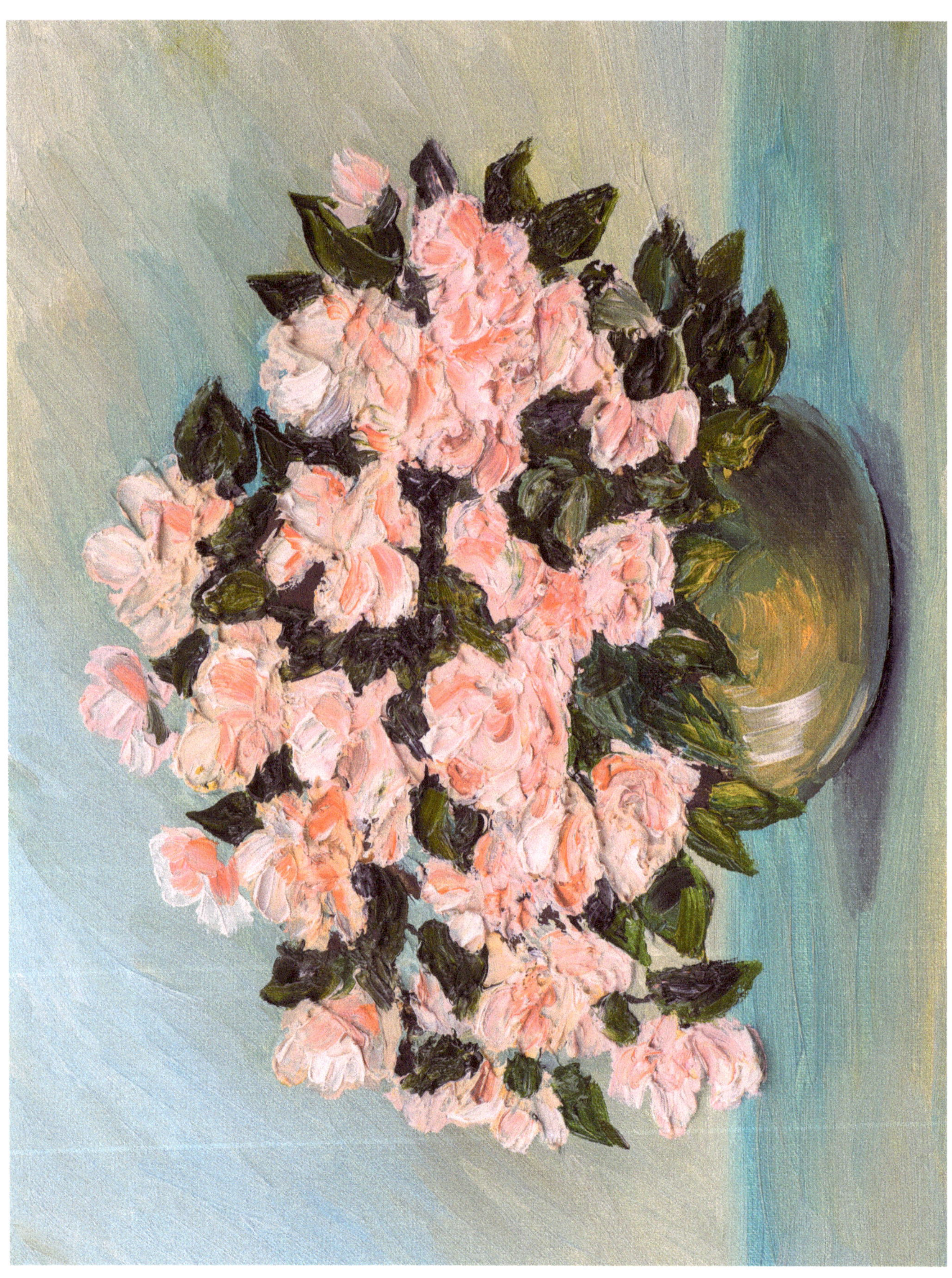

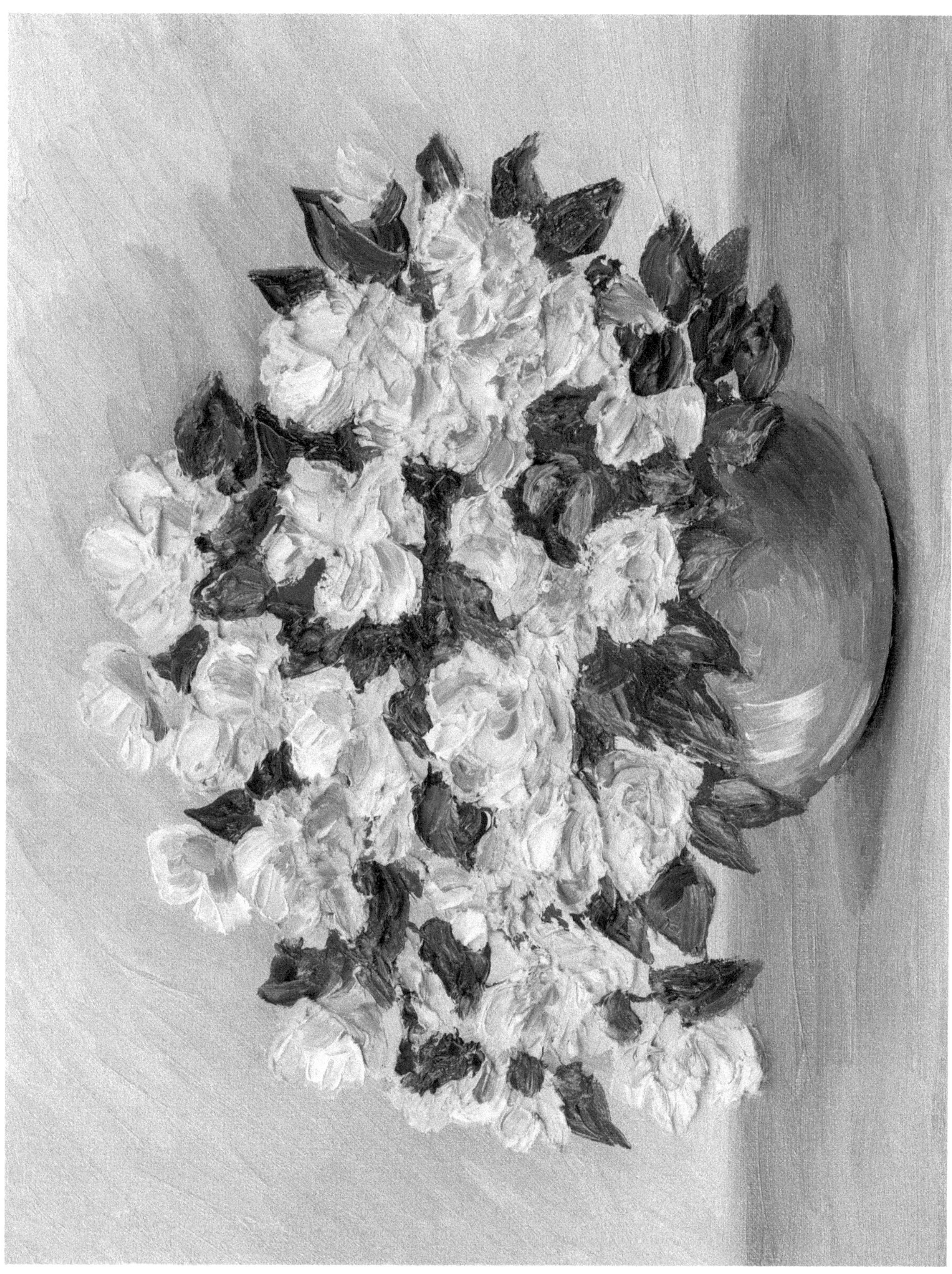

Colored By ______________________________ Date ______________________

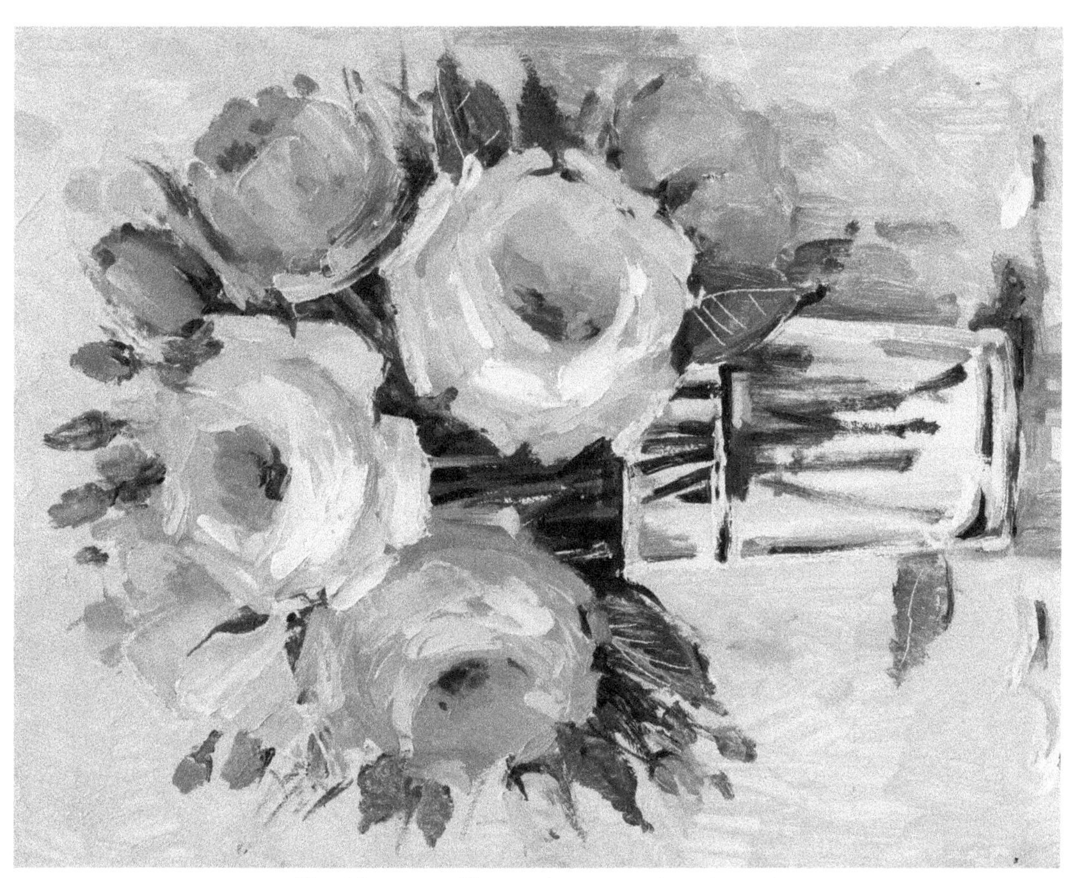

Test Images: Try out your colors here!

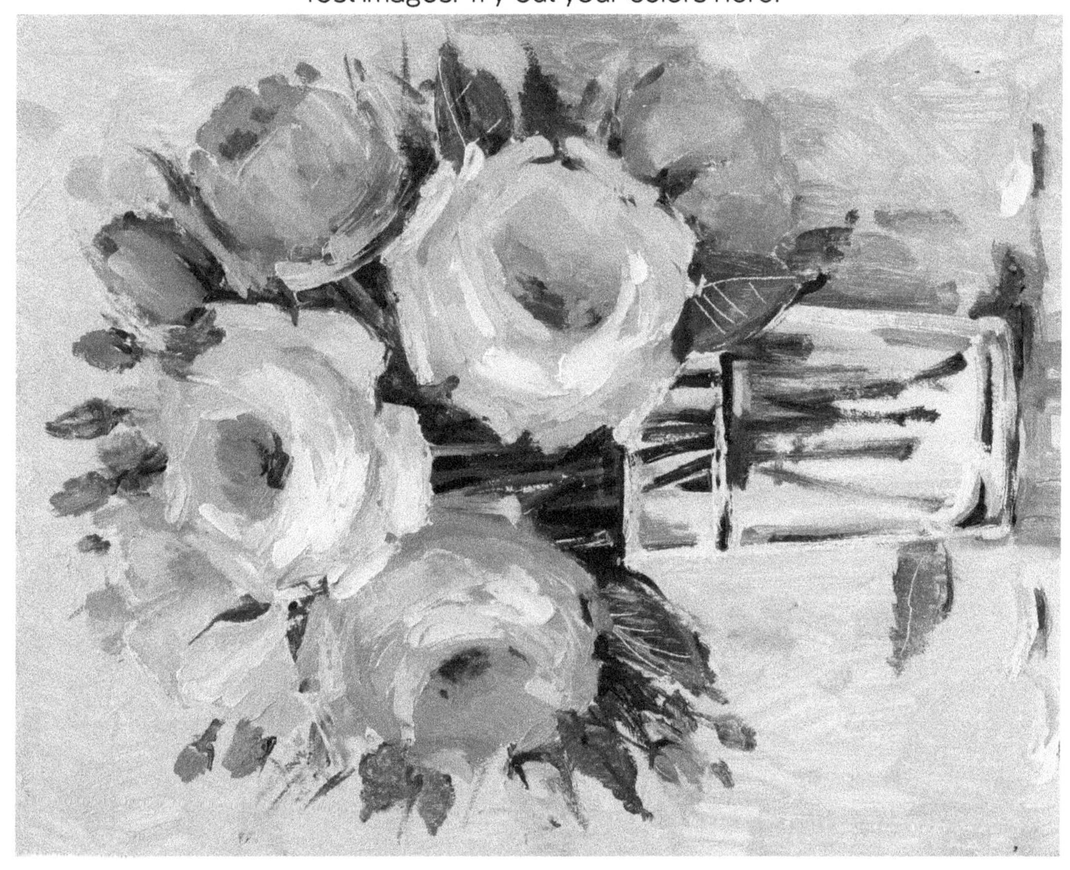

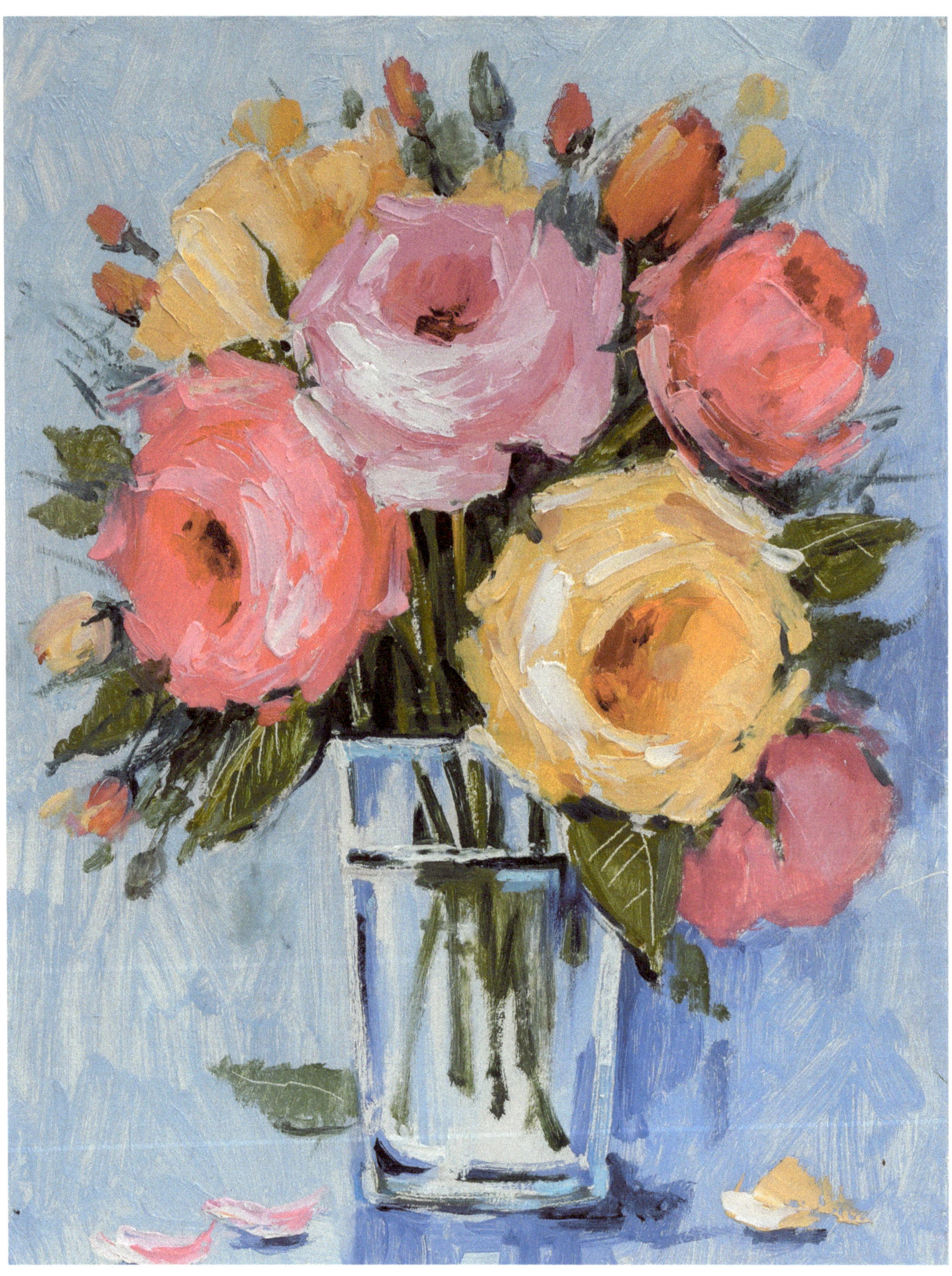

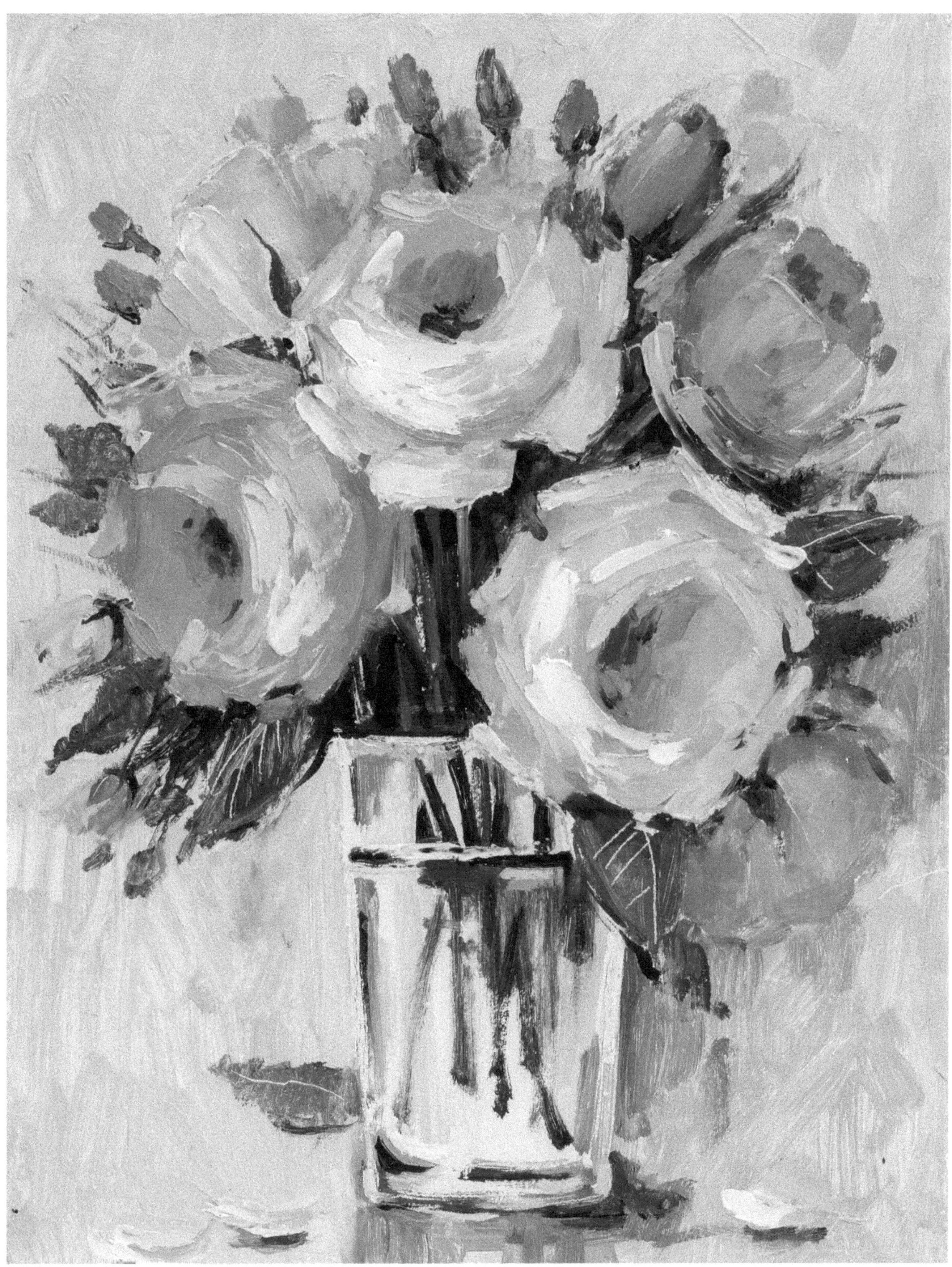

COLORED BY ____

DATE ____

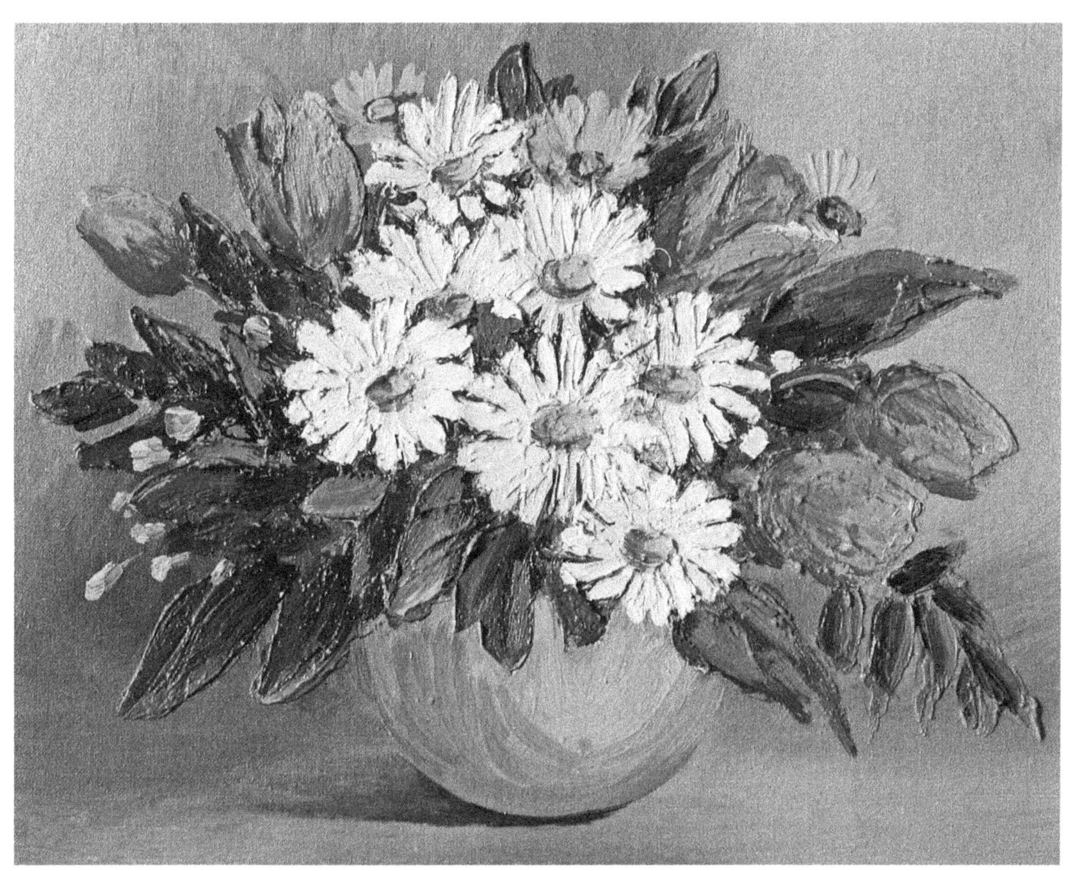

Test Images: Try out your colors here!

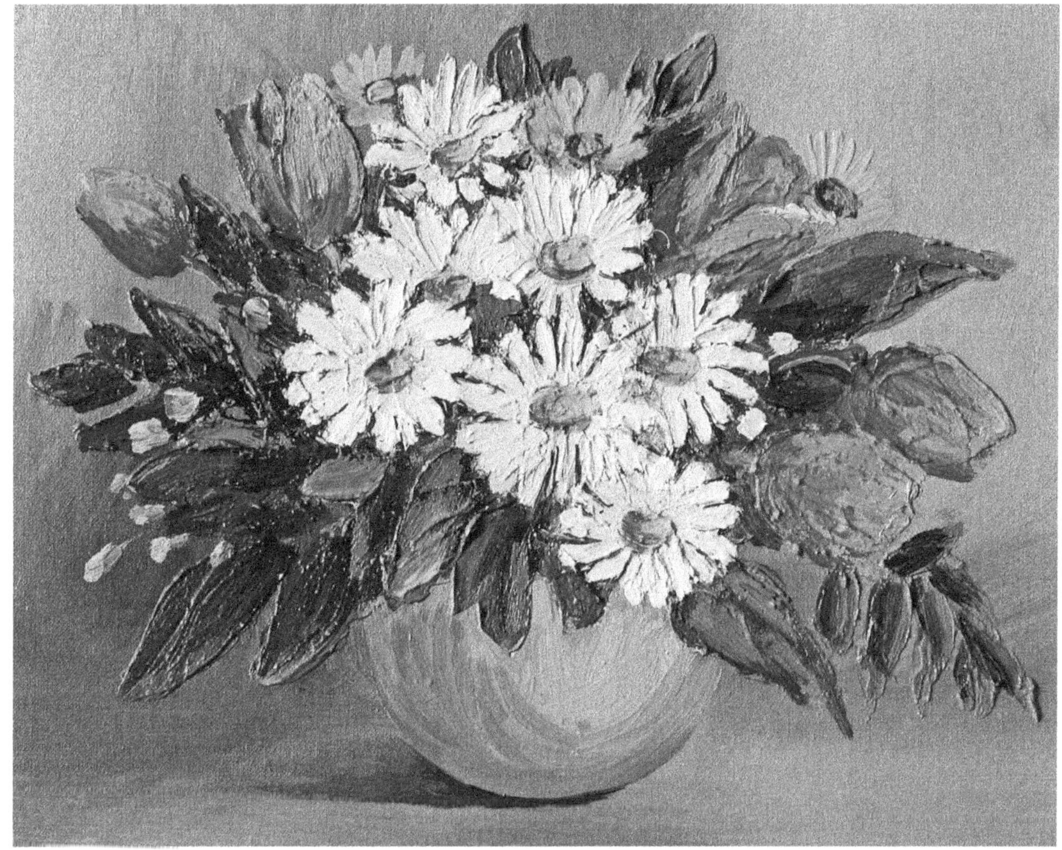

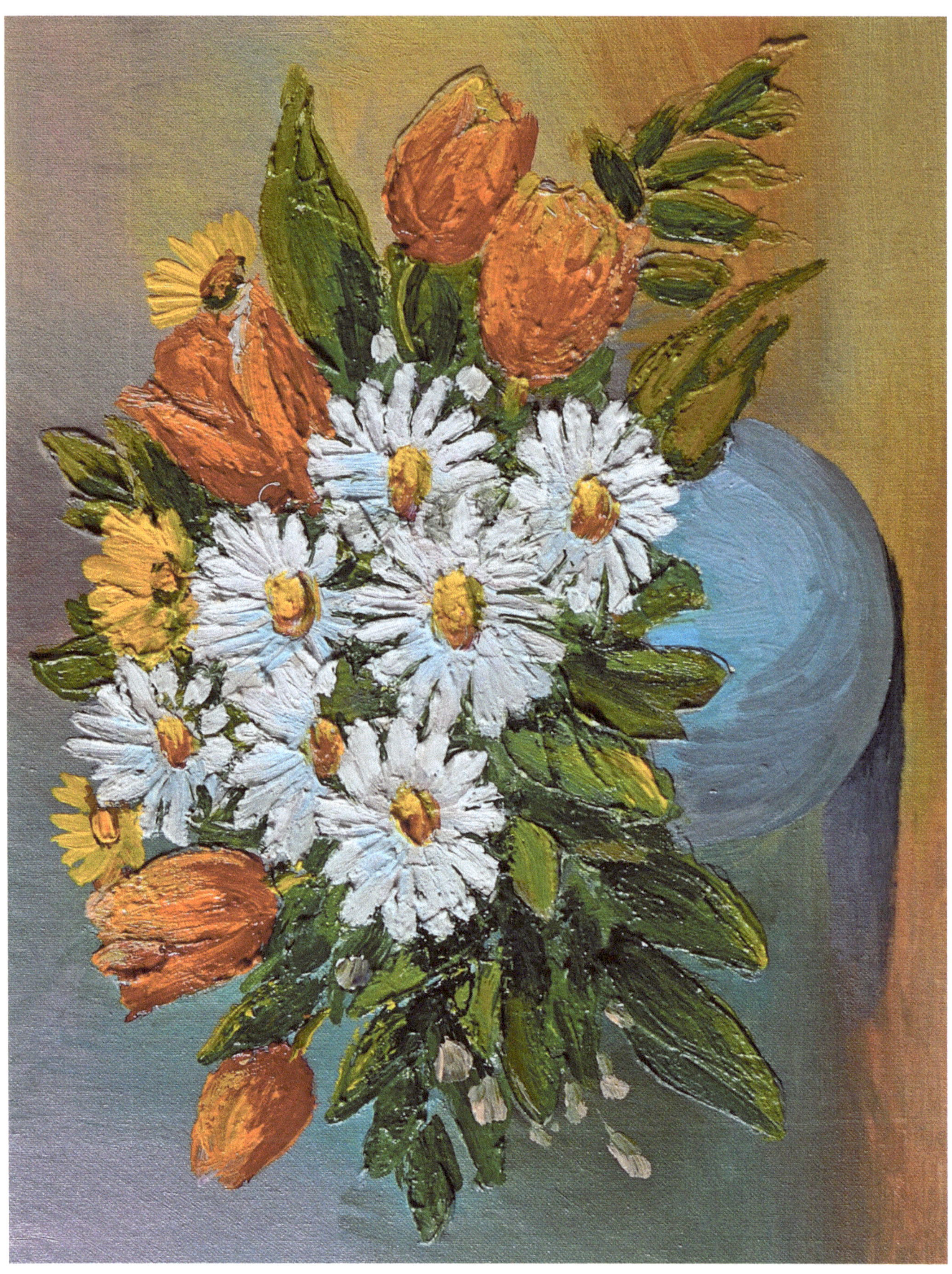

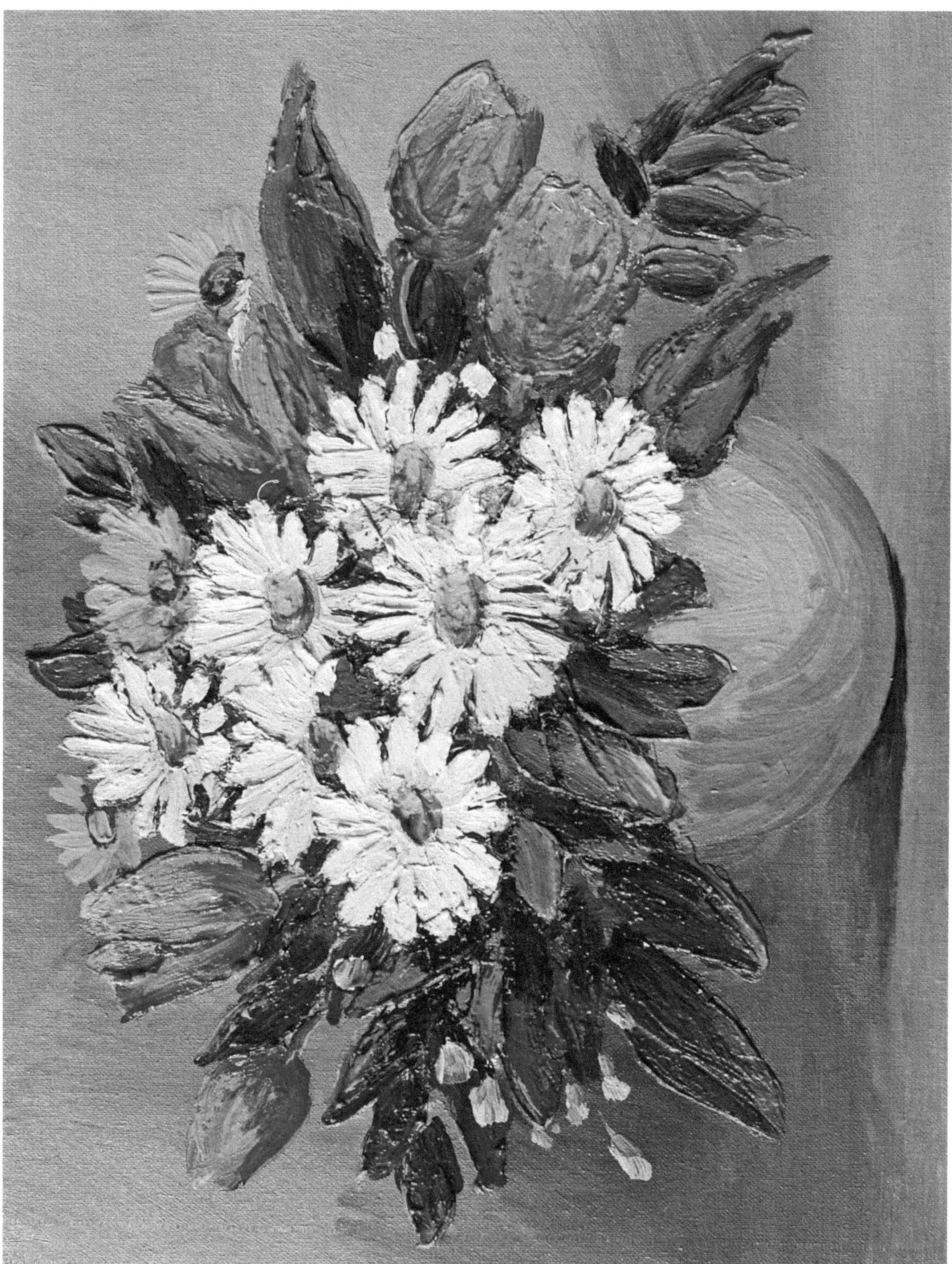

Colored By ______________________________ Date ______________________

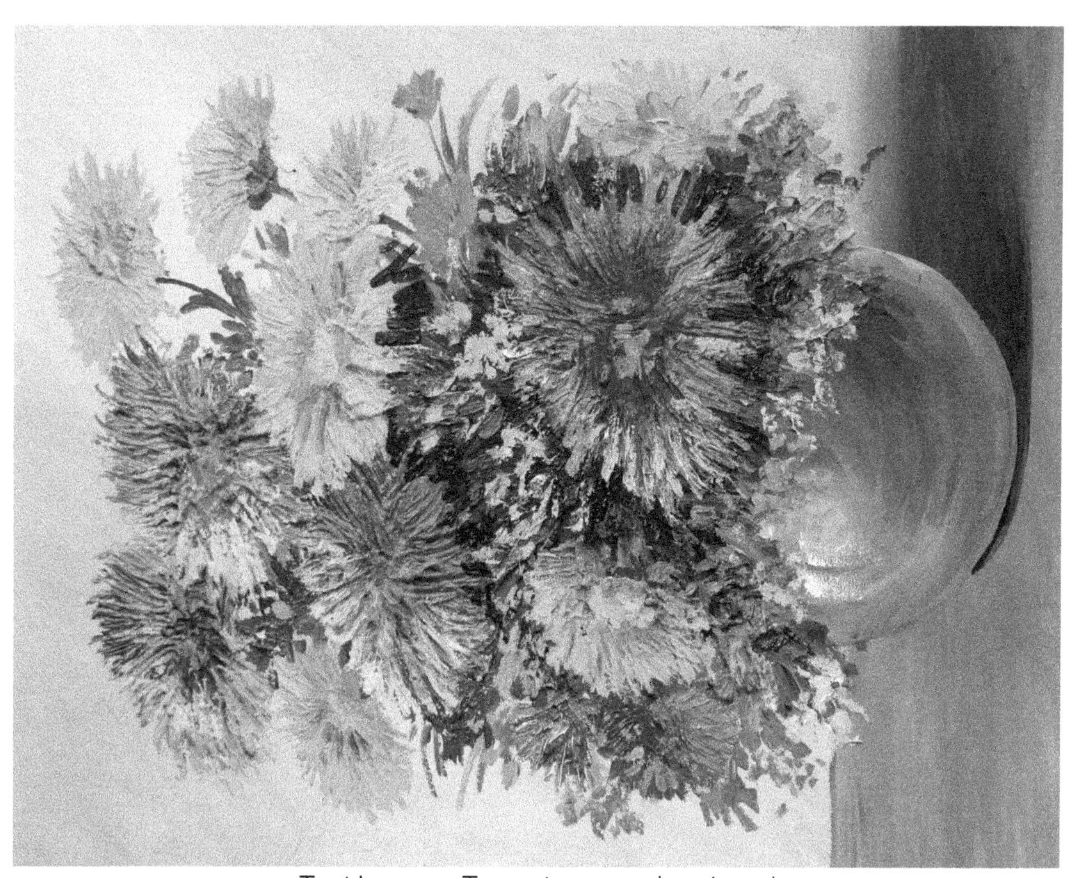

Test Images: Try out your colors here!

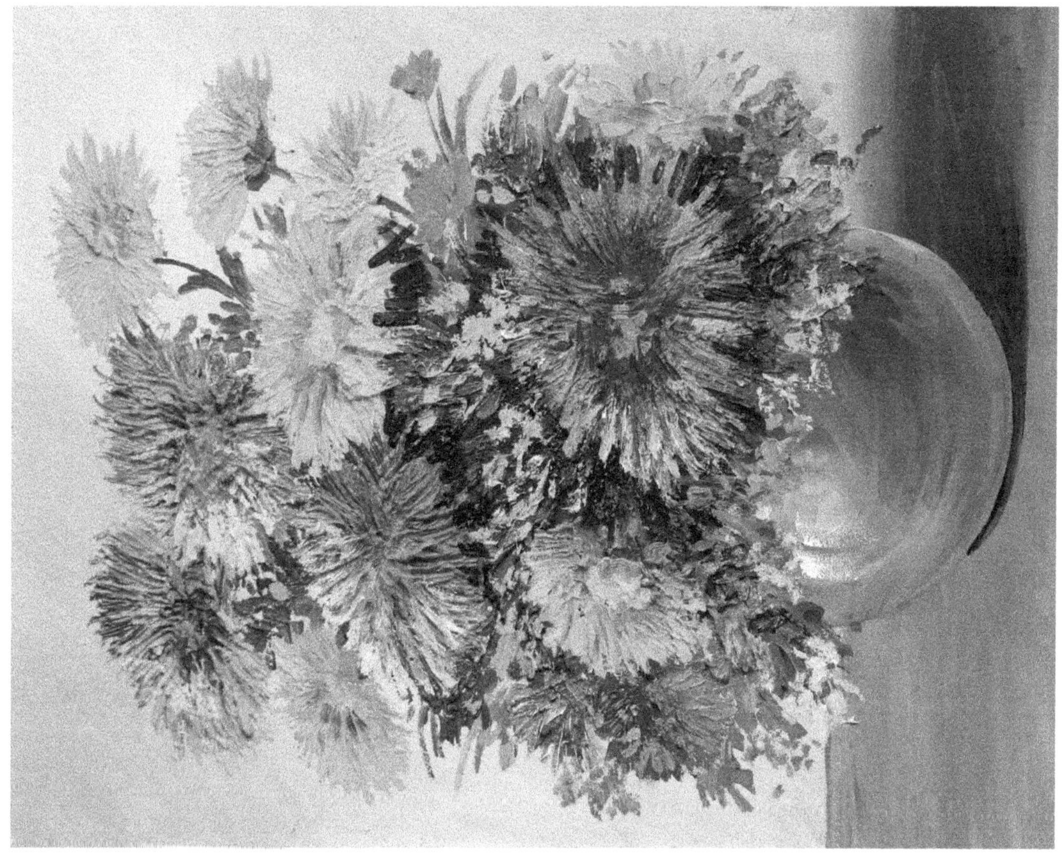

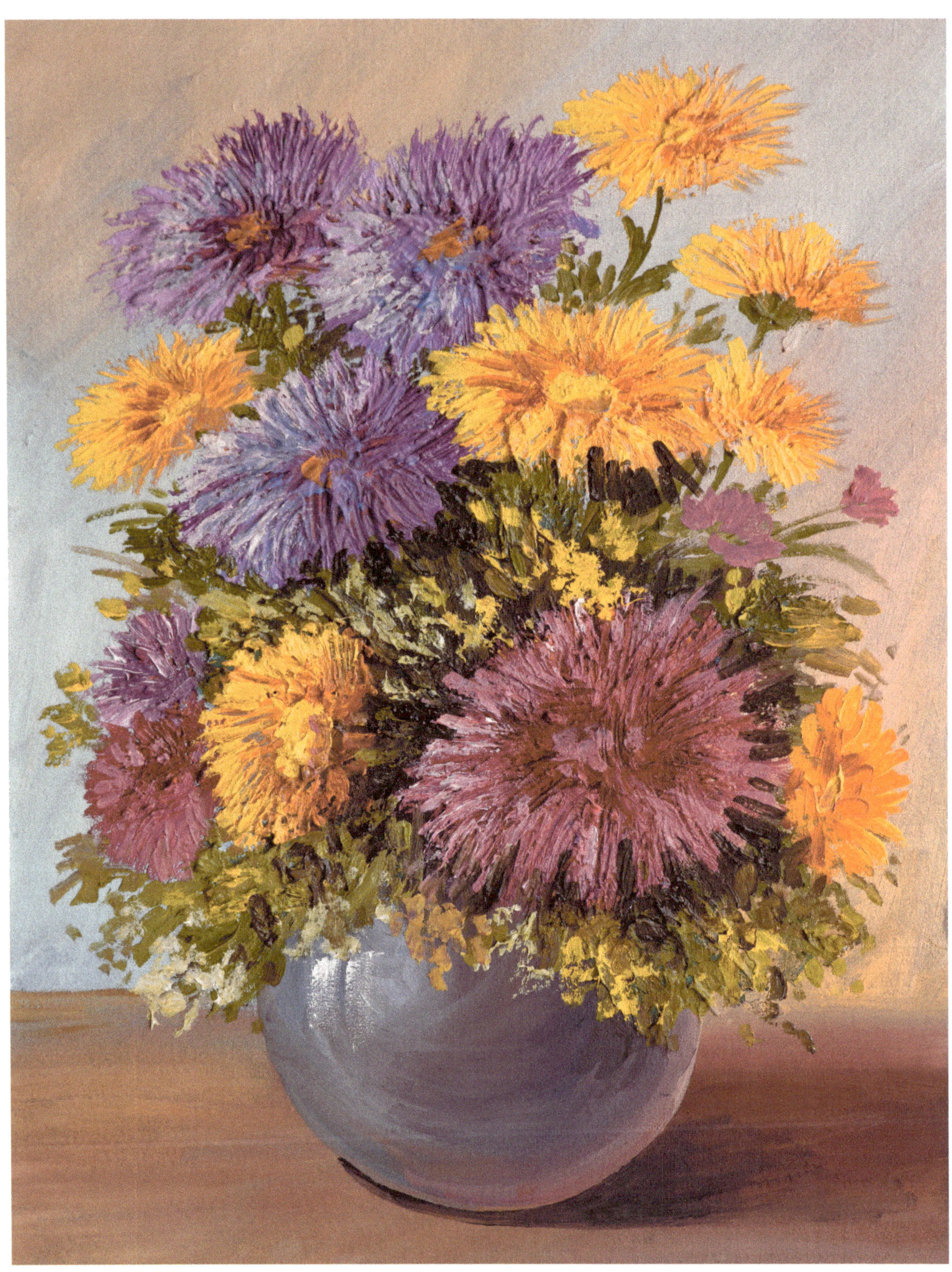

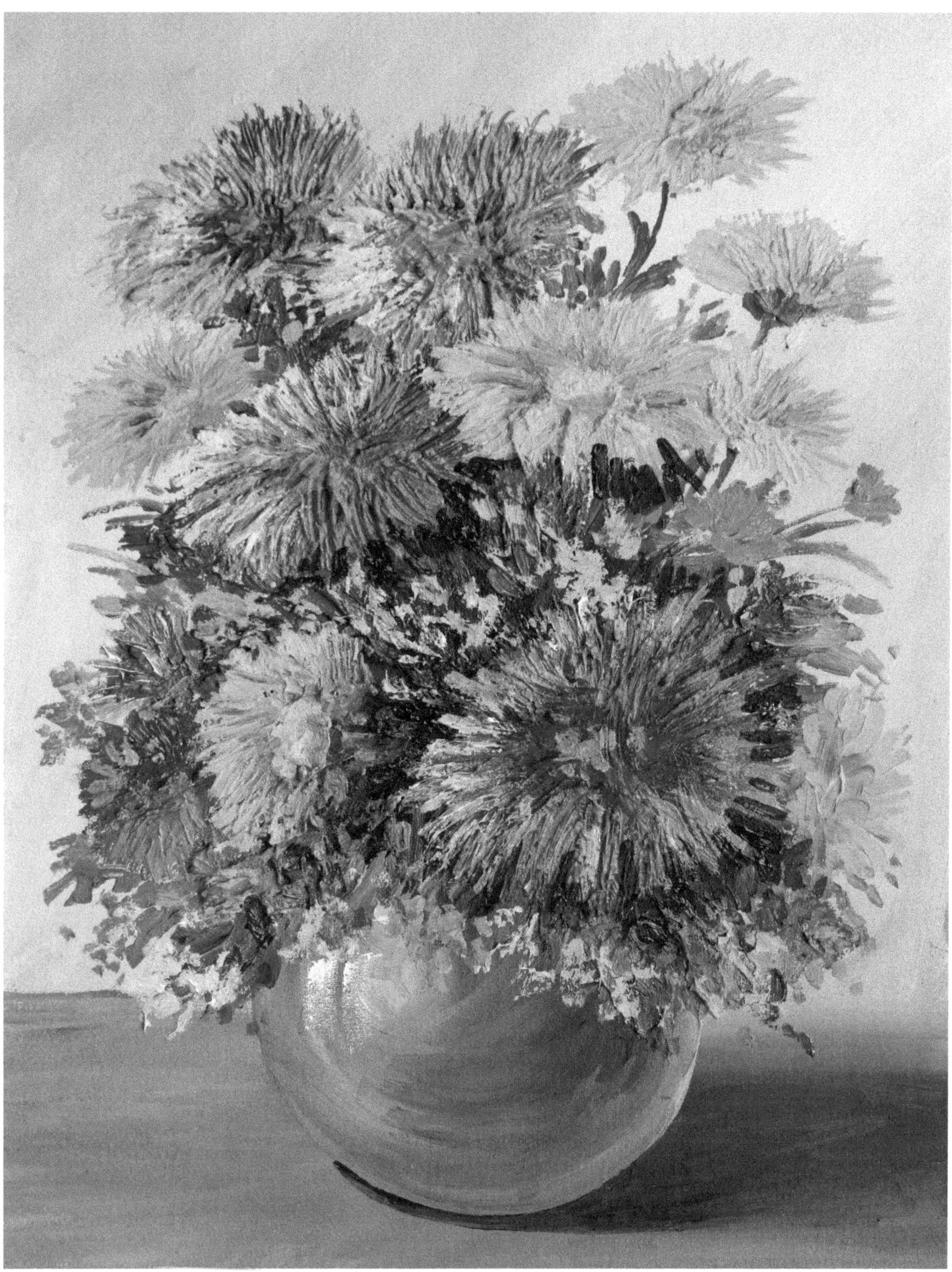

COLORED BY ____________________

DATE ____________________

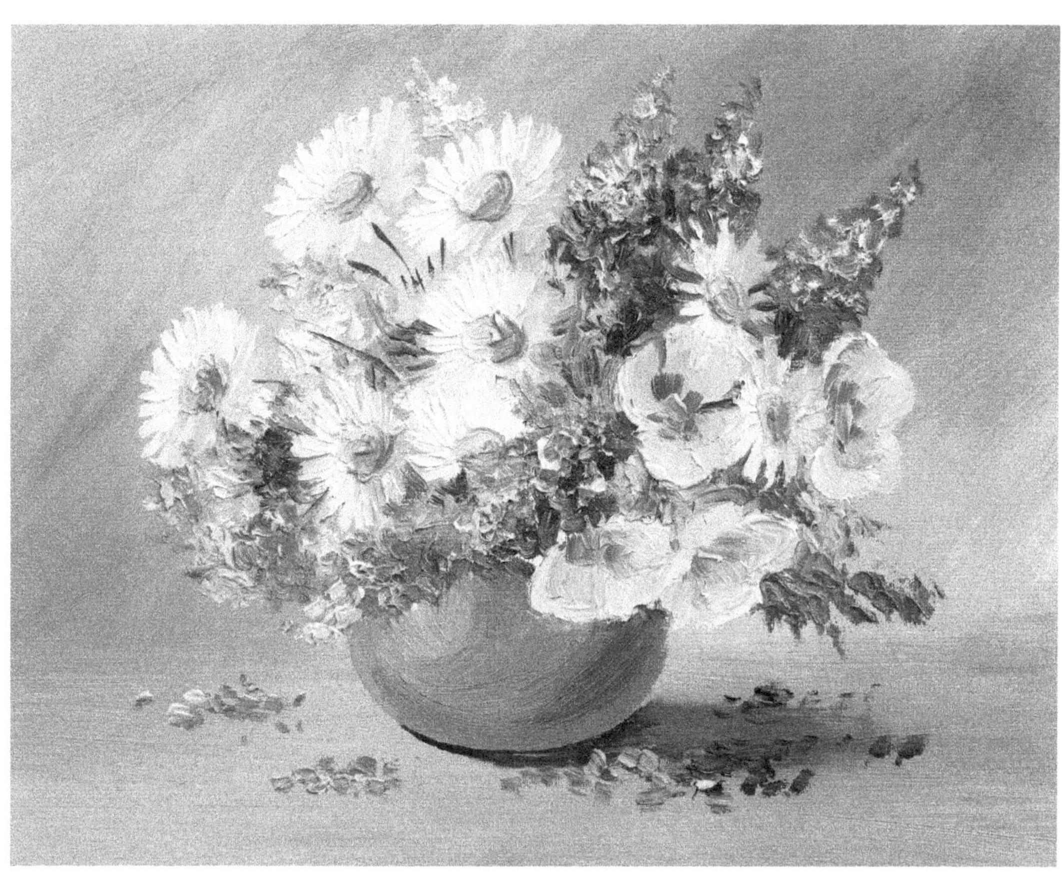

Test Images: Try out your colors here!

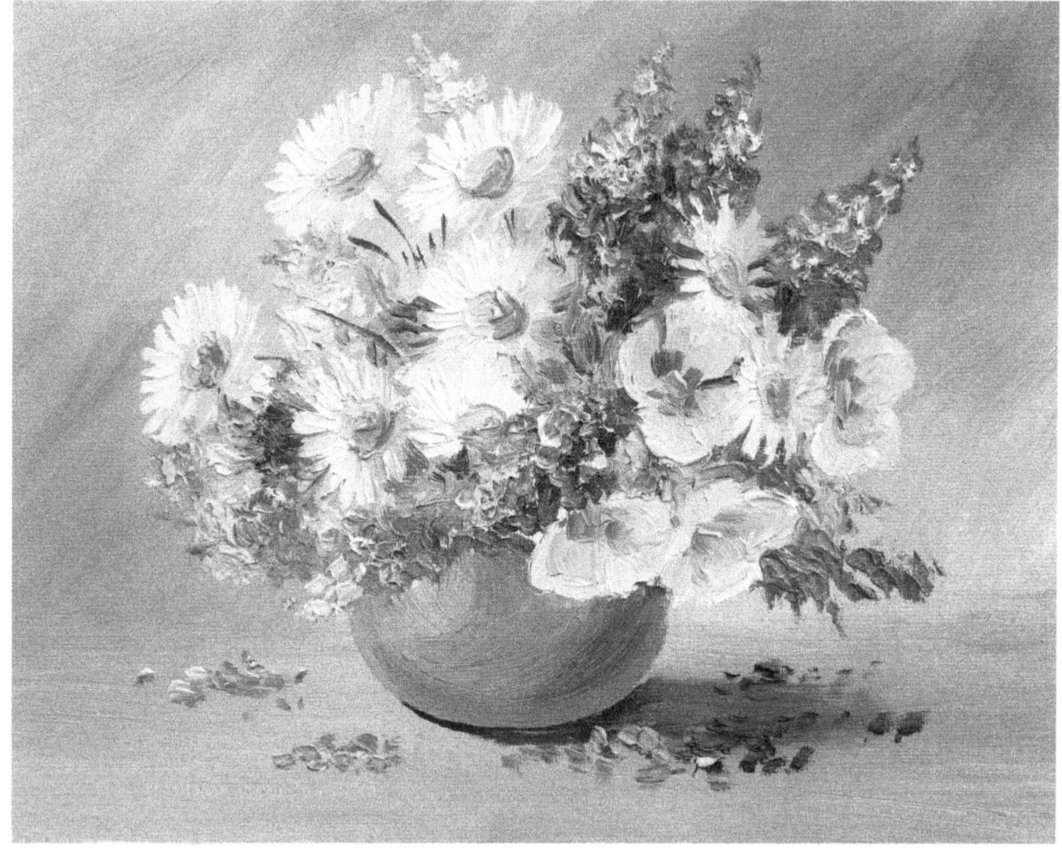

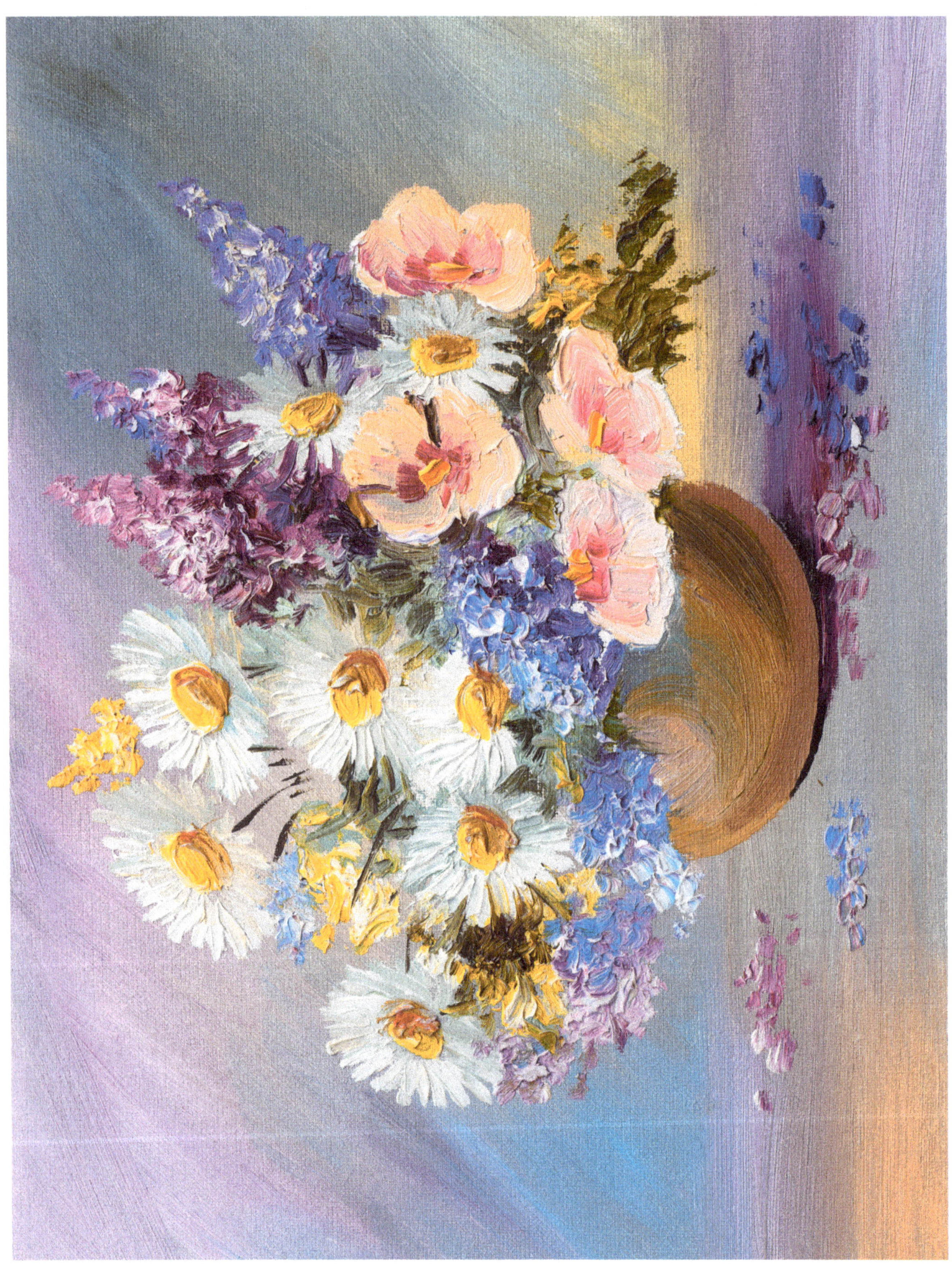

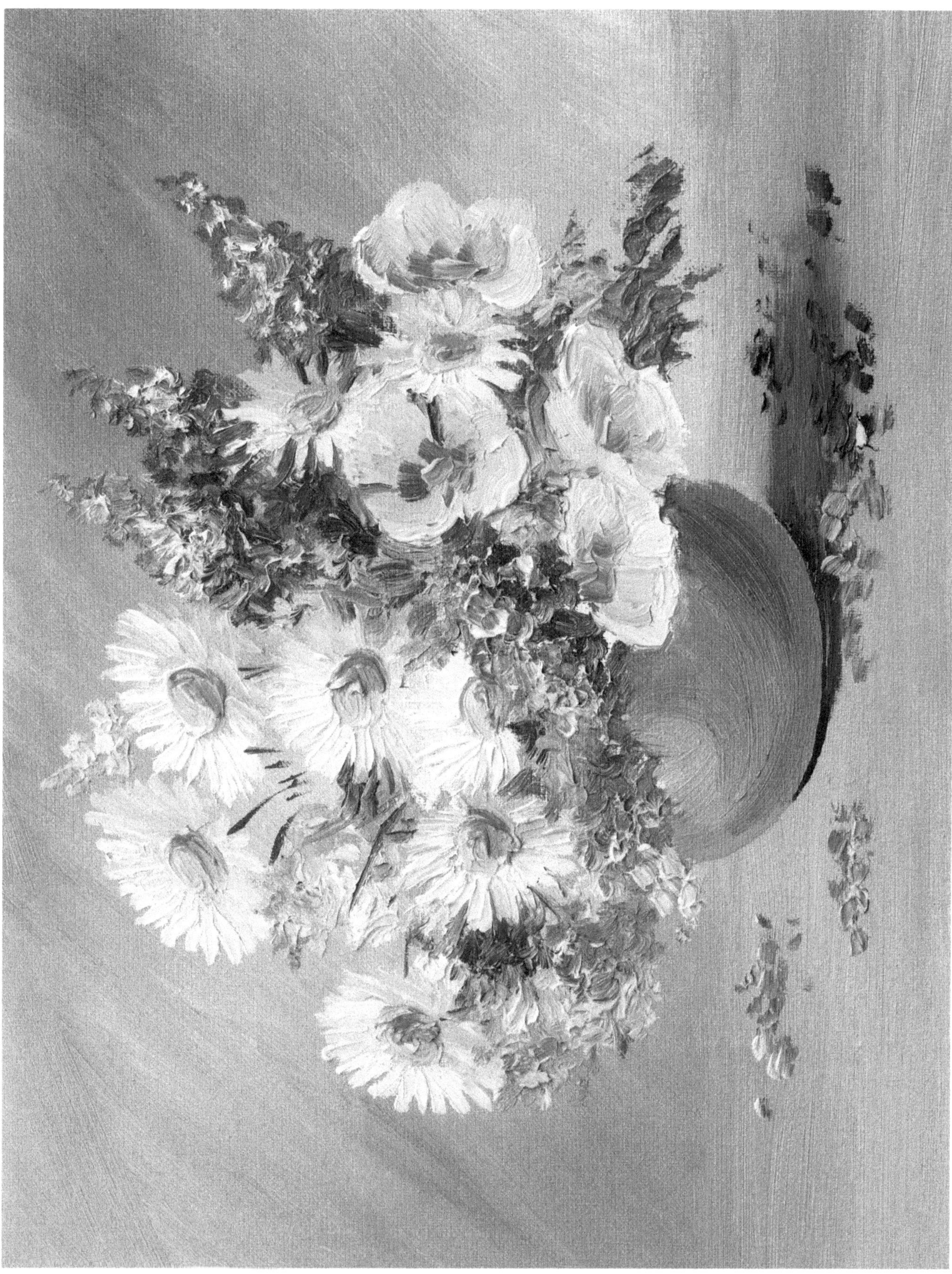

Colored By ______________________ Date ______________________

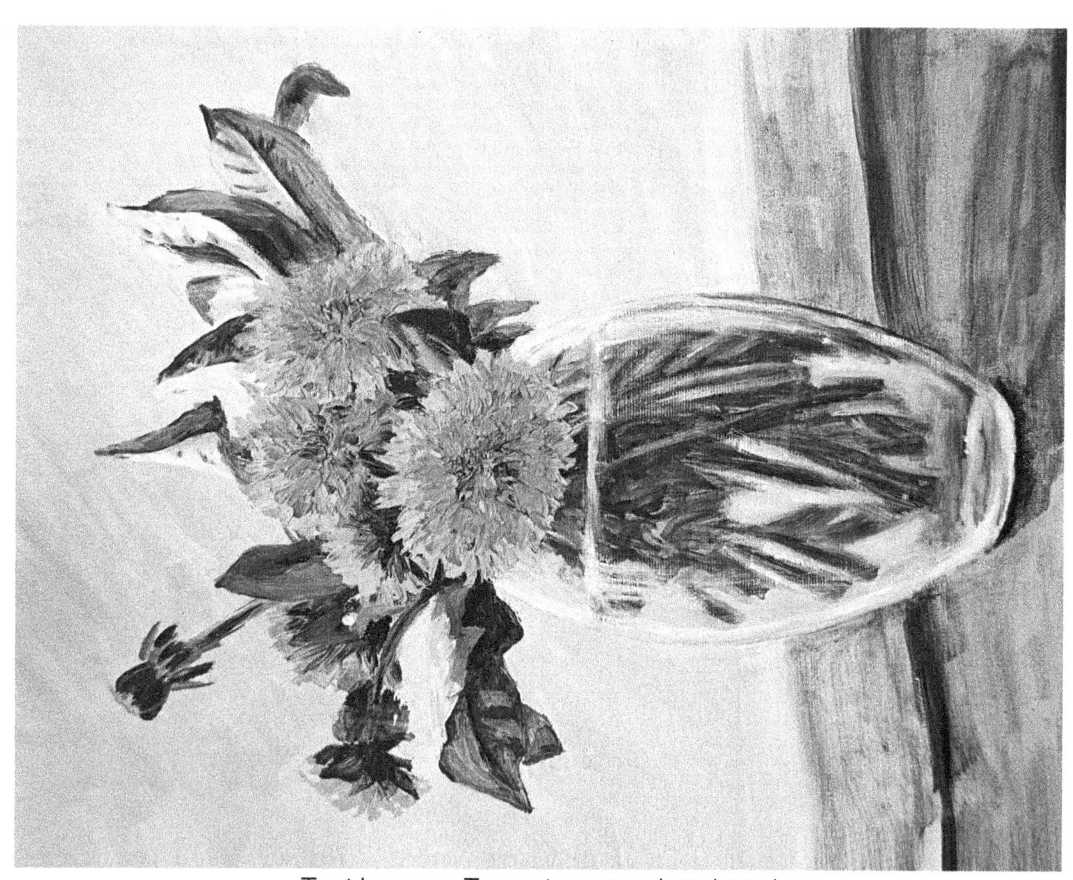

Test Images: Try out your colors here!

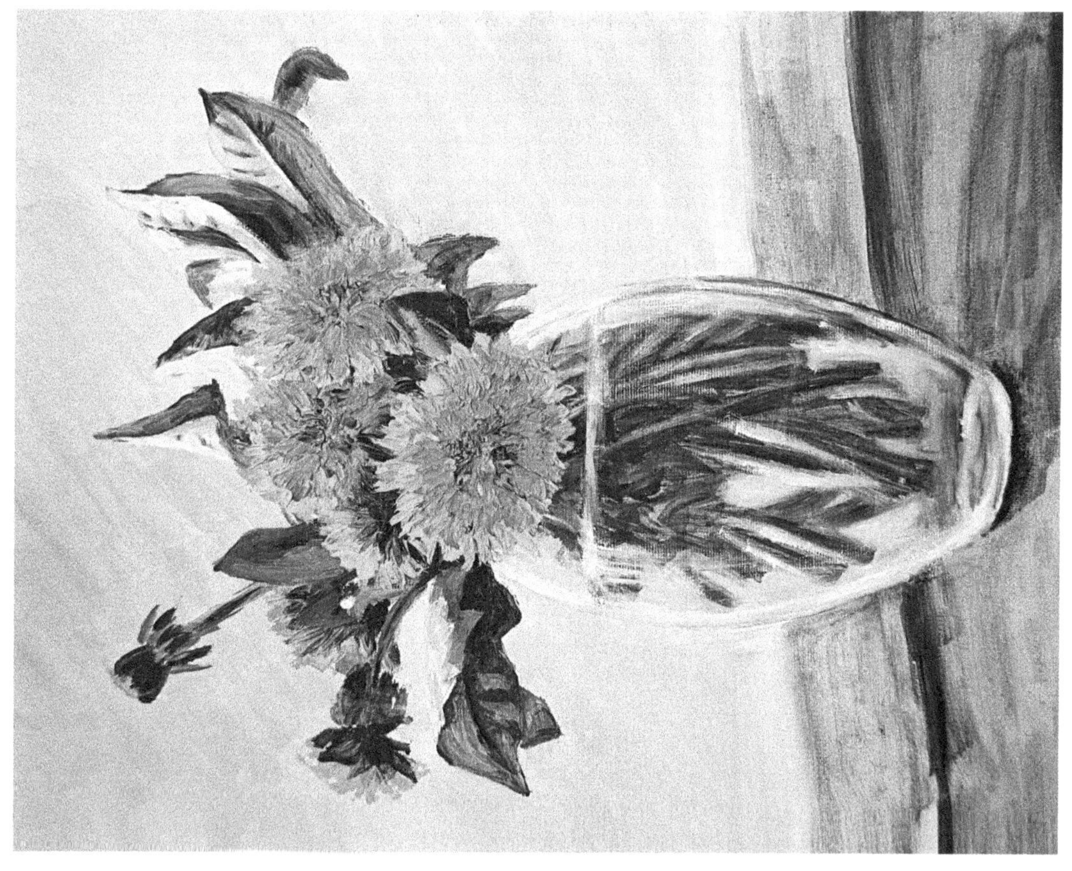

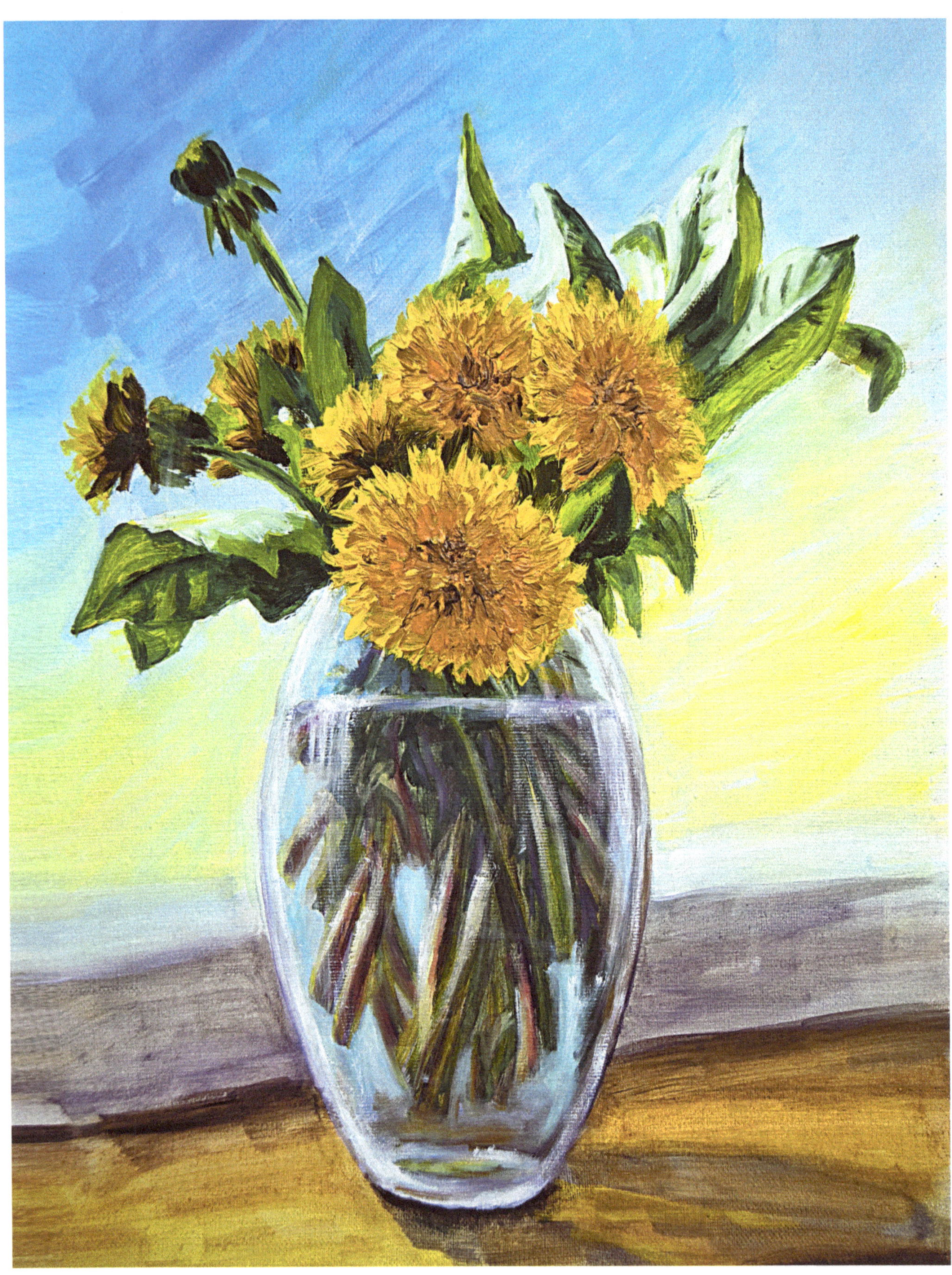

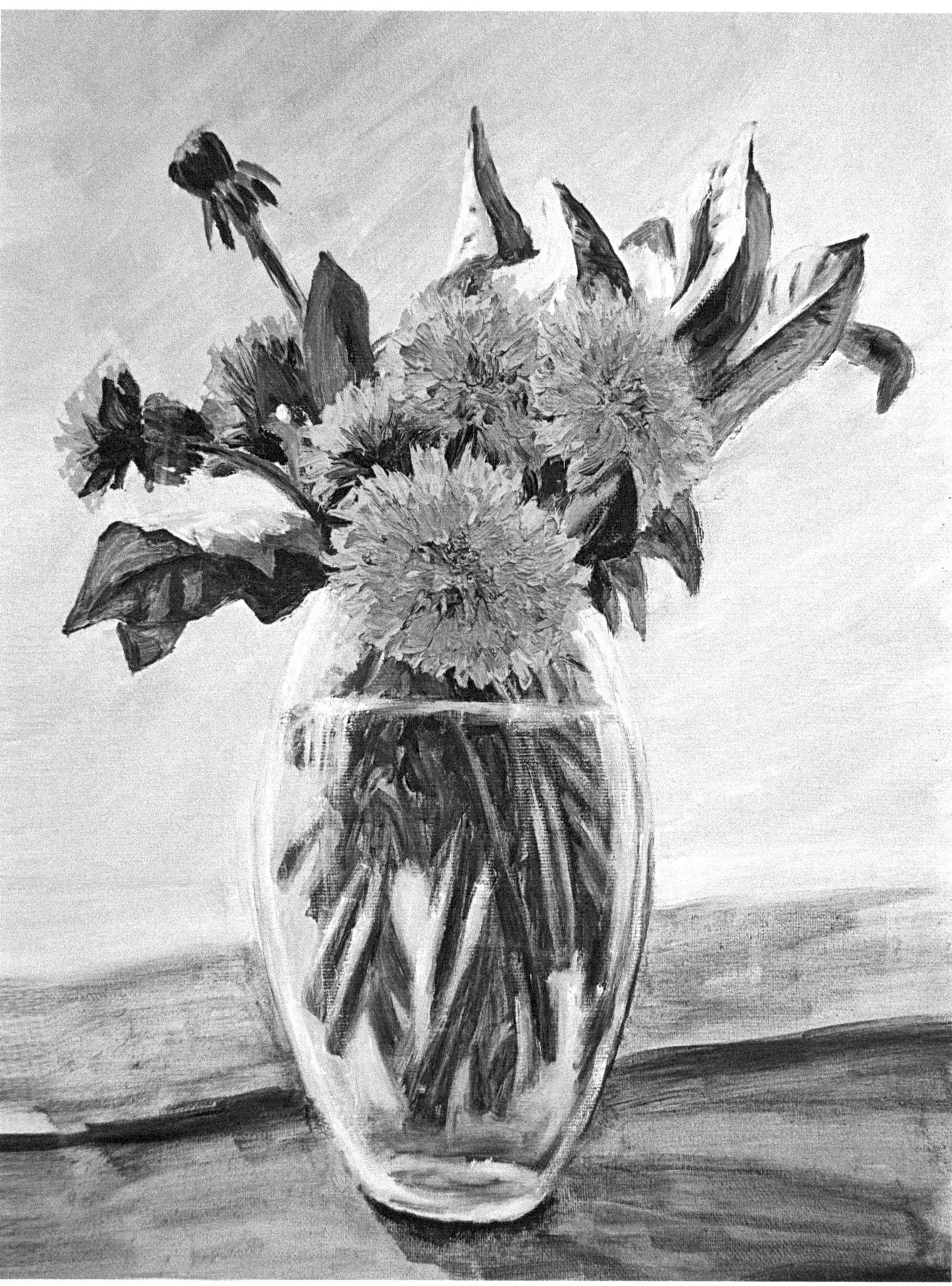

Colored By ____

Date ____

www.ingramcontent.com/pod-product-compliance
Lightning Source LLC
LaVergne TN
LVHW060618110826
845147LV00019B/1048